THE LANGUAGE OF
WORLD WAR II

THE LANGUAGE OF WORLD WAR II

☆ ☆ ☆

*Abbreviations, Captions, Quotations, Slogans, Titles
and Other Terms and Phrases*

COMPILED BY

A. MARJORIE TAYLOR

*Head, Literature Division
Rochester (N.Y.) Public Library*

Revised and Enlarged Edition

THE H . W . WILSON COMPANY
NEW YORK—NINETEEN HUNDRED FORTY-EIGHT

*Each crisis creates its own
vocabulary*—John Mason Brown

PREFACE TO FIRST EDITION

This collection really began with "Praise the Lord and pass the ammunition." When conflicting stories were circulating as to who actually used the phrase at Pearl Harbor, I felt, from the background of my library experience, that the stories should be noted for future reference. So a folder was made for the vertical file under the heading, World War II—Slogans, and soon many other stories joined the "Praise the Lord." As the file grew, other members of the Rochester Public Library staff became interested and having once become slogan-conscious, we found apt phrases, headlines and poster captions in increasing numbers, as we read magazine articles, glanced through the daily newspapers, read books and listened to the radio.

Our material soon seemed to approach book proportion. It was difficult to know just what to include but the final decision was: quotations, slogans, poster captions and song titles (since so many of both of those resembled slogans), initialed government agencies created in connection with the war effort, and initialed women's organizations which were either started in this war or developed during the course of it.

Poster captions came not only from observation but also from the collection of posters in the Rochester Public Library. For song titles we consulted the large collection of songs of this war in the Sibley Music Library of the University of Rochester, which the librarian generously placed at our disposal. For government war agencies we used the *United States Government Manual* published by the Division of Public Inquiries of the Office of War Information.

Many activities which seemed very directly connected with the war effort, such as Blood Bank, Rationing, Victory Gardens etc. were included in an attempt to make this a useful handbook on subjects connected with World War II.

Throughout the book we have listed the sources of our information in the hope that librarians everywhere may be saved hours of research.

We realize that since the material relates to the present war, of necessity it cannot be complete at this time, but there seems to be enough included to answer a real need. And we hope that readers and users of the book will send us new entries as they find them so that a revised edition if any, may be as complete as possible.

To the staff members of the Rochester Public Library and to others who have aided in collecting items, our sincere thanks.

September 7, 1944

A. M. TAYLOR

Preface to Revised Edition

When the first edition of THE LANGUAGE OF WORLD WAR II was published late in 1944, I thought (though I have since been proved to be much mistaken) that I could continue to watch for new terms, collect them, and bring out a reasonably complete revision at the end of the war. I did watch for new terms, and I did collect much additional material, and many people very kindly sent me suggestions for an improved second edition, but so far as a complete edition is concerned, I reluctantly, but of necessity, give up. A complete record of the changes and growth of the language during the course of the war would require years of study and research, and even then some angles would undoubtedly be missed.

As it is true with all phases of knowledge that the more you learn, the more you realize there is to know, so it is with this compilation. The further I went, the more acutely did I realize that I never could manage a complete dictionary of the language of this global war. At the same time, there seemed enough additional material to make a new edition worthwhile. Included with the language are some slang expressions which either originated or gained wide currency during the war. However the book is not intended to be a glossary of slang. There are good books on army slang already available, for example Elbridge Colby's *Army Talk* and Park Kendall's *Dictionary of Service Slang*. But certain slang phrases were heard so often that they seemed to me to be definitely a part of the language of World War II, and it is slang of this type that I have tried to include.

For the help given me so generously by the staff of the Rochester Public Library, and other friends, I express thanks; and for any omissions, I express regrets. I am grateful for, and acknowledge with warm appreciation, the great help I received from the magazine *American Speech*, published by Columbia University Press. Its many articles on G.I. speech and its bibliographies of articles on new words were most helpful. The magazine *American Notes and Queries* was a gold mine of information, especially its featured column "Thumbtack" which aimed to "pin down" new words as they appeared in print. I am grateful to the editor, Mr. Pilkington, for his permission to quote *American Notes and Queries* as source material. To the G. and C. Merriam Company go thanks for permission to quote from their magazine *Word Study*. To John Mason Brown a warm thank you for permission to use as an epigraph a phrase which first appeared in his column "Seeing Things" in the *Saturday Review of Literature*. It seemed so eminently fitting to the book I was compiling.

The book itself I send out in the hope that it may be useful, and as interesting to read as it has been interesting to compile.

A. M. Taylor

October 22, 1947

CONTENTS

THE LANGUAGE OF WORLD WAR II

A: "A" type ships. See note under APA

"A" Award Flag: As the "E" award was given to factories making munitions and war equipment, the "A" award was given for achievement in another field—to factories turning raw crops into food —frozen eggs, evaporated milk, canned goods, etc. The award came into being on September 18, 1943, under the WFA. By the end of 1944, 281 food processing plants were flying the "A" award.—*New York Times Magazine. March 25, 1945. p. 36*

AACS: Army Airways Communications System

AAF: Army Air Forces

AAFAS: Army Air Forces Aid Society

AAFSAT: Army Air Forces School of Applied Tactics.—*New York Times Magazine. July 25, 1943. p. 8*

AAFTAC: Army Air Forces Tactical Center, with headquarters at Orlando, Fla. Conducted a three-fold program: the training of cadres to form the nuclei of new units, the training of individuals in highly specialized duties and the testing of new tactics and techniques under combat conditions. Lectures and classes were held in the AAFSAT (q.v.).—*U.S. Army Air Forces. Official Guide. p. 116*

AAFTAD: Army Air Forces Training Aids Division

AAFTC: Army Air Forces Training Command

AAMC: Army Air Material Command.—*Newsweek. August 26, 1946. p. 54*

Abbeville Kids: AAF slang. Enemy fighters who pressed home the attack with great daring and skill were sometimes referred to as "Abbeville Kids," because in 1943 the pick of the Luftwaffe's fighters were stationed near Abbeville.—*New York Times Magazine. June 4, 1944. p. 12*

ABC Victory Route: See Com Z

ABCA: Army Bureau of Current Affairs (British). Headed by a civilian, William Williams. He tried to get British soldiers to think and talk about what they were fighting for. No equivalent bureau in United States.—*Life. July 12, 1943. p. 87*

ABCD: American, British, Chinese, and Dutch forces. Name given to powers arrayed against Japan.—*Newsweek. November 24, 1941. p. 24-6*

ABDA: Southwest Pacific area. So called by President Roosevelt, from the first initials of the American, British, Dutch, and Australian forces fighting there against the Japanese.—*Newsweek. February 9, 1942. p. 29*

Able: In official language to avoid any misunderstanding in transmission of messages, a "phonetic" alphabet was used, Able for A, Baker for B, etc. The complete alphabet as used by United States forces was Able, Baker, Charlie, Dog, Easy, Fox, George, How, Item, Jig, King, Love, Mike, Nan, Oboe, Peter, Queen, Roger, Sugar, Tare, Uncle, Victor, William, X-ray, Yoke, Zebra. In Navy usage, A, I, N, O and P appear as Afirm (*sic*), Interrogatory, Negat, Option and Prep. For British alphabet see entry under Ack Ack.—*American Speech. December 1946. p. 284; U.S. Civil Aeronautics Administration. Army-Navy-CAA Standard Airport Traffic Control Procedures. p. 21.*

Able Day: See Test Able

A-Bomb: See Atomic Bomb

ABSD: Advance Base Sectional Docks; floating drydocks, built in sections and welded together in the combat area, with a capacity of 56,000-100,000 tons—more than enough to raise the largest battleship.—*Newsweek. June 25, 1945. p. 74*

Absenteeism: See "There is no absenteeism. . . ."

ABSIE: American Broadcasting Station in Europe. Official station of OWI, located in England. OWI Overseas Director Robert E. Sherwood gave the first broadcast over the new station in the spring of 1944.—*Time. May 8, 1944. p. 38.* Announcement was made in June 1945 that it would cease operations on July 4, 1945.—*New York Times. June 3, 1945. p. 2E*

"Absolutely Unnerved and Calm Over the News": A Japanese English-language dispatch recorded by the Federal Communications Commission said that Admiral Kiyoshi Hasegawa, governor-general of Formosa, was in Tokyo at the time of the Japanese announcement of a 1000-plane raid on his territory. He proclaimed that he was "absolutely unnerved and calm over the news."—*Democrat & Chronicle, Rochester, N.Y. October 13, 1944. p. 1*

Accolade Certificate: A certificate suitable for framing sent to the next of kin of all members of the armed forces who died in the performance of duty, whether or not the death occurred in conflict with the enemy.—*National Geographic Society. Insignia and Decorations of the U.S. Armed Forces. 1944. p. 13, 16*

Accredited Correspondent: Journalist, writer, radio correspondent or photographer authorized by the War Department to carry on his work in a theater of operations.—*U.S. Army. ETO. CONAD History. p. 374*

Accurator: New bulletless mechanism to be used in the teaching of long-distance rifle shooting; by combining "piping, joints and elbows" with precision sighting and aligning instruments, simulated distance conditions are provided with the aid of a telescope; operates within the confines of a small room. Invented by Sergeant Vincent Genre.—*American Notes and Queries. May 1944. p. 24*

Ack Ack: Anti-Aircraft Fire. Radio communication required a phonetic alphabet for words which had to be spelled out clearly. In the English alphabet Ack was used for A, whence Ack ack for anti-aircraft fire. Though Able was used for A in the American phonetic alphabet, Americans in England took over the British Ack Ack. For American phonetic alphabet see entry under Able. The British phonetic alphabet was as follows: Ack, Beer, Charlie, Don, Edward, Freddy, George, Harry, Ink, John, King, London, Monkey, Nuts, Orange, Pip, Queen, Robert, Sugar, Tock, Uncle, Victor, William, X-ray, Yorker, Zebra. The British used this alphabet for the first three years of the war; then they switched to the American alphabet (see entry under Able) for the rest of the war.—*British Library of Information, New York City*

ADA: Atomic Development Authority, proposed by Bernard Baruch to exercise control over those aspects of atomic energy inimical to global security.—*Britannica Book of the Year. 1947. p. 840*

A-Day: The day set for landing on Leyte in the Philippines. See also D-Day, S-Day.—*New York Times. January 21, 1945. p. 6E*

ADC: Alaska Defense Command. Known to many of the soldiers who served in it as "All Damn Confusion"—*New York Times Magazine. September 26, 1943. p. 36*

Admiral-General MacNimsey: A fabulous character created by Joseph Driscoll, *New York Herald Tribune* correspondent, to get around censorship regulations. This hero of the war in the Pacific was a combination of the names of General MacArthur, Admiral Nimitz and Admiral Halsey.—*New York Times Book Review. September 10, 1944. p. 8*

Admiral of the Fleet: New rank (5-star admiral) created during World War II. See also General of the Army.—*Saturday Review of Literature. March 10, 1945. p. 5*

ADSC: Advanced Section Communication Zone. The term is pronounced Ad-Sec. See also Com Z

Aero Clubs: Red Cross relaxation clubs for our air forces in Britain. They were later flown by cargo planes from Britain to our forces in France. They could be set up within an hour, complete with ping-pong tables, easy chairs, snack bars, pianos and writing desks.—*New York Times. August 20, 1944. p. 2E, 7E*

AES: Army Exchange Service set up in September 1941 centralized the control of PXs (Post Exchanges) both at home and abroad.—*Newsweek. September 7, 1942. p. 49-50*

AFHQ: Allied Forces Headquarters. Might refer to any theater of war.

AFMIDPAC: U.S. Army Forces, Middle Pacific. Official name for the theater of war which was more commonly called MIDPAC, with headquarters at Ft. Shafter, Hawaii

AFMR: Armed Forces Master Records. Begun in 1942. Solicited records and money to buy records for the armed forces. On the whole, favored classical music in its selection of purchases. See also RFOFM.—*Newsweek. June 14, 1943. p. 84*

AFPAC: U.S. Army Forces, Pacific, top Army headquarters for all the Pacific after the recapture of the Philippines. See also SCAP, USAFFE.

AFRS: Armed Forces Radio Service. Programs for the GI's in Japan and Korea, arranged by General of the Army MacArthur's Information and Education Services.—*Newsweek. October 8, 1945. p. 84*

After Tokyo: Slogan adopted by sailors in the Pacific Fleet, signifying their belief that Tokyo should be the Navy's first objective. —*Newsweek. April 13, 1942. p. 11*

AFWESPAC: U.S. Army Forces, Western Pacific, headquarters for Philippines, Okinawa, etc., set up in 1945 in Manila

AGCT: Army General Classification Test.—*Newsweek. July 5, 1943. p. 47*

AGF: Army Ground Forces

AH Plan: "After Hitler" plan. General Motors Co.'s postwar plans, so called by Alfred P. Sloan, Jr., chairman of General Motors.—*Newsweek. December 15, 1941. p. 50*

AI: Aircraft Interception. Airborne radar device used to locate and intercept enemy aircraft by means of radar data.—*Army and Navy Journal. August 18, 1945. p. 1534*

Aichi 99 Val; Aichi 00 Jake: Nicknames for Japanese planes

"Aid [to Democracies] Will Be Increased—and Yet Again Increased—Until Total Victory Has Been Won": By Franklin D. Roosevelt. Speech delivered at dinner of White House Correspondents' Association, Washington, D.C., March 15, 1941.—*Vital Speeches. April 1, 1941. p. 356*

AIF: Australian Imperial Forces

Airacobra: (American plane) A Bell P-39 fighter plane

Airedales: Slang term for plane handlers on an aircraft carrier. —*Reader's Digest. September 1944. p. 76*

Air Force: Air Force terminology was clarified by a release from ETO of U.S. Army in London, March 20, 1944. Various terms with their meanings follow: AIR-FORCE: Composition unlimited. DIVISION: Composition unlimited, depending on number of wings available for assignment. FLIGHT: Three or more aircraft. GROUP: Three or more squadrons. MISSION: An ordered operation against the enemy, such as dropping bombs, strafing ground troops and ships, taking photographs, etc. SORTIE: Act accomplished by a single aircraft when, on an ordered operation, it entered an area where the enemy's defense usually was active, or on a mission in the course of which the plane was subject to enemy attack. If a reconnaissance plane flew over enemy-held territory it accomplished a sortie. A thousand sorties could mean one operation by a thousand planes, two operations by five hundred planes each, or one plane's execution of a thousand trips. SQUADRON: Two or more flights. WING: Three or more groups.—*American Notes and Queries. April 1944. p. 15*

Airgraph: British equivalent of American V-mail (q.v.).— *American Speech. October 1944. p. 223*

Airhead: The counterpart, in air action, of Beachhead; term used by Maj. Eliot F. Noyes, AAF, speaking before the Soaring Society of America, August 5, 1944, in referring to the behind-German-lines base established by Allied gliders during the Normandy invasion.—*American Notes and Queries. September 1944. p. 85*

Air Holding Station: A small installation operated by medical corps personnel, providing the necessary minimum medical care at a casualty collecting point to patients awaiting air evacuation to the rear.—*U.S. Army. ETO. CONAD History. p. 374*

Airplane Stamps: In Book 3 of ration stamps, issued during the war, there were four sheets of stamps, bearing pictures of guns, tanks, ships and airplanes. The first three of these series were never specified for purchase of goods, but airplane stamps were necessary when buying shoes. For that reason, "airplane stamps" became a commonly heard phrase in 1944 and 1945

Airplanes, U.S.—Names: A long range policy for the naming of military aircraft was adopted by the Joint Aircraft Committee. American and British military and naval services had members on this committee. Aircraft names were submitted to this committee, to insure uniformity, simplicity and meaning. Rules laid down by this committee were: FIGHTERS: Names indicating speed, maneuverability, etc. BOMBERS: Names indicating weight, size, power, etc. PATROL types: Names employing seafaring terms. TRANSPORTS: Names implying transportation, range or load-carrying ability. TRAINERS: Names employing tuition terms, educational institutions, etc. MISCELLANEOUS: Names indicating primary operational functions.—*Army and Navy Journal. January 22, 1944. p. 622*

Airstrip: A hurriedly prepared strip of land for temporary use by landing aircraft, usually fighter planes.—*Newsweek. December 7, 1942. p. 27*

Albacore: (British plane) Fairey reconnaissance plane used as a fleet spotter

Alcan Highway: Highway stretching 1600 miles from Dawson Creek, Canada, to Fairbanks, Alaska. Begun hastily in February 1942 after the Japanese attack on Pearl Harbor brought home to America the strategic importance of Alaska, it was officially opened nine months later on November 20, 1942. The name, quite obviously, comes from the first syllables of Alaska and Canada.   Later the State Department in Washington officially designated it the Alaska Highway.—*Aviation. May 1943. p. 114; Holiday. August 1946. p. 28*

Alcatraz in Technicolor: Naval mobile Base Hospital 3, the first to leave the United States after Pearl Harbor, was located on a South Sea island base so remote from combat and so lonely that the men assigned there nicknamed it "Alcatraz in Technicolor."—*New York Times Book Review. March 25, 1945.   p. 6*, in a review of *"Mob 3" by Captain Robert P. Parsons, U.S.N.*

Alert: An air-raid alarm.—*American Speech. April 1941. p. 144*

Alibist: Name given to the politician in Nazi-controlled countries who is now trying to give the impression that he had never been anything but friendly toward the Allies from the very beginning.—*American Notes and Queries. November 1943. p. 119*

All Clear: Signal given by siren to indicate the end of an air raid, meaning the enemy planes had gone by and people could come out of the air raid shelters

"All His Usual Formalities of Perfidy Were Observed with Scrupulous Technique": By Winston Churchill, in referring to Hitler's attack on and invasion of Russia. Radio address, "The Fourth Climacteric," June 21, 1941.—*Churchill. The Unrelenting Struggle. p. 170*

All-out: This term was originally considered slang (see Webster's Dictionary) defined as "with full vigor, determination or enthusiasm; full pelt."   In World War II, it ceased to be slang and was used in various phrases, such as "the struggle still may be far short of the 'all out' air warfare to come"; "the twelfth raid since Germany began her 'all-out' assaults on London," etc.   "Total" is a synonym of all-out, though usually applied to activities on a larger scale, e.g., an all-out battle but a total war.—*American Speech. February 1941. p. 64*

All Out for America: Song title. Marching song of the U.S.A. Dedicated to our Commander in Chief. Words by John Adams. Music by Mayhew Lake. Sam Fox Pub. Co., c1941

"All We Are and All We Have": By Generalissimo Chiang Kai-shek (Chinese Army).   Message to President Roosevelt, December 9, 1941. Complete message was as follows: "In this tragic hour when you too are assailed by the treacherous aggressor the people of China renew their gratitude to the people of the United States for the understanding and help that have been given us.

"To our now common battle we offer *all we are and all we have* to stand with you until the Pacific and the world are freed from the curse of brute force and endless perfidy."—*Chiang Kai-shek. All We Are and All We Have. (pam.) p. 1*

"All Will Be Well": By Winston Churchill. Speech at the Guildhall, Hull, during a tour of the Northeastern cities of England, November 7, 1941. "I am sure that at the end *all will be well* for us in our island home, all will be better for the world."—*Churchill. The Unrelenting Struggle. p. 291*

Alligator: See L

Alpha (Beach): An arbitrary code name given to the segment of beach in southern France between Toulon and Nice when the Third Division with its attached 36th Engineer Regiment made an assault landing.—*U.S. Army. ETO. CONAD History. p. 374*

Always Ready, Join Today: Poster caption. United States Coast Guard

AMA: Agricultural Marketing Administration. Established by executive order of President Roosevelt February 23, 1942.—*World Almanac. 1943. p. 624*

America Calling, Take Your Place in Civilian Defense: Poster caption. United States Office for Emergency Management. Information Division

"America Cannot Remove Itself from the World": By Wendell Willkie. Speech before Women's National Republican Club, Hotel Astor, New York, January 8, 1941.—*Vital Speeches. February 1, 1941. p. 250*

"America Has Ordered Me to Defend the Philippines. I Must Not Fail America": By General Douglas MacArthur. President Roosevelt recalled General MacArthur (61) from retirement and ordered him to take command of all the armed forces of the Far East, July 26, 1941. MacArthur accepted in words as given above.—*Miller. General Douglas MacArthur, Fighter for Freedom. p. 189*

"America Held a Full House but We Had a Royal Flush": By Admiral Isoroku Yamamoto (Japanese Navy). Yamamoto was a poker player, so the message he sent back to Japan after the attack on Pearl Harbor was couched in poker lingo.—*Times-Union. Rochester, N.Y. May 21, 1943*

"**America Is Not Only the Cauldron of Democracy but the Incubator of Democratic Principles**": By Madame Chiang Kai-shek. Speech to House of Representatives, Washington, D.C., February 18, 1943.—*Vital Speeches. March 1, 1943. p. 301-2*

"**America Is on the March**": By John W. McCormack. Speech at Boston, Mass. on December 31, 1941.—*Vital Speeches. February 1, 1942. p. 244*

"**America Must Unite—Now. America Must Sacrifice—Now. America Must Work—Now**": By Joseph P. Kennedy. Former Ambassador to Great Britain. Radio address, January 18, 1941.—*Vital Speeches. February 1, 1941. p. 231*

"**American Armed Forces Must Be Used at Any Place in All the World**": By Franklin D. Roosevelt. Message to Congress January 6, 1942.—*Newsweek. January 19, 1942. p. 22*

"**America's Holy Grail Lies on Corregidor**": By General Douglas MacArthur. Declaration on the first anniversary of the surrender of the rock fortress in Manila Bay.—*Democrat & Chronicle. Rochester, N.Y. May 9, 1943*

AMET: Africa and Middle East Theater of Operations.—*New York Times. June 10, 1945. p. 2E, 6E*

AMGOT (AMG): Allied Military Government of Occupied Territory. Set up by British and United States armies in Sicily in July 1943, presumably the pattern of military government to be applied elsewhere as Axis territory was taken.—*Time. July 26, 1943. p. 35.* Name shortened to AMG, August 25, 1943, after it was discovered that AMGOT was an unprintable word in Turkish.—*New York Times. August 26, 1943*

Amigo: Spanish word for friend or comrade. Nickname given by Costa Ricans to Henry A. Wallace, Vice President of the United States, in recognition of the good will which they felt he bore toward them.—*Newsweek. March 29, 1943. p. 42*

Ammo: Abbreviated from the word ammunition and used very generally instead of the longer word in World War II.—*Nation. November 9, 1940. p. 447*

Amphibious Operations: Military operations during which the objective was approached by combined efforts of land, sea and air forces

"Amphibious Operations of a Peculiar Complexity and Hazard": By Winston Churchill. Speech delivered to House of Commons, London, June 8, 1943.—*Vital Speeches. June 15, 1943. p. 516*

Amphtrac: See L

Amvets: See AVC

ANGAU: Australian-New Guinea Administrative Unit. When the Australian-mandated islands of the Bismarck Archipelago fell to the Japanese in February 1942, Australia reorganized the administration of its remaining overseas territories. Southeastern New Guinea (Papua)and the former German possessions to the north were combined under Army control in the Australia-New Guinea Administrative Unit.—*Newsweek. May 8, 1944. p. 45*

"The Angels": Nickname of the 11th Army Airborne Division.—*Times-Union. Rochester, N.Y. August 25, 1945*

Angels of Bataan: Name given to U.S. Army nurses who served so courageously and unselfishly in the Bataan campaign and were afterward, until the liberation of Manila, subjected to three years of fearful misery as prisoners of the Japanese.—*American Notes and Queries. March 1945. p. 182*

ANMB: Army and Navy Munitions Board. Ordered supplies and granted priorities; WPB (q.v.), however, had final authority over allocations and could veto any demand of ANMB.—*Newsweek. August 10, 1942. p. 44*

Ann: The unaffectionate name given to the Anopheles mosquito, the insect that carries malaria, and against which the Army conducted a drastic campaign.—*Newsweek. October 23, 1944. p. 80*

Anschluss: Nazi term derived from the phrase *sich anschliessen*, meaning to join oneself. Used by the Nazis after the conquest of Austria (March 1938), with the implication that Austria had rallied freely to the Third Reich. Later used in English to describe the act of grabbing something which does not belong to you.—*New York Times Magazine. May 14, 1944. p. 2*

ANSCOL: Army-Navy Staff College

Anson: (British plane) Avro reconnaissance plane and bomber

Anti-G Suit: See G-Suit

Antipersonnel Mine: Introduced by the Germans in the fall of 1939. Its chief feature was an arrangement whereby the mine on being tripped was boosted out of the ground to about the height of a man's waist before exploding. It was really a bomb which sprayed a wide area with shrapnel.—*Reader's Digest. December 1942. p. 83*

Anvil: Code name for operation against southern France. Planned at the Quadrant Conference (q.v.). See also Dragon.—*General Marshall's Report. 1945. p. 18*

Any Bonds Today?: Song title. Words and music by Irving Berlin. Copyright by Henry Morgenthau, Jr., and widely used to stimulate the sale of war bonds and stamps

"Any Man or State Who Fights on Against Nazidom Will Have Our Aid": By Winston Churchill. Pledging support to Russia on the occasion of Germany's invasion of Russia; an address broadcast June 22, 1941.—*Churchill. Unrelenting Struggle. p. 172*

ANZAC: Australian and New Zealand Army Corps. Also nickname given to members of this corps; in World War I, specifically those who served in vicinity of the Gallipoli Peninsula. Though the term did not originate in World War II, it was widely used

Anzio Amble: A fast shuffle from one shelter to the next. Other terms which undoubtedly originated on the Anzio beachhead were Anzio anxiety (jitters, from the strain of danger); Anzio foot (when the scream of a shell suddenly turns you on another course); Anzio walk (jumping, twitching, dodging shells).—*American Speech. April 1945. p. 150*

Anzio Annie: A German rail gun that used to drop 10-inch shells into the famous Beachhead at Anzio.—*Saturday Review of Literature. November 3, 1945. p. 7*

Anzio Beachhead: Allied troops were landed on the Italian beach at Anzio, January 22, 1944, in an attempt to panic the Germans into pulling out of Cassino. The operation was a strategic failure. The Germans, with long range artillery, kept the beachhead under almost constant fire.—*Life. May 1, 1944. p. 31; Newsweek. June 5, 1944. p. 23*

APA: Auxiliary Personnel, Attack. Designation for Navy ships that carried troops to all the combat landings, from Africa to Okinawa. To distinguish among the many types of vessels in the fleet, the U.S. Navy employed a system of letter-designations. Many of these letter-designations began with "A," "L" or "P." The "A" stands for Auxiliary and was applied to all ships that serviced the fighting ships, fleet oilers, aircraft repair ships, and others. The APA is one of the most interesting of this "A" group. See also L; P.—*New York Times Magazine. October 21, 1945. p. 49*

Apache: (American plane) North American P-51 fighter plane

APM: American Peace Mobilization. Worked actively for United States neutrality prior to Germany's invasion of Russia. After the invasion in June 1941, the organization advocated aid to all nations fighting Germany. In August 1941, the APM changed its name to American People's Mobilization.—*Newsweek. August 4, 1941. p. 14*

Arctic Whiteout: A menace in far northern flying. Arctic whiteout is a condition of the snow country wherein all visible land features are camouflaged, blending earth and sky so that the horizon and all landmarks are indistinguishable. This condition was described by Leonard J. C. Hedine of the U.S. Weather Bureau at Winnemucca, Nev., and he recommended that the term Arctic whiteout be adopted as an officially recognized term for use in airway reports.—*Democrat & Chronicle, Rochester, N.Y. April 20, 1946. p. 1*

"Are We Through and Downhearted? Listen, You, We've Just Started": By Lieutenant Colonel Robert Herlong of Johnston, S.C., after his command had wiped out half a Nazi armored division.—*New York Times Magazine. January 7, 1945. p. 15*

Area Bombing: A widespread bombardment over a whole district to make it untenable by the enemy, an attempt to hit every part of a predetermined section of land. Also called saturation bombing.—*American Speech. December 1945. p. 299*

Armed Services Editions: Pocket-size books printed in a special format for the use, primarily, of men in the armed forces overseas. Sponsored by the Council on Books in Wartime, these books began to come from the presses in September 1943. They were designed to be strictly "expendable" and were printed in size small enough to go in pockets and in types easy to read. The range of titles was very wide. From September 1943 to September 1947, 122,923,388 volumes were issued to the Army and Navy. At the peak, 155,000 copies of 40 titles were produced every month. The total number of titles issued was 1324.—*Publishers' Weekly. Nov. 2, 1946. p. 2607-8; June 14, 1947. p. 2937*

Army Flash: In towns along the Atlantic seaboard, airplane spotter could say to telephone operator "Army Flash" and then be connected with the nearest air-raid information center.—*Newsweek. October 20, 1941. p. 34*

Army "Lids": Radio operators, so called because they "talk through their hats."—*Newsweek. March 10, 1941. p. 39*

Army-Navy "E": After Pearl Harbor and its demand for increased war production, there developed an awareness that our fighting forces and industry were partners. From the resolve to work and fight together came the Army-Navy Production Award, our fighting forces joint recognition of exceptional performance on the production front. —*E. K. Co. Kodak Flies the Battle Flag of War Production (pam.) no paging*

ARO: Airborne Range Only. Radar ranging set for use with various gun computors.—*Army and Navy Journal. August 18, 1945. p. 1534*

ARP: Air Raid Precautions, a branch of civilian defense. British ARP has been in effect since September 1938.—*Science News Letter. November 11, 1939. p. 311*

Arsenal of Democracy: See "We must be the great arsenal. . . ."

Arsop: See RSOP

Aryan: Scientific name applied to some of the peoples of Caucasian race and of the Indo-European language group. The Nazis transformed the term into an elastic expression embracing not only the tall, fair, blue-eyed Nordics but all active sympathizers with the Nazi regime—even short, black-haired Japanese.—*New York Times Magazine. May 14, 1944. p. 2*

A.S.F.: Army Service Forces. Originally called Services of Supply (S.O.S.), name was later changed to Army Service Forces, to conform with Army Ground Forces and Army Air Forces.—*Time. March 22, 1943. p. 51*

Ash Can: Depth bomb.—*American Speech. December 1944. p. 280*

Ashcan Patrol: Slang phrase to designate mine layers, units of the U.S. Army. The name was derived from the shape of the mines

ASTP: Army Specialized Training Program

ASV: Airborne Surface Vessel Detection. Airborne radar devices used to locate surface vessels and surfacing submarines.—*Army and Navy Journal. August 18, 1945. p. 1534*

"At the Price of Our Honor We Could Only Purchase a Precarious Peace Which Would Be Revocable": By Edouard Daladier at the outbreak of war in Europe. A speech made to the Chamber of Deputies, September 2, 1939.—*Vital Speeches. September 15, 1939. p. 712*

ATC: Air Transport Command. Started in June 1941, under name of Ferrying Command. Main function was to fly Lend-Lease aircraft to the United Kingdom. In April 1942, the Troop Carrier Command (TCC) was organized under the name of ATC, principal mission being to fly troops into combat. But the Ferrying Command grew so vastly and took on so many new duties after the United States entered the war, that it took over the name of the ATC and the old ATC became the TCC.—*New York Times Magazine. August 15, 1943. p. 15*

ATCOM: Atoll Commander in Pacific operations. Ulithi islands in the Pacific were taken over for an advanced base by U.S. troops in September 1943. For almost a year it was a military secret. Asor island in the group was the headquarters of the Atoll Commander, Commodore Oliver Owen Kessing.—*Time. August 6, 1945. p. 31*

Atheists in Fox Holes: See No atheists in fox holes

Atlantic Charter: In August 1941 Roosevelt and Churchill met on a battleship at sea and together wrote out the eight-point list of war aims that became known as the Atlantic Charter.—*Newsweek. April 23, 1945. p. 38*

Atlantic Wall: Name given to line of coastal defenses set up by the Nazis in France along the Channel coast for repelling the expected invasion of Europe by the Allies

Atomic Age: Name given to the period after August 6, 1945, the date on which the first atomic bomb was dropped on Hiroshima, Japan.—*American Speech. October 1946. p. 222*

Atomic Bomb: A bomblike device containing U235, one of the three physical forms of the element uranium, which, unlike the other kinds of uranium, has the faculty of splitting when an atomic particle known as a neutron strikes it and lodges within it. U235 in splitting gives off more neutrons and scatters them in all directions to break up more atoms, thus releasing more neutrons. Consequently a single starting neutron can set off a whole mass of U235, setting up a chain reaction and releasing enormous quantities of power. If the power is released quickly enough, the explosion is something like two million times as great as that of a similar amount of TNT.

Atomic bombs were released over Hiroshima, August 6, 1945, and over Nagasaki, August 9, 1945. The destruction of these two cities was so drastic that the Japanese came to terms and signed the un-conditional surrender presented to them by the Allies.—*Newsweek. August 20, 1945. p. 34*

Atomic Bomb Nicknames: The first, or Hiroshima bomb, was nicknamed "Little Boy." The second, or Nagasaki bomb, was called "Fat Boy." A third, which might have been used had the war con-tinued, was called "Big Boy."—*Newsweek. September 17, 1945. p. 44*

ATS: Army Transport Service

A.T.S: Auxiliary Territorial Service. The Auxiliary Territorial Service was the largest of Great Britain's three women's services at-tached to the fighting forces: the WRENS (q.v.), the W.A.A.F. (q.v.), and the A.T.S. A.T.S. was organized in 1938. Girls were recruited to replace soldiers as clerks, cooks, drivers, messengers, store keepers, etc. —*Anderson. British Women at War. p. 14-18*

ATTA Girls: Nickname given to British Women of the Air Transport Auxiliary—*Newsweek. December 1, 1941. p. 45*

"Attack and Attack": By Major General George S. Patton, Jr. Before American troops sailed for North Africa in the largest amphi-bious combat operation of the war General Patton gave the men a personal slogan, "We shall attack and attack until we are exhausted and then we shall attack again."—*Democrat & Chronicle. Rochester, N.Y. November 16, 1942*

Attack—and Vengeance!: Slogan of Torpedo 8 squadron. Pre-vious to the battle of Midway June 4, 1942, the slogan had been "At-tack." Afterwards, on June 12, 1942, the slogan was changed to "At-tack—and vengeance!"—*Wolfert. Torpedo 8. p. x*

"Attack, Attack, and Attack Again, Even When You Are on the Defensive": Motto of General Sir Harold R. L. G. Alexander (British Army).—*Newsweek. August 31, 1942. p. 25*

Aufbau: Monthly newspaper of German exile press; edited by Manfred George (New York City).—*Saturday Review of Literature. July 17, 1943. p. 3-4*

The Auk: Nickname of General Sir Claude Auchinleck, at one time Commander in Chief of the British forces in the Middle East.— *Current Biography. 1942. p. 46; Time. June 28, 1943. p. 26*

Aunt Jemima: During the war a high explosive was mixed with flour and smuggled to Chinese saboteurs behind the Jap lines. The mixture was called "Aunt Jemima."—*Newsweek. June 24, 1946. p. 17*

Auntie Mol: At the Yalta conference this nickname was given to Foreign Commissar Molotov, presumably to distinguish him from "Uncle Joe" Stalin.—*Newsweek. February 26, 1945. p. 42*

AUS: Army of the United States

Austus: Said to be a football game invented in Australia in 1943 by American and Australian soldier teams; the name was formed from the abbreviations of Australia and United States.—*American Notes and Queries. September 1944. p. 85*

Avalanche: Code name for invasion of Italian mainland.—*General Marshall's Report. 1945. p. 18*

AVC: American Veterans Committee. Organization for World War II corresponding to American Legion of World War I. Often called Amvets

Avenge December 7: Poster caption. United States Office of War Information. Division of Public Inquiries

Avenger: (American plane) Grumman TBF light bomber plane

AVG: American Flyers (Volunteer Group) under Brigadier General Claire Lee Chennault, in China. Also called Flying Tigers. Organized in the fall of 1941. This group ceased to be a unit of the Chinese army, July 4, 1942, and became a part of the United States Army Air Forces, 23d Pursuit Group.—*Newsweek. April 6, 1942. p. 20; July 6, 1942. p. 20; Time. June 8, 1942. p. 30; June 15, 1942. p. 23*

AWVS: American Women's Voluntary Services. Founded in 1940 by Mrs. Alice T. McLean. A permanent, national, voluntary organization which worked closely with all existing agencies and sought to supplement their work.—*World Almanac. 1943. p. 135*

Axis: An alliance entered into by two or more major powers to demonstrate their solidarity of interest and to insure collaboration and mutual support in foreign policies; specifically, the Rome-Berlin axis of the fascist bloc;—from an application by Benito Mussolini in a speech at Milan on November 2, 1936.—*Webster's New International Dictionary. 1943. p. xcvii*

B-2: GI term for strange planes, from the phrase "be too bad if they are not friendly."—*New York Herald Tribune, September 11, 1944*

"B2H2" Plan: Ball-Burton-Hill-Hatch resolution calling for United Nations' cooperation in waging the war, planning post-war rehabilitation, and setting up an international police force to keep the peace. Nicknamed "B2H2" by Washington reporters. Resolution was presented to the Senate by the four Senators: Joseph H. Ball, Harold H. Burton, Lister Hill, Carl A. Hatch.—*Newsweek. March 29, 1943. p. 25*

"The B-29's Are Changing the Name of Tokyo Harbor to 'Bomb' Bay": By Walter Winchell on a Jack Benny radio program December 3, 1944

BABS: Blind Approach Beacon System. System for approaching landing field by radar means.—*Army and Navy Journal. August 18, 1945. p. 1534*

Baby Blitz: Name given by Londoners to renewed bombings in the spring of 1944. Londoners called it the Baby Blitz but it was only "Baby" by comparison with the 2,000- and 3,000-ton assaults by Allied bombers on German cities.—*Newsweek. April 10, 1944. p. 24*

Baby Flat-top: Navy's name for a craft classed as a combatant carrier converted or built from a merchant hull. On July 16, 1943, there was released in the newspapers a story of an attack by a "baby flat-top" on eleven U-boats. See CVE

Baby Leave: Furloughs applied for by British Tommies who had been stationed overseas for two or three years and who wanted to return to England to become fathers.—*American Notes and Queries. October 1944. p. 101*

Back the Attack—Buy More Than Ever Before: Slogan selected to advertise the Fifth War Loan Drive, June 1944.—*New York Times Magazine. June 11, 1944. p. 20*

Back the Attack—With War Bonds: Slogan used to advertise the Third War Loan Drive, September 1943.

Bad Show: See Good Show

Baedeker Raids: Phrase used in the English press on April 29 or 30, 1942. German officials made the statement that the Luftwaffe in attacking Bath, Norwich, etc., were deliberately aiming to destroy buildings of high historic interest, as listed in the Baedeker guide books. Official German bulletin described these as "reprisal raids"— reprisals for raids on Cologne and Lubeck. English newspapers accordingly styled the raids immediately following (on Exeter, Norwich, York, etc.) as "Baedeker Raids." *American Notes and Queries. December 1942. p. 138*

Bail Out: To leave an airplane in mid-air and come to earth by parachute

"Bail-out" Ration: Smallest and most compact of all emergency rations, this was composed of a bar of D-Ration (q.v.) chocolate, dextrose tablets, concentrated bouillon, and chewing gum. It weighed only 8¼ ounces and would fit into the shirt pocket of an airman or paratrooper. See also C-Ration, K-Ration.—*Hoffmann. Feeding Our Armed Forces. p. 56*

Bailey Bridge: A hooked span likened to a "huge Meccano set," used to advantage by the allies in North African operations and now identified as one of the important pieces of equipment for the invasion of the Continent; invented by Donald Coleman Bailey, English civil engineer (CP dispatch from London, February 23, 1944).— *American Notes and Queries. March 1944. p. 181*

Baka: Japanese rocket bomb piloted by a "suicide" pilot. American forces gave these kamikaze suicide planes and pilots the nickname Baka (Japanese for stupid or foolish). Other less formal nicknames were Booby Wagon, Loony Joe, and Highpockets.—*Newsweek. May 7, 1945. p. 46*

Baksheesh: AAF slang for an easy mission; no enemy encountered

BAL: British Anti-lewisite. Ointment for treatment of eye injury from lewisite gas; a secret formula developed in England in 1942. Tests show it to be effective in treating arsenic dermatitis, systemic arsenic and mercury poisoning.—*Newsweek. October 15, 1945. p. 86; December 10, 1945. p. 100*

Bale Out: British spelling for Bail Out (q.v.)

Balloon Cargo: Air Force slang for collapsible cargo requiring loading in the upper holds of vessels. Most Air Corps cargo was balloon cargo.—*American Speech. October 1945. p. 226*

Balloon House: Concrete igloo home, offered as possible answer to housing shortage since they can be built at the rate of 200 in 90 days. The basic construction tool is a balloon which builders inflate, then spray with sand and concrete. The balloon is then deflated and removed, leaving a shell of solid concrete.—*Newsweek. November 24, 1941. p. 44; Popular Science. March 1942. p. 68*

Balloon Juice: Nickname for helium.—*New York Times Magazine. November 21, 1943. p. 39*

Balls of Fire: See Foo-fighters

Baltimore: (American plane) Martin A-30 bomber plane

Bamboo Network; or, Bamboo Network Fresh Air Broadcasting Company: A program of broadcasts recorded in the CBI theater of operations from actual engagements and activities and then broadcast in the U.S.A. over the Blue Network.—*Newsweek. September 25, 1944. p. 96*

Bams: The almost universal term used by GI's to refer to women marines. The derivation is not printable! (So I was told, but "any marine could tell you." Ed.)

Banana Dollar: Japanese dollar (now worthless) in Singapore; so called because of the banana design on the notes. (AP dispatch from Singapore, September 10, 1945.)—*American Notes and Queries. September 1945. p. 87*

Band: A range of wave lengths or frequencies (radar).—*Army and Navy Journal. August 18, 1945. p. 1534*

Bandit at Four Angels: Radar code language. "Bandit" meant identified enemy aircraft, and "Angels" indicated feet in thousands; thus "Bandit at four angels" would mean to a pilot "Enemy plane sighted at 4000 feet."—*Newsweek. September 10, 1945. p. 92*

Bandits: AAF slang for enemy planes

Banshee: (American plane) Douglas A-24. First dive bomber to be ordered by the Air Forces. The Banshee is an Army version of the Navy's SBD Dauntless

Banzai: (Japanese "ten thousand years"). The victory cry of Japanese warriors.—*New York Times Magazine. December 2, 1945. p. 22*

BAR: Browning Automatic Rifle.—*American Speech. December 1946. p. 246*

Barrack Wacky: See Shell-shock

Barrage: Concentrated artillery fire, usually aimed to strike in front of advancing infantry troops to protect them and to drive the enemy back. An anti-aircraft barrage is a barrier of fire sent up to intercept the flight of enemy planes

Bash: Slang. See entry under Kriegie

Basilisk: One of the names given to Reinhard Heydrick, former deputy director of the German State Secret Police.—*Newsweek. June 15, 1942. p. 39*

Basin-hat: English term for a metal helmet. Also called bassinet and battle bowler.—*American Speech. February 1944. p. 6*

Bastards: See Robot Bombs

Bat: Radar-guided bomb developed by U.S. Navy; it is guided electronically from a mother plane and follows its target until it strikes.—*American Notes and Queries. April 1946. p. 7*

"Bataan": Word chosen by General Douglas MacArthur as the code designation for Japanese surrender negotiations.—*Times-Union. Rochester, N.Y. August 16, 1945.* Bataan was also the name of the transport plane in which MacArthur arrived in Japan, there to direct the occupation and surrender.—*Democrat & Chronicle. Rochester, N.Y. August 30, 1945*

Bataan Death March: See March of Death

"Bataan Has Fallen, but the Spirit That Made It Stand—a Beacon to All the Liberty-Loving Peoples of the World—Cannot Fall!": Radio report of the fall of Bataan, from the tunnel on Corregidor, by Third Lieutenant Norman Reyes, one of Colonel Romulo's assistants.—*Romulo. I Saw the Fall of the Philippines. p. 302*

"Bataan Was Starved into Collapse": By General Douglas MacArthur. Statement on first anniversary of the fall of Bataan.—*Times-Union. Rochester, N.Y. April 9, 1943*

Battered Helmets: See "We lift our battered helmets. . . ."

Batting the Breeze: Slang meaning "talking things over." Same as Shooting the breeze

Battle Bowler: See Basin-hat

Battle for a Road: Name given to the region through which the Ledo (or Stilwell) Road was being built in Burma. The road was a military necessity, and the fighting that made the road possible brought with it the liberation of Burma.—*Miller. History of World War II. p. 62*

"The Battle of Britain Is About to Begin": By Winston Churchill. Speech delivered before the House of Commons, June 18, 1940.—*Vital Speeches. July 1, 1940. p. 562*

"Battle of the Atlantic": By A. V. Alexander, First Lord of the Admiralty. Said of Nazi raids on shipping: "We must impress upon both employers and workers that in facing the Battle of the Atlantic, now opening, we need every ounce of their energy in ever-increasing production." When he spoke thus, on March 5, 1941, the Battle of the Atlantic already was well under way.—*Newsweek. March 17, 1941. p. 27*

Battle of the Bulge: On December 16, 1944, the Germans in a counter-attack against the invading forces drove westward into Luxembourg and Belgium, establishing a salient 40 or 50 miles deep into the Allied front. A fierce battle resulted as the Allies worked to cut off these German troops and regain the lost territory. The German advance into Belgium was called the Bulge, and later the whole action was termed the Battle of the Bulge.—*New York Times. January 7, 1945. p. 1E; Democrat & Chronicle. Rochester, N.Y. December 22, 1945*

The Battle of the Laboratories: Name given by President Truman to the race between Allied and Nazi scientists to perfect the atom bomb.—*Newsweek. August 13, 1945. p. 30*

Battleship: Navy's nickname for a discharge certificate.—*Fox. Blind Adventure. p. 181*

Bazooka: Nickname given by soldiers to a new anti-tank gun. Used rocket method of propulsion, was operated by two men. One soldier loaded and aimed it, and the other, who fired it, carried it on his shoulder. Army officials declared it capable of destroying any enemy tank.—*Popular Mechanics. August 1943. p. 12.* Name came from a similarity (in soldiers' eyes) of the gun to the freak musical instrument invented by Bob Burns and used by him on the radio.—*Notes and Queries. May 19, 1945. p. 215; American Speech. December 1946. p. 245*

B Bag: A column in the soldier newspaper *Stars and Stripes* where letters from soldiers are printed. A good place in which to air grievances.—*New York Times Magazine. March 18, 1945. p. 24*

"B.B.B." Program: Best Berlin Broadcast. Title of a radio program broadcast from Berlin by Robert H. Best, formerly a South Carolina journalist. Mr. Best at first concealed his identity under the name of Mr. Guess-Who and in his broadcasts referred to himself as a "crusader" and urged his listeners to form a militant anti-war, anti-Roosevelt, and anti-Jewish party. He was indicted for treason July 26, 1943 by the District of Columbia Grand Jury. Robert Best was arrested at Villach in February 1946, in the British-occupied zone of Austria by Allied authorities and turned over to American officers for return to the United States to stand trial as a traitor.—*Christian Science Monitor magazine. July 18, 1943. p. 6; Newsweek. February 25, 1946. p. 67-8*

Be a Marine . . . Free a Marine to Fight: Poster caption. United States Marine Corps Women's Reserve

Be the Woman behind the Man behind the Gun. Buy War Stamps Here Today: Poster caption

Beachhead: A position established and fortified on enemy territory by an invasion force.—*American Speech. April 1942. p. 121-2.*

Beam: A constant unidirectional radio signal transmitted from a flying field for the guidance of pilots. 'On the beam' became used as a slang expression meaning on the right track, right, sane; 'off the beam' meant off the track, wrong, insane.—*American Speech. February 1943. p. 63*

Bearded Lady: British slang for a searchlight whose rays were diffused. See also Paul Pry.—*Nation. November 9, 1940. p. 446*

Beast of Belsen: Josef Kramer, former commander of the Belsen concentration camp, notorious for the frightful atrocities committed there.—*American Notes and Queries. October 1945. p. 104*

Beat-up: Army slang phrase applied to anything damaged, worn out or of unimpressive appearance. Of a person it meant one who was completely tired or exhausted. This latter use was also common among civilians

Beat Up: R.A.F. slang meaning to dive on a friendly flying field for practice, a gesture of triumph or sheer joie-de-vivre.—*American Speech. February 1941. p. 76*

Beat Your Gums: Slang phrase meaning to talk a lot.—*American Speech. April 1945. p. 147*

Beaufighter: (British plane) Bristol fighter plane. Somewhat of a cross between the Blenheim and the Beaufort

Beaufort: (British plane) Bristol bomber, reconnaissance and general purpose plane. Used as a mine layer for the Coastal Command

Beaver: Nickname for the LCM-3, popularized by workers at the Warren City Manufacturing Company, Warren, Ohio, who regarded the barge as "sturdy, hard-working, fast-traveling"; and its landing ramp, they said, "like a beaver's tail, slaps down at the moment for action."—*American Notes and Queries. July 1944. p. 54*

Beaverburgers: See Hamburgers

Because We Care: Slogan chosen by retail merchants for use in a newspaper campaign for the Victory Loan of October 29 to December 8, 1945.—*Democrat & Chronicle. Rochester, N.Y. August 31, 1945*

Become a Nurse, Your Country Needs You: Poster caption. United States Public Health Service

Bedpan Commando: Slang for medical corps man.—*American Speech. April 1945. p. 147*

Beedle: Nickname of Lieutenant General Walter Bedell Smith, Eisenhower's Chief of Staff.—*New York Times Magazine. January 21, 1945. p. 26. Saturday Evening Post. June 8, 1946. p. 9* gives nickname as Beetle

Beehives: Pronged packages of explosives constructed on the principle of a bazooka shell; used by the British in blasting the Japanese out of Mandalay, placed over the tunnels and caves in which the enemy was hiding out.—*American Notes and Queries. April 1945. p. 7*

Bee Ko—"Plain Mister Bee": Japanese nickname for the American B-29 Superfortress (according to the Japanese news agency Domei).—*American Notes and Queries. May 1945. p. 22; Newsweek. May 28, 1945. p. 37*

Beep: See Jeep

Beepers: Nickname for drone-controlled planes. In August 1946, two drone B-17 bombers were flown by remote control from Hilo, Hawaii, to California, the longest completely unmanned flight to date.—*Democrat & Chronicle. Rochester, N.Y. August 7, 1946. p. 1*

Beetle Tanks: Midget crewless (radio-controlled) Nazi tanks, said to make twenty miles an hour; used first in Russia and then at the Anzio beachhead.—*Newsweek. March 13, 1944. p. 28*

"Beginning of the End": By Winston Churchill. In a speech given at the Lord Mayor's dinner at the Mansion House, London, November 10, 1942, Churchill said: "Now, this is not the end. It is not even the beginning of the end. But it is, perhaps, the end of the beginning." This is very similar to a statement made in an unsigned article in the *Economist* of June 1942: "Although this is not the end, it can be the beginning of the end." Shakespeare also used a similar phrase "That is the true beginning of our end" in *A Midsummer Night's Dream* (Act V, Sc. 1), and in 1815 the French statesman Talleyrand said in regard to the Hundred Days period during which occurred the Battle of Waterloo, "It is the beginning of the end" (C'est le commencement de la fin).—*Economist. June 13, 1942. p. 813; Vital Speeches. November 15, 1942. p. 66; New York Times Magazine. October 31, 1943. p. 2*

La Belgique Independante: Weekly Belgian magazine in exile; published in Britain.—*Saturday Review of Literature. July 17, 1943. p. 5*

Belgium: Monthly Belgian magazine in exile; published by Belgian Press Association (New York).—*Saturday Review of Literature. July 17, 1943. p. 5*

Belly Tank: Auxiliary gasoline tank under the belly or wing of a plane. It could be released if necessary to lighten the load.—*Britannica Book of the Year. 1946. p. 833*

Berlin Will Rise Again: Song heard sung in a Berlin night club soon after VE-day. The lyrics predicted the resurrection of practically everything except Adolf Hitler.—*Democrat & Chronicle. Rochester, N.Y. June 12, 1945. p. 1*

Bermuda: (American plane) Brewster A-34 SB2A bomber plane

"Better Buy One Bomber Than Be Buried on Bataan": Slogan of the United States and Filipino troops under General Douglas MacArthur during the siege of Bataan. Troops agreed to contribute as much as a month's pay per man to a "Bomber for Bataan" fund.—*Time. March 9, 1942. p. 20*

Betty: Name of a Japanese bomber plane.—*Newsweek. December 25, 1944. p. 10*

BEW: In July, 1941, President Roosevelt created a Board of Economic Defense, somewhat on the order of the Ministry of Economic Warfare (British). On December 17, 1941, the name was changed to Board of Economic Warfare, BEW or EWB. See also OEW.—*Newsweek. March 16, 1942. p. 31-2*

Big Ben: Navy name for the aircraft carrier Franklin.—*Newsweek. May 28, 1945. p. 42*

Big Boy: See Atomic Bomb nicknames

The Big E: Nickname given by its crew to the aircraft carrier Enterprise. When sailors of the Essex tried to steal the nickname for their newer, larger carrier, and tried to call the Enterprise "The Little E," Enterprise men (being proud of their ship's achievements, definitely not in the "little" class) beat them up.—*Newsweek. October 22, 1945. p. 64*

Big Friends: AAF slang for bombers. See also Little Friends

Big Inch; Little Big Inch: A pipeline 1,254 miles long which during the war carried an endless stream of oil (500,000 barrels daily) from Texas to the Atlantic Seaboard.—*Newsweek. September 24, 1945. p. 72*

Big Time Operator: Prisoner of war slang for a prisoner who traded various items until he finished with more than he started with. —*Democrat & Chronicle. Rochester, N.Y. February 22, 1945*

Big Wheel: Air Force slang for anyone with a little authority. —*American Speech. October 1945. p. 226*

Bigot: An arbitrary general code word to denote highly secret material, such as invasion plans.—*U.S. Army. ETO. CONAD History. p. 374*

Bing Bang Corner: Dover, the most bombarded region of England, was known as "Bing Bang Corner." See also Hell's Corner.— *New York Herald Tribune. May 20, 1944*

Bird of Paradise: Another name for the discharge button. See also Ruptured Duck.—*American Speech. April 1946. p. 153*

Biscuit Blast: Damage caused to teeth when hungry soldiers crunched down on nutritious but refractory "dog biscuit" in the army's K-ration; term coined by Captain Sam V. Pecora, of Beaumont, Texas, and other dental officers (AP dispatch from Normandy, July 4, 1944).—*American Notes and Queries. July 1944. p. 54*

Black Cats: Nickname for Navy Catalina Flying Boats, so called because of their black paint and nocturnal habits. Another nickname was Dumbo. They were used to spot enemy radar. See also Ferret.—*Joint Board, OSRD, War Dept., Navy Dept. Electronics Warfare. 1945. p. 32; Newsweek. April 9, 1945. p. 10*

Black Caviar: Soldiers' name for globular ball powder produced in East Alton, Ill. Made by a new process under water, it was turned out in one fifth the time required to make ordinary smokeless powder.—*American Notes and Queries. August 1943. p. 70*

Black Devils: Reported to be the Nazi name for the joint American-Canadian First Special Service Force, trained not only in snow, amphibious, and mountain warfare but in infantry tactics; a limited and picked group—cowpunchers, miners, trappers, lumberjacks (AP dispatch from southern France, August 21, 1944).—*American Notes and Queries. August 1944. p. 70*

Black Market. This term cropped up in European dispatches in 1939. It referred to the practice of hoarding goods and selling them above ceiling prices. The dishonorable practice of black markets in Europe dates back before the war in the juggling of international currencies (notably in the period of Germany's inflation, 1923-1924). However, the term became a household word, and black markets a very real menace to the "man in the street" and to his wife and family during World War II

Black Marketeer: Person selling in black markets. Term appeared as a headline in *PM* May 3, 1943

Black Widow: (American plane) Northrop P-61 fighter plane

Blacketeer: A person who operates a black market.—*Time. March 9, 1942. p. 29*

Blackout: A blacking out of lights of an area, village, town or city as protection against enemy aircraft and bombing. The blackout in London was lifted in April 1945 after 2,061 nights of dangerous and distressing darkness. In the United States practice blackouts were held at intervals so that areas would be prepared in case bombing threatened and real blackouts should be made necessary. See also Brownout, Dimout. The term Blackout also signified fainting, resulting from dive-bombing, and later, fainting from other causes.—*New York Times, April 29, 1945. p. 7E; New York Times Magazine. December 2, 1945. p. 22; American Speech. April 1942. p. 122*

Blackout practice was widespread in this global war, called by other names in countries other than English-speaking: Arabia—Atimme (pronounced Ah-timm-ah with accent on first syllable); Belgium—Occultation (French) and Occultatië (Flemish); Bohemia—Zatemniti; Chile—Obscurecimiento; China—In Cantonese dialect the transliterated form is pronounced Dun faw gwoon tsai (combining the characters for *light* and *control*); Costa Rica—Oscurecimiento or Obscurecimiento; Czechoslovakia—Zatemněni'; Denmark—Mørkelaegning; Estonia—Pimendus; Finland—Pimennys; France—Obscurcissement (in France the English term *blackout* was used in conversational French); Germany—Verdunkelung; for a practice blackout the word was Verdunkelungsübungen; for a partial blackout—beschränkte Verdunkelung; for blackout measures—Verdunklungs-massnahmen; Greece—Photósvesis; Japan—Toka kansei, or Shōtō ("Put out the lights!"); Mexico—Obscurecimiento; Netherlands—Verduistering; Norway—Mörklegning; Peru—Apaga luces; Poland—Pelne zaciemnienie (meaning full dimout); Portugal—No word that could be literally translated "blackout" has yet been coined. Pôr a cidade ás escuras ("to put the city in the dark") was the phrase in common use; Puerto Rico—Obscurecimiento; Russia—Zatemnénie; Spain—Obscurecimiento; colloquially it might be Apagón; and historically, in florid language, one might use the old and traditional Spanish expression hora de queda; Sweden—Mörkläggning; Switzerland—Verdunkelung; Turkey—Pasif korunma için karartma; Yugoslavia—Zamračenje (pronounced Zah-mrah-tchay-nyai).—*American Notes and Queries. October 1942. p. 99-100; December 1942. p. 142*

British phrase for drawing the blackout curtains was "one does the blackout."—*American Speech. December 1944. p. 294*

Blank-Eyed Dragon: Nickname of General Adrian Carton De Wiart. He was serving as Winston Churchill's personal representative to Chiang Kai-shek and was given the nickname by the Chinese. He lost an eye before World War I, and wears a black patch, hence the nickname.—*New York Herald Tribune News Week. August 27, 1944. p. 9*

Blastard: See Robot Bombs

Bleater: Prisoner of war slang meaning an habitual complainer.—*Democrat & Chronicle. Rochester, N.Y. February 22, 1945*

Blenburger: See Plane Nicknames

Blenheim: (British plane) Bristol medium bomber reported to have been used as a special night fighter

BLIP: Term applied to "echo" presented on cathode ray tube (radar).—*Army and Navy Journal. August 18, 1945. p. 1534*

Blister Club: See Walkout Club

Blitz or "The Blitz": The bombing of Britain which lasted from August 1940 until the end of May 1941. The term came from *Blitzkrieg,* a German word meaning literally "lightning-war," thus warfare waged at almost lightning speed.—*New York Times Magazine. October 3, 1944. p. 29*

This word was used also as a verb, to attack in the manner of the blitzkrieg. Instances of its use as a verb were noted in *American Speech. April 1941. p. 145*

Blitz Buggy. See Jeep

Blitz to Obliteration: See "It will be a long campaign. . . ."

Blitzkrieg: This German term appeared in the *Nation* on September 10, 1938, p. 240, with definition "lightning stroke." The word hit the popular imagination and appeared in innumerable forms and meanings—airblitz, blitzlizzies, blitz-rhythm and many others.—*Words. April 1940. p. 59; June 1941. p. 41-42; American Speech. February 1940. p. 110*

BLO: Bombardment Liaison Officer (pronounced "blow"). His function on a ship was the control of spotting and transmission of information to "Guns" (the gunnery officer) who then worked out the fire problems and corrections.—*Newsweek. November 13, 1944. p. 39*

Bloc(k): Code name for a television transmitter attached to a plane which enabled one to see what was going on 200 miles away. It was developed by the U.S. Navy in cooperation with the Radio Corporation of America and was used in life-saving and in actual battle.—*Britannica Book of the Year. 1947. p. 840*

Block Captain: A Civilian Defense officer in charge of the air wardens of a city block. It was his duty to head up Civilian Defense work, see that things went properly in air raid alarms, and to take care of any emergencies that might arise

Blockbuster: A large, highly effective bomb, powerful enough to wipe out a block—not a city block as meant in America, but rather a large modern building, as the British say 'a block of flats' or 'a block of offices.'—*American Speech. December 1944. p. 293; February 1944. p. 8*

Blood Bank: Blood plasma (whole blood from which the red cells have been separated, and which can be kept indefinitely) is of inestimable value in war time. French physicians had a plan for collecting blood from civilian donors in every province. In Spain twenty or more transfusion centers were in operation in 1938. In January 1941 the American Red Cross announced plans for a giant blood bank, which was planned to furnish thousands of liters of blood plasma solution to the British Red Cross for the treatment of war victims.—*Hygeia. February 1941. p. 107; Science News Letter. October 8, 1938. p. 232*

"Blood, Sweat, and Tears": By Winston Churchill. Speech in House of Commons May 13, 1940. After receiving a commission from the King to form a new administration, Churchill said "I would say to the House, as I said to those who have joined this government: 'I have nothing to offer but blood, toil, tears, and sweat.' "—*Churchill. Blood, Sweat and Tears. p. 276*

A similar phrase may be found in John Donne (1611) and Lord Byron (1823). Compare Donne—"Anatomie of the World," 1st Anniversary, line 430-31: "Mollifie it with thy teares, or sweat, or blood." Compare also Byron—"Age of Bronze," line 620-21: "Year after year they voted cent. for cent., Blood, sweat, and tear-wrung millions—why? for rent!"

Churchill himself used a similar phrase in his book *The Unknown War: the Eastern Front* (c1931, Scribner). On the first page, in reference to the Czarist Russian armies, he said "their sweat, their tears, their blood bedewed the endless plain."

An early American use appears in the writings of Thomas Branagan (1774-1843), an ardent opponent of slavery who ridiculed those "fair devotees" of philanthropy who, while declaiming against slavery, felt no qualms about using its products, but supped their tea, "sweetened . . . by the sweat, the blood, the tears of their own tender sex. . . ."—*American Notes and Queries. November 1943. p. 124-5*

Another example may be found in the life of the Marquis de Lafayette. In argument concerning the excessive taxes, he wrote: "The millions that are being dissipated are raised by taxes. . . . All these millions . . . are the price of the sweat, the tears, and it may be the blood of the people. . . ." *Latzko. La Fayette. p. 124-5*

The Bloodhound: Nickname of General Archibald Wavell (British general).—*Current Biography. 1941. p. 902*

"A Bloody Monument to Divided Responsibility": By Colonel Hugh J. Knerr, retired, onetime GHQ Army Air Force chief of staff. Above is his characterization of Pearl Harbor.—*American Mercury. June 1942. p. 648*

Bloody Nose Ridge: On Peleliu Island.—*Newsweek, October 2, 1944. p. 34*

Blue Circuit: The second of three USO Camp Shows circuits in the United States. The Blue Circuit was made up of "Tabloid Troupes" who could play anywhere. Small, mobile variety units, they performed indoors or out, with or without theaters. See also Hospital Circuit, Victory Circuit, and Foxhole Circuit.—*Newsweek. July 31, 1944. p. 60*

Blue Letter Mail: Letters which soldiers may not have wanted their immediate superiors to read (for censorship) were handled by the Base Censorship Detachment of Military Intelligence. Soldiers could send two of these a month.—*Newsweek. March 27, 1944. p. 57*

Blue Points: In rationing of food, "blue points" (paper coupons first, later tokens, small blue fibre discs) were necessary when buying certain processed foods, canned fruits and vegetables. See also Red Points

Blue Star Brigade: Name given to volunteers who sold war bonds from door to door in the Seventh War Loan Drive May-June, 1945.—*New York Times. May 20, 1945. p. 2E, 6E*

Bob Hopes: Bob 'Opes—nickname given to robot bombs by Cockney children in London. Apparently no connection with Bob Hope, American comedian. The children themselves explained it as "Bob down and 'ope for the best."—*American Notes and Queries. March 1945. p. 191*

Bobbing: In radar, the fluctuation of an echo on a scope because of alternating interference and reinforcement of returning waves reflected from objects.—*Army and Navy Journal. August 18, 1945. p. 1534*

Bobcat: (American plane) Cessna AT-8 and 17 trainer plane

Bogey: In radar code, an unidentified enemy aircraft.—*Newsweek. September 10, 1945. p. 92*

Bolo: (American plane) Douglas B-18 medium bomber plane

Bolona: A bombless night. The Germans devised the term, not an adaptation of baloney but made up of parts of two German words—bombenlose nacht, meaning bombless night.—*American Speech. February 1944. p. 8*

"Bomb and Keep Bombing until Brest Surrenders": Orders from General Dwight Eisenhower to pilots of American war planes.—*Democrat & Chronicle. Rochester, N.Y. September 4, 1944. p. 1*

Bomb Bay: That portion of the fuselage in an airplane where the bombs are lodged.—*American Speech. December 1945. p. 299*

Bomb-Boogie: Title of a new jitterbug dance.—*Newsweek. February 8, 1943. p. 69*

Bomb, Burn, Destroy: Anglo-American high command in secret sessions at Quebec, August 1943, planned ways to "bomb, burn and ruthlessly destroy" both Germany and Japan. Announcement of decision was made by Brendan Bracken, British Minister of Information. —*Democrat & Chronicle. Rochester, N.Y. August 20, 1943. p. 1*

Bomb Happy: See Shell-shock

Bomb Rack: Mechanism for holding and releasing bombs.— *Democrat & Chronicle. Rochester, N.Y. September 8, 1940*

Bomb Run: The course from a predetermined point on the ground (called "initial point" or I.P.) to the point where the bombs were released.—*American Speech. December 1945. p. 300*

Bomb Sight: Delicately adjusted optical mechanism for aiming bombs in rectification with air speed and trajectory.—*Democrat & Chronicle. Rochester, N.Y. September 8, 1940*

Bombardier: One who bombs, especially from aircraft. A previously obsolete word adapted to modern warfare. 'Bomb' was once synonymous with shell.—*American Speech. October 1942. p. 202, 203*

Bombardment: Nickname of Major General Harold L. George, Chief of the United States Army Air Transport Command.—*Current Biography. 1942. p. 292*

Bombay: (British plane) Bristol bomber and transport plane

Bomber's Moon: A moon full enough to give light for bombing operations.—*American Speech. December 1945. p. 300*

Bomphlet: Propaganda leaflet dropped by air in enemy territory. Word was coined by A. P. Herbert (British author). Bomphleteer was the term applied to airmen engaged on the pamphlet raids in the early days of the war.—*American Speech. February 1944. p. 8*

A Bond in Every Kitchen; Preserve Your Freedom, Too: Slogan used by Women's Division of the War Finance Committee of Rochester, N.Y. in the Third War Loan Drive. Advertising in downtown booths featured bonds in glass fruit jars. The drive came in the autumn at canning time.— *Democrat & Chronicle. Rochester, N.Y. September 28, 1943. p. 16*

Bondadiers: Nickname given to volunteer workers in Third War Loan Drive. Term appeared in a news story August 26, 1943.— *American Notes and Queries. September 1943. p. 87*

Bonds: United States defense bonds were issued by the United States Government to raise money for defense. In April 1942, the name was changed to U.S. War Savings bonds, but they were commonly called just "War Bonds." After VE and VJ days, the name was again changed, and they were called "Victory Bonds."

Boobed It: R.A.F. slang. He boobed it meant "he made a mess of it."—*American Speech. February 1941. p. 76*

Booby Trap: Webster's dictionary defines this as a school boy trick—"a trap made by placing a receptacle containing water over a door in such a way as to drench any person as he opens the door." As used in World War II, it was any sinister trap used by the Nazis and Japanese to kill Allied soldiers. It took many forms, one being mines placed under bodies of dead or wounded soldiers. The mines would explode when the bodies were moved

Booby Wagon: See Baka

Books Are Bullets: Phrase coined by Council on Books in Wartime (q.v.) Quoted in *Saturday Review of Literature*, March 27, 1943. p. 20. Also used as title of a weekly radio program (1943) headed by Bennett Cerf.—*Saturday Review of Literature. March 6, 1943. p. 17*

Books Are Weapons in the War of Ideas: This phrase was chosen by the Council on Books in Wartime (q.v.) as their official slogan. *Ballou. A History of the Council on Books in Wartime. p. 6*

Books Cannot Be Killed by Fire . . . Books Are Weapons in the War of Ideas: Poster caption. United States Office of War Information. Division of Public Inquiries

Boot: Nickname for an apprentice seaman, so called from the puttees which he wears

Boot Camp: Training process for Marines. Marine inductees are called "Boots" and "it is Marine Corps custom to send them all through a grim process called 'boot camp.' "—*Bailey. Boot; a Marine in the Making. Foreword*

Boot Hill: Hill 89, last stronghold of the defeated Japanese army on Okinawa; so called by Colonel M. M. Finn, commander of the Thirty-second Regiment of the Seventh Division, because so many booted Japanese toes could be seen sticking up from the soil.—*American Notes and Queries. June 1945. p. 39*

Boot Training: Course of training given to Navy recruits at the various United States Naval Training Stations

Boston: (American plane) Douglas A-20A. Designed as a medium bomber, it was used with great success for both fighting and bombing

Botha: (British plane) Blackburn reconnaissance torpedo-carrying bomber plane

Bottleneck: An impasse in production or movement of men or matériel.—*New York Times Magazine. December 2, 1945. p. 22*

Boy Browning: Nickname of Major General Frederick A. M. Browning (British Army).—*Current Biography. June 1943. p. 1*

Boyington's Bastards: Nickname for the famous Black Sheep squadron under Lieutenant Colonel Gregory Boyington, Marine flying ace.—*Newsweek. September 24, 1945. p. 33*

The Brass: Slang term for officer. "GI" almost invariably denoted an enlisted man. Officers were usually called "the brass" or, if of high rank, "the big brass."—*American Speech. December 1946. p. 248*

Brassed Off: See Browned Off

Breakneck Ridge: Name given to a ridge on Leyte Island in the Philippines.—*New York Times. November 19, 1944. p. 2E, 6E*

Bridgehead: A position established at a bridge or ford of a river in offensive or defensive action against the enemy.—*American Speech. April 1942. p. 122*

Briefing Room: Room in which pilots are "briefed," i.e. receive their instructions for air raids over enemy territory

"Brighter and Solid Prospects Lie before Us": By Winston Churchill. Speech in House of Commons, June 1943, after his return from North Africa.—*Newsweek. June 21, 1943. p. 23*

"Bring Back Daddy" Clubs: Two hundred or more such clubs, scattered over the country, were organized to send appeals to the House and Senate Military Affairs Committees to have the fathers returned from Germany. Many of the appeals were sent in on baby shoes. These shoes were turned over by the House and Senate members to relief and welfare organizations.—*Newsweek. January 21, 1946. p. 62*

Britannia: Nickname of Commander Mildred H. McAfee. So called because she "rules the Waves."—*Newsweek. October 5, 1942. p. 40*

British War Relief Society: Organized in December 1939 for the sending of aid of various kinds to civilians in Britain.—*Survey. September 1942. p. 232*

Brock's Benefit: Destroyers closing in on the German battle-cruiser "Scharnhorst," were said to have given her a "Brock's Benefit of a tracer" (Brock's Crystal Palace fireworks were once a fabulously popular London spectacle). The battle with the "Scharnhorst" took place December 26, 1943.—*Saturday Evening Post. March 25, 1944. p. 9; American Notes and Queries. April 1944. p. 8*

Brotherhood of Bi-Ocean Bipeds: Club formed by American infantrymen who served in the Panama Zone. Membership was limited to those men who tramped from the Atlantic to the Pacific over the Isthmus.—*American Notes and Queries. February 1946. p. 176*

"Brothers Our Country Is in Your Hands": By Marshal Timoshenko (Russian army).—*Mehring. Timoshenko, Marshal of the Red Army. p. 137*

Brown Shirts: See note on SA under SS

Brown Underground: Reported to be a Nazi organization of loyal party members formed to conduct postwar resistance and the propagation of Nazi philosophy. *American Notes and Queries. March 1945. p. 182*

Browned Off: R.A.F. slang meaning fed up. Other similar phrases were Brassed off—very fed up, and Cheesed off—utterly disgusted. Browned off originated in the British Army in India about 1932. Cheesed off was probably suggested by browned off, the link being the brown rind of cheese, and brassed off was originally a naval term, derived from the excessive and continuous polishing of the ship's brasswork. Cheesed off in the R.A.F. became the favorite of the three phrases.—*Reader's Digest. May 1940. p. 39; American Speech. February 1941. p. 76; Nineteenth Century. April 1944. p. 184*

Brownie: Slang term for a person who was always asking and answering questions in an army class to impress the instructor; also a person who stayed after class to try to insinuate himself into the teacher's good graces.—*American Speech. April 1945. p. 147*

Brownout: Blackout regulations were eased in New York City in November 1943, but many firms were undecided as to how far to go in lighting up. The *New York Herald Tribune* (November 3, 1943) in a headline referred to the "'Brilliancy' of Brownout." Brownout, obviously enough, was a mild form of Blackout.—*American Notes and Queries, November 1943. p. 127*

BTO: Bombing through overcast. Radar equipment which made it possible for bombers to locate targets, no matter how adverse were the weather conditions. The British pilots called their set "Stinky." Our nickname was "Mickey."—*Newsweek. August 20, 1945. p. 42*

Bubble Dancing: Army slang for dishwashing.—*Good Housekeeping. December 1942. p. 11*

Bucats:. See CATS

Buccaneer: (American plane) Brewster A-34 SB2A light dive bomber plane

Buck Rogers: See VT Fuse

Buck Slip: A general term in the Army and some commercial firms for a slip of paper on which certain information is requested from another department or office. The information is usually returned on the same slip. Term probably came from the phrase "passing the buck."—*American Speech. October 1945. p. 226*

Bucking for Section 8: The verb 'to buck' in army slang meant to work hard to qualify for a higher rank, an assignment, a transfer, to cram for an examination, etc. A soldier who made many mistakes or continually got into trouble was said to be "bucking for Section 8"

(discharge for military ineptitude). See also Section 8.—*American Speech. October 1941. p. 164; April 1945. p. 147; Colby. Army Talk. p. 34-5*

Buddy Sheet: Term used at Infantry Officer Candidate School, Fort Benning, Georgia, to designate the more formal Student Rating Form, on which each student numerically rated and commented on all the other students in his section. The word "buddy" was used ironically, for the men were encouraged to be entirely frank in the reports, which were confidential.—*American Speech. December 1945. p. 263*

Buffalo: (American plane) Brewster F2A fighter plane

Buffaloburger: "Hamburger" made of buffalo meat; popularized in New York City to help solve wartime meat shortages (buffalo, as game, was not rationed).—*American Notes and Queries. July 1945. p. 54*

Buffaloes: Huge armored amphibious vehicles capable of carrying soldiers and weapons

Bug: See Jeep

Bulge: Area retaken by Germany in a counterattack on the western front. See also Battle of the Bulge

The Bull: Nickname of Lieutenant General Simon Bolivar Buckner, Jr.—*Newsweek. July 2, 1945. p. 33*

The Bull Moose: Nickname of Lieutenant Colonel Julian Frisbie (United States Marine Corps).—*Hersey. Into the Valley. p. 63*

Bumble bomb: See Robot Bomb

Buna: A synthetic rubber developed in Germany, made by polymerization of butadiene.—*Webster's New International Dictionary. 1943. p. xcviii*

Bundles for America: On January 26, 1942, Mrs. Latham, head of Bundles for Britain (q.v.), announced a nation-wide organization to be known as Bundles for America. This organization was to supply knitted garments and comfort kits to members of the U.S. Armed Services and the Merchant Marine. This organization was suggested by the President's Committee on War Relief Agencies in Washington. Bundles for America took over the work formerly carried on by Bundles for Bluejackets (q.v.).—*New York Times. January 27, 1942. p. 15*

Bundles for Bluejackets: On November 24, 1941, Mrs. Latham, head of Bundles for Britain (q.v.), announced a separate organization to be known as Bundles for Bluejackets, to aid sailors of the U.S. Navy and the Merchant Marine. The organization had been functioning since July 1941 as a division of Bundles for Britain. The new group was to concentrate principally on sending to sailors garments knitted according to Navy specifications. Functions of this group were later taken over by Bundles for America (q.v.).—*New York Times. November 25, 1941. p. 29*

Bundles for Britain: Mrs. Wales Latham organized a group of women to aid Britain; registered the above name for the group with the State Dept. Mrs. Winston Churchill acted as honorary sponsor. New York Bundles for Britain Headquarters opened January 15, 1940.—*New Yorker. April 19, 1941. p. 23*

Bunk Fatigue: The art of resting on one's bed. The term was compounded of "bunk" for bed and "fatigue" which is the Army's term for labor as distinguished from military training.—*American Speech. December 1945. p. 261*

Buqwees: Name for evacuees in the Philippines.—*Wolfert. American Guerrilla. p. 23*

Burma Road: The road from Burma to China, used as a military supply route. Figuratively it came to mean any supply route of similar nature or importance.—*American Speech. December 1942. p. 271*

Burp Gun: Practically any type of German automatic or semi-automatic small arm was apt to be described as a burp gun, presumably from the resemblance of shots or short bursts of fire to hiccoughs. *American Speech. December 1946. p. 246*

Bushido: (Japanese) Code of honor, particularly of warriors.— *New York Times Magazine. December 2, 1945. p. 22*

Bushmasters: Members of the Bushmaster Regiment—158th Infantry—so called because of its superior ability and high success in jungle fighting.—*American Notes and Queries. June 1944. p. 38*

Buster: In radar code, "to buster" meant to fly at normal speed: "to gate" meant to fly at the greatest speed possible.—*Newsweek. September 10, 1945. p. 92*

Butt-End Charlie: Nickname for tail gunner in a bombing plane. Sometimes called "Tail-end Charlie."—*New York Times Magazine. September 27, 1942. p. 16-17; Collier's. December 25, 1943. p. 15-16*

Butterfly Bomb: A bomb with wings that opened up as soon as the bomb was released and acted like a parachute to slow its descent —*American Speech. April 1946. p. 140*

Buttoned Up: Army slang for "orders carried out." In British slang it meant "thoroughly prepared."—*Saturday Review of Literature. October 4, 1941. p. 9; American Speech. February 1941. p. 76*

Buy a Share in America: Poster caption. For sale of defense bonds. United States Treasury Department

Buzz: AAF slang for diving low over an area

Buzzbombs: See Robot Bombs

By the Numbers: In training, certain fundamental operations. such as putting on a gas mask, were taught by the numbers—at the count of one, the carrier was unfastened, two the mask was removed, and so forth. To do anything "by the numbers" came to mean to do it in a practiced, routine, semi-automatic manner.—*American Speech. December 1946. p. 251*

"Bye-Bye—Buy Bonds": By Phil Baker. On "Take it or leave it" radio program Sunday nights, 1942-1945, Phil Baker signed off with above slogan

CAA: Civil Aeronautics Administration. Civil Aeronautics Authority was established under the Civil Aeronautics Act of 1938. Reorganized in 1940. Now within the framework of the Department of Commerce and has been separated into Civil Aeronautics Board and Civil Aeronautics Administration. See also WTS.—*World Almanac. 1943. p. 633*

CAB: Civil Aeronautics Board. See note under CAA

CAC Library: Civil Affairs Center Library. Located "somewhere in England," it served British and American officers preparing for activity in connection with civilian affairs in territories to be occupied by allied forces.—*Library Journal. July 1944. p. 571-2, 586*

Cactus: Code name for operations on Guadalcanal.—*Newsweek. March 5, 1945. p. 34*

Cadets for Naval Aviation Take That Something Extra . . . Have You Got It?: Poster caption. United States Navy Department

Cake à la Stalag: A "cake" recipe published in a prisoners of war news sheet. "Take some large biscuits, raisins, cocoa and milk. Bash down the biscuits to a powder, add raisins, mix with water and bake. Mix cocoa to a paste and spread on when cooked. Decorate with mixed milk powder."—*American Red Cross. Prisoners of War Bulletin. August 1943. p. 9*

CALA: Combined Administrative Liquidating Agency. Organization left in Paris after SHAEF (q.v.) was disbanded. Its task was to copy and microfilm thousands of SHAEF documents for each participating country.—*Newsweek. July 23, 1945. p. 40*

CAM: Catapult Aircraft Merchantship. Adopted by the RAF, to accompany and afford protection to convoys. The ship was equipped with Hurricane fighter planes, which were catapulted off, to battle with enemy bombers attacking the convoy. The pilots of these Hurricanes were called catafliers or catafighters.—*Cosmopolitan. August 1943. p. 14*

Camoufleur: One who took part in camouflage, applied it or used it. For some examples of work of camoufleurs, see article in *Time. August 6, 1945. p. 27*

Can Do!: Popular slogan of the Seabees. See also We Build, We Fight

Canary: Slang term for gas mask. Gas masks were also called dicky-birds and nose-bags.—*American Speech. February 1944. p. 8*

Canol: A coined word, abbreviated linking of the two words Canada and oil—Canadian oil development project, initiated early in 1942 when the decision to build the Alcan Highway made it feasible. —*Roads and Streets. December 1943. p. 48-9, 85; American Speech. April 1944. p. 96*

CAP: Civil Air Patrol. Established under the Office of Civilian Defense on December 9, 1941, with Major General John F. Curry of the Army Air Corps as national commander.—*Newsweek. January 5, 1942. p. 38*

Capital: Code name for operation in which the forces of Admiral Mountbatten and General Stilwell were given the mission of investing northern and central Burma.—*General Marshall's Report. 1945. p. 27*

Capitulation: See "There is no such word. . . ."

Caraburgers: See Hamburgers

Caravan: (American plane) Curtiss C-76 transport plane

CARE: Cooperative for American Remittances to Europe. A non-profit organization, approved by The President's War Relief Control Board. Organized by 24 American agencies engaged in foreign relief. A $15 remittance paid for a package of food to be delivered to a recipient in one of the famine devastated countries of Europe in the postwar period

Careless Talk May Cost His Life, Don't Talk about Aerodromes or Aircraft Factories: Poster caption. Great Britain

Carpet: See Radar Countermeasures

Carpet Bombing: A bombing attack which attempted to clear the way for advancing ground troops.—*Britannica Book of the Year. 1946. p. 832*

Casey Jones Mission: A flight undertaken by U.S. airmen over Japan against railroad installations.—*American Notes and Queries. July 1945. p. 54*

Cassino Corridor: See Purple Heart Valley

CAT: Civilian Actress Technician. Civilian actresses were hired by the Army Special Services Division to participate in and assist in the production of Soldier Shows (q.v.). Only women with a college education and with previous theatrical experience were eligible. —*Information contributed by a former War Department officer*

Cat: See Plane Nicknames

Cat Fever: Nickname given by Navy personnel in Norfolk, Va., to a "new infection" that swamped the city early in December 1943; three days of high fever followed by subsiding temperature, a clammy feeling, and nausea. A revival of a term given by Navy men, in the tropics during the First World War, to a grippal fever. The term was in general use throughout the Navy. "A cat fever patient is a sailor who isn't feeling well. . . The cat, in case you're uncomfortable about it, is short for catarrh. It has nothing to do with cats and in fact very little to do with catarrh."—*American Notes and Queries. January 1944. p. 149; McCracken. Baby Flat-top. p. 64*

Catafighters, Catafliers: See CAM

Catalina: (American plane) Consolidated OA-10 PBY patrol bomber (Flying Boat) plane

CATS: Civil Air Training School. Students at the Boston CATS were nicknamed Bucats, and at the University of Pennsylvania Upcats or Catsup.—*Christian Science Monitor Magazine. December 23, 1944. p. 14*

Cat's Eyes: Nickname of RAF night-fighter pilots; they received several months' special training and diet to help them see in the dark.—*Newsweek. April 14, 1941. p. 42*

Catsup: See CATS

CAVU: Ceiling And Visibility Unlimited

Caydet: (American plane) Boeing PT-13 and 17 N2S1 and 3 trainer plane

CBI Theater: China-Burma-India Theater of Operations.— *New York Times. June 10, 1945. p. 2E, 6E*

CBS: See Conad

CCC: Commodity Credit Corporation. Created by act of Congress in 1935; amended in 1941 and functions extended to June 30, 1943. The Corporation was primarily a lending institution making loans principally to producers, to finance the carrying and marketing of agricultural commodities.

Extended by President Roosevelt until January 1, 1944. Its borrowing power was increased by the measure, and the president was given a free hand in retail food price subsidies.—*Democrat & Chronicle. Rochester, N.Y. July 17, 1943. p. 3; World Almanac. 1943. p. 610*

CCRC: Combat Crew Replacement Center

C.D.D.: The army abbreviation for Certificate of Disability Discharge. This information was furnished to the Grosvenor Library by the U.S. Army induction service office in Buffalo, N.Y.

"Cease Firing, but if Any Enemy Planes Appear Shoot Them Down in Friendly Fashion": Word passed by Admiral William F. Halsey, Jr. After the Japanese surrender, orders to cease hostilities were sent to the Allied troops. As a British task force was hoisting victory pennants a Kamikaze darted out of the clouds toward the ship. A fighter plane shot it down. On the American ships also the Kamikazes kept pecking away, a fact which led to the above message relayed by Halsey to his troops.—*Newsweek. August 27, 1945. p. 25*

CED: Committee for Economic Development. Organized in the summer of 1942 to work on plans for postwar employment problems in an effort to avert a postwar depression. The Committee was composed of a board of 26 trustees, 12 regional chairmen, approximately 100 district chairmen and more than 1700 community chairmen. It was completely independent and self-financed. Basic responsibility for the committee rested with its Board of Trustees. Its activities were carried out by two major divisions—The Field Development Division and The Research Division.—*Library Journal. August 1944. p. 625-8, 630*

Ceiling: An upper limit (extended from the aeronautical use of the term). Used in reference to top prices placed on goods by the United States Government, in an attempt to prevent inflation. For examples of usage in this sense, see *American Speech. December 1941. p. 307-8*

CFEP: Committee on Fair Employment Practice. Established to eliminate discriminatory employment practices.—*World Almanac. 1944. p. 38*

CGIBT: Commanding General India-Burma Theater—*New York Times. January 20, 1946. p. 2E, 6E*

CGMTO: Commanding General Mediterranean Theater of Operations.—*New York Times. January 20, 1946. p. 2E, 6E*

CGUSFET: Commanding General United States Forces, European Theater.—*New York Times. January 20, 1946. p. 2E, 6E.* A demobilization directive was sent to these three offices (CGIBT, CGMTO and CGUSFET) by General Eisenhower in January 1946

Chairborne Troops: AAF slang for non-flying AAF personnel

Charlie Noble: Marine slang for smoke pipe from a ship's galley.—*Time. July 19, 1943. p. 69*

Chase-me-Charlie: Off the coast of Italy in 1943, British fighter pilots ran into a new German weapon trained on Allied shipping. It was a small glider with a bomb for a body. Directed by remote control from a launching plane, the device assumed attack position and hurtled itself at the target, where it exploded. The British named it "Chase-me-Charlie." Had they known it was the forerunner of the robot bombs (q.v.), they probably would have taken it more seriously.—*Newsweek. June 4, 1945. p. 90*

Chatterbox: R.A.F. slang for a machine gun.—*Nineteenth Century. April 1944. p. 183*

Chatter-bug: A civilian who spread military information. Term was coined by Harold Nicolson, Parliamentary Secretary to the Ministry of Information (England—1940).—*American Speech. February 1944. p. 8*

Chato: (Russian plane) A fighter plane which made a good showing against German and Italian planes in Spain

Cheesed Off: See Browned Off

Chetnik: The name adopted by the Yugoslav guerillas. It comes from an old Turkish word "chete" or band.—*New York Times. April 7, 1946. p. 2E, 6E*

Chicken: A slang term widely used in the armed services, both as noun and adjective. It signified anything mean, petty or annoying, especially as applied to regulations; unnecessary discipline or regimentation; a person who adhered too closely to army rules and regulations or misused or abused his authority, especially in minor or petty matters.—*American Speech. April 1945. p. 147; December 1945. p. 261; December 1946. p. 248*

Chicken Colonel: A full colonel, rank designated by silver eagles (chickens) on his shoulders. A colonel's eagles were called "chickens" in World War I, as noted in a popular song of the day— "I'd rather be a private with a chicken on my knee than a colonel with a chicken on my shoulder"

Chickens: In radar code, Allied fighters.—*Newsweek. September 10, 1945. p. 92*

The Chief: Nickname of Sir Arthur W. Tedder, Vice-Chief of the Air Staff, British aviation officer.—*Current Biography. 1943. p. 758*

Chigger: See Jeep

Chin Turret: A gun turret mounted beneath the nose of a bomber.—*Britannica Book of the Year. 1944. p. 770*

China Incident: Japanese-coined expression for Japan's attack on China. On the night of July 7, 1937, the Japanese held large-scale maneuvers in the vicinity of Lukouchiao, or Marco Polo Bridge, a railway junction. One of the Japanese soldiers was alleged to be missing and when the Japanese demand to search for him was refused, firing started. The Chinese endeavored to settle it as a local incident and withdrew the garrison from Lukouchiao. The Japanese not only refrained from withdrawing their troops but also brought reinforcements from Mukden. The fighting spread and on August 13 hostilities broke out in Shanghai. The undeclared war was called the "China Incident."—*China Handbook. 1937-1943. p. 350*

China's Sorrow: Phrase used to describe the Yellow River, which veered off its course in 1938 (as it does periodically, causing great devastation and loss of life) after the Chinese had blasted dikes to hold back the Japanese. An engineering job was started in January 1946 to turn the river back on its course.—*New York Times. January 27, 1946. p. 2E, 6E*

Chinese Dragon: Nickname given to aerial mines which made sharp explosions like firecrackers.—*American Speech. February 1944. p. 8*

Chindits: Name given to his raiders by General Orde Wingate. "He called his men 'Chindits' after the Chinthey—the mythological beast, half lion, half griffin, statues of which stand guard over Burmese pagodas to ward off evil spirits."—*Rolo. Wingate's Raiders. p. 9-10*

Chinese Lenin: Nickname of Mao Tse-tung, Chinese political leader. *Current Biography. 1943. p. 490*

Chislings: Suggested name for quota chiselers, firms failing to conform to production quotas set up by WPB.—*Time. February 16, 1942. p. 14*

Chocolate Drop Hill: On southern Okinawa. Figured in the fighting there during the week of May 13-20, 1945. See also Conical Hill, Flat-top Hill, Tombstone Ridge.—*New York Times. May 20, 1945. p. 2E, 6E*

Chowmobile: Trailer-type canteen pulled by a tractor and serving hot meals.—*New York Times Magazine. December 2, 1945. p. 22*

Chutist: A parachutist.—*American Speech. December 1942. p. 271*

CIAA: See OCIAA

Ciande: Civil Information and Education Section of Allied Headquarters. Three days after the occupation of Japan began CIANDE, under Brigadier General Ken R. Dyke, took on the job of overseeing the Broadcasting Corporation of Japan.—*Time. April 1, 1946. p. 58*

C.I.C.: Counter-Intelligence Corps; a spy-catching outfit that operated at the front.—*Schwarzwalder. We Caught Spies. p. vii*

The Cigar: Nickname of Major General Curtis E. LeMay, addicted to cigar smoking.—*Time. August 6, 1945. p. 29*

CINCAFPAC: Commander in Chief Army Forces, Pacific.—*New York Times. January 20, 1946. p. 2E, 6E*

CINCPAC: Commander in Chief of the Pacific Fleet.—*New York Times. February 4, 1945. p. 6E*

CINCPOA: Commander in Chief of the Pacific Ocean Area.—*ibid*

CINCUS: Naval Commander in Chief, United States

Circuit (slang): See entry under Kriegie

Circuit Riders by Air: U.S. Air Transport Command's flying chaplains. Head of the ATC's chaplains was Lieutenant Colonel Clement A. Siwinski, a Catholic of Lincoln, Neb., who flew some 125,000 miles.—*Newsweek. March 26, 1945. p. 86*

Civilian Defense Week: November 11-16, 1941. Proclaimed by President Roosevelt. Nation wide observance was planned to stimulate public interest in civilian preparedness.—*Newsweek. November 17, 1941. p. 40*

Clara: See Moaning Minnie

Clear, Lucid Thinking: See "The times call for clear, lucid thinking. . . ."

Clem, Kilroy, etc.: New folklore has grown up around a fabulous figure in the overseas replacement depots. He goes by various names, such as Clem, Kilroy (q.v.), or perhaps a dozen others. Probably a real person to begin with, the tales soon reached proportions beyond what could have happened to one person. The name Kilroy seems more popular on the west coast than Clem. "Smoe" was a similar figure who appeared in cartoons at Army Air Field, Sioux Falls, S.D. "Luke the Spook," another variation, is said to have come into being at the Boeing factory in Seattle, Wash.—*American Notes and Queries. January 1946. p. 152; New York Times Magazine. January 6, 1946; Newsweek. December 17, 1945. p. 18*

Cloak and Dagger: Phrase generally used as an adjective, applied to a person "engaged in some form of activity that is at once secret, exciting, dangerous, and highly important"; reminiscent of the popular notion that a Borgia always carried a dagger beneath his cloak; in use in the Army, particularly the British Army.—*New York Herald Tribune, July 20, 1944; American Notes and Queries. July 1944. p. 54*

Clutter: Radar term for the image on radar scope caused by noise, permanent echo or jamming.—*Army and Navy Journal. August 18, 1945. p. 1534*

CMP: Controlled Materials Plan. New system of the War Production Board to control production and flow of materials. Introduced in November 1942, to replace PRP (Production Requirement Plan). See also PURP.—*Newsweek. November 16, 1942. p. 66*

Coastal Base Section: See CONAD

Cobra: Nickname of Reinhard Heydrick, former deputy director of the German State Secret Police.—*Newsweek. June 15, 1942. p. 39*

Coffee Grinder: "Coffee grinder" is a portable radio set which sends out SOS signals; so nicknamed because it resembles an old-fashioned coffee mill. These machines were installed as an added safety equipment on life boats of vessels plying the war zones.—*Times-Union. Rochester, N.Y. June 24, 1943. p. 1*

Coffin Corridor: As the Allied troops were driving on across France toward Paris in August 1944, there was still a narrow route in Normandy along which the German Seventh Army expected to be able to withdraw to a safer position at the Seine. When the gap was closed by Allied advances 100,000 to 200,000 German troops were forced to turn for a battle to the death. Newspaper accounts of the action named the locality "Coffin Corridor."—*Democrat & Chronicle. Rochester, N.Y. August 15, 1944. p. 1A*

The Coise of the Panama Jungle Coast Artillery: United States Army nickname for radio station PCAN. "Coise" is Brooklynese for Curse.—*Newsweek. September 8, 1941. p. 46*

Collaborationist: General term applied to all who were suspected of collaborating with the enemy in any way

Collision Mats: Slang for pancakes.—*Word Study. April 1944. p. 3*

Colmar Pocket: The popular term applied to the German-held salient in the Vosges mountains which included the city of Colmar. This salient was liquidated by a Franco-American offensive in the first week of February 1945.—*U.S. Army. ETO. CONAD History.* *p. 375*

Colonel Blimp: A cartoon character created by David Low, used to designate any elderly, stupid and highly conservative man. A British film was made around the character of Colonel Blimp.—*American Speech. February 1944. p. 8*

Colonel Britton: Identified as Douglas E. Ritchie, director of the BBC European news service and British radio propagandist who later became General Dwight D. Eisenhower's spokesman on Europe's airways; credited with making (in 1941 and 1942) the letter "V" and the opening bars of Beethoven's Fifth Symphony symbols of resistance to the enemy. His identity was one of the war's most closely guarded secrets. (About the letter "V," see also note on Victor de Laveleye under V-for-Victory, a conflicting source.)—*American Notes and Queries. May 1945. p. 22*

ComAirForward: Commander of all shore-based aircraft in the forward areas of the Central Pacific. Major General Willis H. Hale was appointed to this job in May 1944.—*Newsweek. May 8, 1944.* *p. 22*

Combat Fatigue: A neurosis resulting from combat conditions. —*Britannica Book of the Year. 1945. p. 771*

Combat Infantryman Badge: Approved November 15, 1943, for officers and men "whose conduct in combat is exemplary." Exemplary was later (October 17, 1944) changed to read satisfactory— "satisfactory performance of duty in ground combat against the enemy." See also Expert Infantryman Badge.—*Army and Navy Journal. October 28, 1944. p. 242*

Combined Operations: This term means a landing operation in which, owing to actual or expected opposition, it is essential that the fighting services take part together, in order to strike the enemy with the maximum effect, at the chosen point and at the chosen moment.—*Saunders. Combined Operations. p. vii*

Come on, Rochester! We're in It—Let's Win It. Buy More War Bonds: Poster caption. Rochester, N.Y.

Comin' in on a Wing and a Prayer: Song title. Lyric by Harold Adamson, music by Jimmy McHugh. Robbins Music Corporation. c1943

Commando: (American plane) Curtiss C-46 R5C transport plane -

Commandos: A group of picked men from the British Armed Services who operated under Combined Operations Command. A combined operation was a landing operation in which it was essential that the fighting services take part together in completely synchronized action. To help the services do this a Combined Operations Command was formed. Its chief function was to train officers and men of the armed services in the conduct of amphibious warfare. It was also the task of the Command to plan and execute all kinds of raids.

The term Commando (according to *Webster's Dictionary*) dates back to the Boer war and in South Africa means a military body or command; also an expedition or raid. To readers of war news of World War II, it meant a group of British soldiers trained to carry out sudden raids on Nazi-held territory, and in general to set the pattern for the planned invasion of Nazi-held Europe. See also Rangers. —*Saunders. Combined Operations. p. vii, 1-4; American Speech. April 1944. p. 81-90*

Com Z: Communications Zone, the non-combat area of a theater of operations, especially ETO. The Com Z commander was responsible for getting supplies to the right places in the right quantity. Trucking routes which carried the supplies to armies in the ETO were variously known as Red Ball Express, White Ball, Green Diamond, Little Red Ball, and ABC Victory Route.—*Newsweek. April 2, 1945. p. 48*

Comsubspac: Commander, Submarines Pacific.—*New York Times Magazine. June 3, 1945. p. 10*

CONAD: Continental Advance Section. Originally called Coastal Base Section with the security abbreviation of CBS.—*U.S. Army. ETO. CONAD History. p. 1*

Concentration Camp: An area, usually enclosed by barbed wire and heavily guarded, for the forcible retention of political prisoners, enemy aliens, military prisoners, etc.

Conchie: Slang for conscientious objector to military service— *Good Housekeeping. February 1941. p. 113*

Condition: Verb, to train, to inure.—*New York Times Magazine. December 2, 1945. p. 22*

Condition Black: "Degrees of danger in this war are described in shouted warnings of CON-DISH-SHUN YELLOW, RED, BLACK, etc. 'Condition Red' means enemy planes are approaching.

'Condition Black' is the most imperative of all; it means enemy landing parties are approaching."—*Huie. Can Do! the Story of the Seabees. p. 35 note*

Conical Hill: On southern Okinawa. Figured in the fighting there during the week of May 13-20, 1945. See also Chocolate Drop Hill, Flat-Top Hill, Tombstone Ridge.—*New York Times. May 20, 1945. p. 2E, 6E*

Conk: AAF slang for sudden stopping of engine during flight

Consolidate a Position: To erect fortifications and establish communications lines to supply and protect armed forces in a newly captured position.—*Times-Union. Rochester, N.Y. May 3, 1940*

Constellation: (American plane) Lockheed C-69 transport plane

Construction Battalions: See *Seabees*

Convoy: Line of supply; more recently, an armed escort.— *New York Times Magazine. December 2, 1945. p. 22*

Convoy Bible: See WIMS

Convoy Jitters: See Shell-shock

Cooler (slang): See entry under Kriegie

Coordinator of Information: In July 1941, Colonel William J. Donovan was appointed Coordinator of Information. His bureau was created "to collect and assemble all information and data which may bear upon national security." This bureau became known as the Donovan Committee. See also OWI.—*Newsweek. June 22, 1942. p. 30*

Corduroy: See Kilroy

Cornell: (American plane) Fairchild PT-19 and 23 trainer plane

Coronado: (American plane) Consolidated PB2Y patrol bomber (Flying Boat) plane

Coronet: Code name for the second phase of a planned Japanese invasion which was to have taken place in the spring of 1946. See also Olympic. This invasion was made unnecessary by capitulation of Japan in August 1945.—*General Marshall's Report. 1945. p. 84*

Corps des Volontaires Françaises: Women's division of the army of the Fighting French. (French equivalent of the WAC).— *Newsweek. July 12, 1943. p. 6*

"Corregidor Needs No Comment from Me": Statement from Australia by General Douglas MacArthur. He went on to say "Through the bloody haze of its last reverberating shot I shall always seem to see the vision of its grim, gaunt and ghostly men."—*Time. May 8, 1944. p. 66*

Corsair: (American plane) Vought-Sikorsky F4U fighter plane

Cossac: Chief of Staff to the Supreme Allied Commander. At the Casablanca conference in January 1943, Lieutenant General Sir Frederick E. Morgan was appointed Chief of Staff to the Supreme Allied Commander, though it was eleven months before a Supreme Commander was selected. The initials of the new designation spelled out "Cossac," and Cossac became the code name of the headquarters in London.—*Saturday Evening Post. June 8, 1946. p. 10*

Council on Books in Wartime: A group of sixty publishers met in June 1942 and voted to establish a Council on Books in Wartime for the duration of the war. The aim in general was "to achieve the widest possible use of books contributing to the war effort of the United Peoples." The Council was formally organized in July 1942 and included also booksellers, librarians and other allied interests in the book world. Activities included Armed Services Editions (q.v.), radio broadcasts, newsreel films, selection of Imperative books (q.v.), providing speakers for forums, booklists and magazine and newspaper publicity.—*Publishers' Weekly. December 25, 1943. p. 2300-13*

Counter-Radar: See Radar Countermeasures

Coventrize: To bombard (an open city) into ruins. Reported in the Winchell column about November 25, 1940, as in use by Germans to describe aerial attacks such as that carried out on the night of November 14-15, 1940, against the English city of Coventry; used in Walter Winchell radio broadcast December 1, 1940.—*American Speech. April 1941. p. 146*

CPA: Central Pacific Area. The old peacetime Hawaiian Department became CPA for a couple of years, then late in 1944 or early in 1945, a new command called MidPac (U.S. Army Forces Middle Pacific) was set up. The Marianas were called WPBC (Western Pacific Base Command) and the Hawaiian Islands were called CPBC (Central Pacific Base Command), both being subordinate to the Mid-Pac headquarters in Hawaii

CPA: Civilian Production Administration, set up as successor agency to the WPB (q.v.).—*New York Times, October 21, 1945. p. 2E, 6E*

CPO: Committee on Period One (q.v.)

CPT: Civilian Pilot Training. See WTS

"The Crafty, Cold-Blooded, Black-Hearted Italian": By Winston Churchill. Adjectives applied to Mussolini. Radio broadcast February 9, 1941.—*Churchill. Blood, Sweat and Tears. p. 454*

Crafty Fox of Harar: Haile Selassie won this nickname early in his career.—*Newsweek. January 27, 1941. p. 26*

C-Ration: In 1940 the Army Subsistence Research Laboratory offered Ration "C" for trial—a ration in six cans, two for each meal. Three of the cans were meat units. The other three contained concentrated biscuits, ingredients for a drink (soluble coffee and sugar), and five pieces of hard candies. In all, the six cans added up to 3,500 calories of well balanced and varied food. See also "Bail-out" Ration and K-Ration.—*Hoffmann. Feeding Our Armed Forces. p. 51*

Cracking Good Show: See Good Show

Crash Boat: A marine rescue boat, for rescuing aircraft personnel and sometimes planes making forced landings at sea.—*American Speech. October 1945. p. 226*

Creative Pause: A term coined by German propagandists to describe the lull in fighting after the Nazi conquest of Crete; and applied to other similar cessations of fighting.—*American Speech. December 1942. p. 271*

Creeping Crud: See Jungle Rot

Crewmaker: (American plane) Boeing AT-15 trainer plane

Crocodile: A flame-throwing device used by the British in conjunction with the Churchill tank; capable of throwing a "geyser of fire" 450 feet. See also Lifebuoy.—*American Notes and Queries. September 1944. p. 85*

Crossroads: See Operation Crossroads

Crowcass: Central Registry of War Criminals and Security Suspects. Using crime detection machines, this organization succeeded in ferreting out hundreds of German war criminals.—*Democrat & Chronicle. Rochester, N.Y. November 6, 1945*

Crump Dump: R.A.F. slang term applied to the Ruhr district in Germany where so many crump holes or bomb craters had been made by the R.A.F.—*Nineteenth Century. April 1944. p. 184*

Crump Hole: British slang for the crater made by explosion of an aerial torpedo.—*Nation. November 9, 1940. p. 447*

Crusade for Living: See World War II

Crying Towels: See TS Cards

Curfloozie: A word coined by the *New York Daily News.* After curfew order was put into effect in February 1945, the midnight closings of restaurants, places of entertainment, etc., threw onto the streets (especially in the large cities) thousands of GI's (and women) with nowhere to go. This gave rise to a serious social problem which many felt far outweighed any advantage the curfew order may have had. It was in this connection that the *Daily News* coined the word "curfloozie."—*Newsweek. March 26, 1945. p. 44*

"The Curse of Garibaldi Has Veritably Fallen" on both Mussolini and his son-in-law Count Ciano: By Winston Churchill. Speech broadcast to the world, August 31, 1943. In 1864 Garibaldi, in a letter acknowledging a sword and telescope presented to him during his visit to England that year, predicted disaster to the Italian who should destroy the friendship between Italy and Great Britain.—*Churchill. Onwards to Victory. p. 132*

CV: Regular aircraft carrier of about 27,000 tons.—*New York Times. October 14, 1945. p. 2E, 6E*

CVB: Super-carrier of 45,000 tons.—*ibid*

CVE: Escort or "baby" carrier ("Baby Flat-top").—*ibid*

C.W.A.A.F.: See R.C.A.F. (W.D.)

C.W.A.C.: Canadian Women's Army Corps. Authorized on August 13, 1941, to release "A" and "B" category soldiers for active service. Originally auxiliary to the Canadian army, it was made an integral part of the army on March 13, 1942. Popularly called Quacks.—*Whitton. Canadian Women in the War Effort. p. 15-16*

CWS: Chemical Warfare Service.—*Newsweek. October 15, 1945. p. 82*

D.A.: Slang term for delayed action bomb.—*Saturday Review of Literature. October 4, 1941. p. 9*

DADOS: Deputy Assistant Director of Ordnance Stores.—*Newsweek. May 15, 1944. p. 26*

Daffy: See Plane Nicknames

"Damnedest Crime Ever Committed Against America": Off-the-record statement made by General George C. Marshall, Chief of Staff of the United States Army, referring to the fact that the rail-wage dispute became so serious that the government had to take over the railroads.—*Newsweek. January 10, 1944. p. 56*

DANA: Initials of the Deutsche Allgemeine Nachrichten Agentur (German General News Agency), sponsored by U.S. news-papermen as a successor to the DNB, which was controlled by the Nazis.—*Britannica Book of the Year. 1947. p. 840*

"A Date Which Will Live in Infamy" (Referring to December 7, 1941, the date of the Japanese attack on Pearl Harbor) : By Franklin D. Roosevelt. Message to Congress. December 8, 1941

Dauntless: (American plane) Douglas A-24 SBD light dive bomber plane

Day of Infamy: See A Date Which Will Live in Infamy

D. C. Speaker: A mythical character created June 15, 1943, by Kent Cooper of the Associated Press. "D. C. Speaker" was quoted when the news was obtained from authentic sources which could not be disclosed.—*Newsweek. July 26, 1943. p. 73-5*

D-Day, H-Hour: Used to designate in unspecific terms the day and hour of a forthcoming operation. Broad time limits might be known within which the operation would take place, but not the exact time. With these designations detailed plans were made. Then, when circumstances warranted, the units to be involved were informed of the exact day and hour. The letters were chosen because they were the first letters in Day and in Hour. They were first used in orders issued for planning the St. Mihiel offensive by the A.E.F. September 7, 1918. However they only came into everyday usage in World War II.— *Time. June 12, 1944. p. 2.* D-Plus Ninety, for example, referred to a date ninety days after D-Day; simple military dating system used in plotting operations beyond an unspecified D-Day. See also Love-Day. —*American Notes and Queries. September 1944. p. 85*

DDT: Dichloro-Diphenyl-Trichlorethane. A disinfectant which was successful in wiping out typhus among American troops overseas. See also NMRI-448.—*American Notes and Queries. June 1944. p. 39*

Dear Johns: Name given by soldiers to letters from wives or sweethearts "calling it all off." Name came from a current radio pro-

gram made up of letters addressed to "Dear John."—*Democrat &*
Chronicle. Rochester, N.Y. August 17, 1945

Dear Lootenant Letters: Name given by aviators in German
prison camps to letters announcing that the girl at home had married
someone else. In one camp, Stalag Luft III, the girls' pictures were
pinned up under the caption "Stand-ups."—*Newsweek. April 2, 1945.
p. 46*

Death March of Bataan: See March of Death

"Death to the German Invaders": By Premier Josef Stalin. In
an order of the day commemorating the 25th anniversary of the Red
Army, Stalin called on his troops to give the Germans "no rest by day
or by night," to "annihilate them if they refuse to lay down their arms,"
and sounded the rally cry of "Death to the German Invaders."—*Democrat & Chronicle. Rochester, N.Y. February 23, 1943. p. 1*

Death's Head: Nickname given to Colonel General Hermann
Von Hoth (German army).—*Newsweek. October 26, 1942. p. 28-9*

Death's Head Units: See SS

Decisions, Not Discussions: See "We need decisions. . . ."

Deep Dunkers: A little-known and exclusive official submarine
servicemen's organization. Established in the spring of 1943, its objective was the recognition of officers and men not qualifying for
medals, which usually were awarded only to skippers. Membership
was restricted to crews whose ships, on war patrol, had (1) sunk an
enemy ship of more than 1,000 tons; (2) damaged a major ship, such
as a carrier or battleship; or (3) performed a mission (usually secret)
of comparable importance.—*Newsweek. October 2, 1944. p. 21*

"Defense" Biscuits: See K-Ration

Defense Bonds: See Bonds

Defiant: (British plane) Bolton-Paul fighter plane

Degaussisation: The process of demagnetizing a ship to protect it against floating magnetic mines.—*American Speech. February
1944. p. 9*

**"Democracy Thrives When the Areas of Liberty Are Expanding
and Dies When They Are Contracting":** By Wendell Willkie.
Speech delivered in Toronto, Ontario, Canada, March 24, 1941.—*Vital
Speeches. April 15, 1941. p. 409*

Denazify: Referring to the educational program of occupation forces to orient the Germans away from Hitlerian doctrines.—*New York Times Magazine. December 2, 1945. p. 22*

DE's: Destroyer Escorts—new type of warship introduced by United States Navy in March 1943. DE's special job was to guard merchant-ship convoys.—*Newsweek. March 15, 1943. p. 21*

Depth Bombs: Three hundred pounds or more of high explosives in a thin shell with an adjustable hydrostatic mechanism to touch it off at any desired depth under the sea. Pitched or rolled from fighting ships, particularly destroyers, it was the nemesis of submarines. Direct hits were unnecessary. Water-transmitted shock of nearby explosion was sufficient to buckle plates of submarines or damage steering or elevating apparatus.—*Democrat & Chronicle. Rochester, N.Y. September 8, 1940*

Desert Demon: Nickname of Field Marshal Erwin Rommel (German general).—*Current Biography. 1942. p. 701*

Desert Fox: Nickname applied to Field Marshal Erwin Rommel (German general) because of his exploits against the British in the African desert campaign of 1942.—*Hart. Hitler's Generals. port. f. p. 72*

Desert Rats: Name given by Mussolini to the British Seventh Armored Division, in contempt on his part, but borne with pride by them, because of their record in Africa.—*Newsweek. March 4, 1946. p. 6*

Devastator: (American plane) Douglas TBD light bomber plane

DF: Direction Finder. Developed by the Navy, DF made it possible to locate instantly and automatically radio-using German submarines from shore, plane or ship. Its peacetime use would be to guide rescuers to the source of an SOS, to rescue castaways and ships in distress.—*Newsweek. January 21, 1946. p. 83*

DFD: Dogs for Defense. Non-profit organization to enroll and train dogs for use in the armed services. DFD was founded just after the Japanese attack on Pearl Harbor and was officially recognized by the War Department in April 1942. It had a marching song and also a nickname "Wags." DFD was founded by Mrs. Milton Erlanger, nationally famous as a trainer and shower of dogs. She began her work

for the Army in 1942.   She wrote the war dog training manual, and
under her direction five training centers were established.—*Collier's*
January 2, 1943.   p. 32; Time.   February 22, 1943.   p. 44; Newsweek
January 28, 1946. p. 44

The Diaper Revolution: Refers to the uprising of Yugoslavian
grammar school children in protest against the Prime Minister, Cvet
kovitch, who signed a pact with Hitler.—*St. John.   From the Land of*
Silent People. p. 6

Diaper Run: See War Brides

Dice an Area: An air corps expression meaning to make a pho
tographic map, 7" x 11".—*New York Times Magazine. May 21, 1944*
p. 8E

Dicky-bird. See Canary

"Die, but Do Not Retreat": Slogan coined by Stalin for the
Russian armies: "Umeraite No Ne Otstupaite."—*Time.   January 4*
1943. p. 23

"Die for Mussolini and Hitler—or Live for Italy": The con
cluding words of the Roosevelt-Churchill joint message to the Italian
people, July 16, 1943 were: "The time has come for you to decide
whether Italians shall die for Mussolini and Hitler—or live for Italy
and for civilization."—*Democrat & Chronicle.   Rochester, N.Y. July*
17, 1943. p. 2

The Difficult We Do Immediately.   The Impossible Takes a
Little Longer: Slogan of United States Army Air Forces.—*News*
week.   March 8, 1943.   p. 34.   See also The Impossible We Do at
Once
     A similar idea has been attributed to Charles Alexandre de Calon-
ne, French minister of finance under Louis XVI. The tale goes that
Marie Antoinette once asked him for something, saying it would perhaps be difficult. He replied "Madame, si cela n'est que difficile, c'est
fait; si cela est impossible, nous verrons."—*Biographie Universelle.*
v. 6. p. 567

Dilbert: Cartoon character created by Robert C. Osborn
Along with "Dilbert" he created another character, a wacky me
chanic, "Spoiler." Dilbert and Spoiler became known to naval combat fliers the world over as horrible examples of what *not* to be.—
Newsweek.   December 31, 1945. p. 74

Dim-out: A dimming of lights, or partial blackout, especially along the coast where bright lights would offer a background against which passing ships would be silhouetted, making them easy prey for U-boats. See also Blackout, Brownout.—*American Speech. October 1942. p. 204*

Dinah: Nickname for Japanese plane

Ding How: Slang phrase meaning swell, okay or all right. First used by the Flying Tigers. It came from a Chinese phrase meaning "very good."—*Word Study. April 1944. p. 4*

Dirty Gertie of Bizerte: One of many phrases in rhymed couplets coined by GI's about girls. Many of these appeared in songs, but many of the songs are unprintable

Dish It Out with the Navy! Choose Now While You Can: Poster caption. United States Recruiting Board

Dit Happy: Slang for 'batty' because of copying too much radio code.—*American Speech. April 1945. p. 147*

Ditch: Slang term used as a verb by aviators, it meant to bail out of a disabled plane over an ocean and take to a dinghy.—*New York Times Magazine. June 4, 1944. p. 12*

Divarty: Slang term for Division Artillery.—*American Speech. February 1947. p. 55*

Dive Bombing: Diving at a steep angle so that the bomb released would have greater velocity than one dropped from a plane in level flight. Dive bombers were specially constructed to stand the strain of air speed greater than the maximum speed in horizontal flight. —*Newsweek. May 27, 1940. p. 21*

Divide and Conquer: Hitler's strategy of conquest.—*Newsweek. January 12, 1942. p. 21*

Division: See Air Force

DNB: Deutsches Nachrichten Buro. Official Nazi German news agency. This name was adopted in 1933, when the Wolff Agency and the Telegraphen Union were merged.—*Desmond. The Press and World Affairs. p. 66, 236*

Do as I Do: Marshal Timoshenko's watchword. It has become a slogan.—*Mehring. Timoshenko, Marshal of the Red Army. p. 90*

Do It Yesterday Arnold: Nickname of General Henry Harley Arnold, Commanding General of the United States Army Air Forces. —*Current Biography. 1942. p. 35*

Do More Than Your Best with What You've Got: Credo of Admiral Ernest J. King.—*Newsweek. March 16, 1942. p. 31*

Dodo: Air Force slang for a cadet before he starts solo flying. From the dodo bird which could not fly.—*American Speech. October 1945. p. 226*

Dog, Dogface, Doggie: Variant nicknames for the infantry. Origin of this term is obscure, but consensus seems to be that the infantryman leads a dog's life as compared with other branches of the army. The War Department does not approve of this name but the infantry seems to have accepted it very widely. The expression occurs in many songs.—*New York Times Magazine. December 10, 1944. p. 36*

Dog-fight: Slang term for a fight to the death in the air.— *Saturday Review of Literature. October 4, 1941. p. 9*

Dog Tags: Name for identification tags which soldiers wear on a chain around their necks.—*Word Study. April 1944. p. 2*

Doghouse Battalions: (German) Court-martialed air officers doing penance by infantry duty.—*New York Times Magazine. May 21, 1944. p. 8E*

Dolly Sister: With the May 20, 1943, ban on unessential motoring, the "Dolly Sister" combination—a policeman on a motorcycle with an OPA inspector riding in the sidecar—was reported again in evidence on city streets and highways in the eastern states.—*American Notes and Queries. June 1943. p. 37*

Domei: Official Japanese news agency

Donovan Committee: See Coordinator of Information

Don't Be a Spare. Be a Spar: Slogan for recruiting women for Coast Guard service. On posters the words were printed on a picture of a spare tire

"Don't Fire until You See the Slant of Their Eyes": By Lieutenant Mortimer K. Smith, Jr. (United States Army, 405th Bomber Squadron, 38th Bomber Group).—*Democrat & Chronicle. Rochester, N.Y. July 15, 1943*

Don't Get Excited. Take a Deep Breath. Then Breathe Peacefully: Placard found on the wall in German corps headquarters, in Strasbourg, when French troops burst in and found the German commander and his staff still packing.—*Democrat & Chronicle. Rochester, N.Y. November 28, 1944. p. 4*

Don't Let It Happen Here! Your Production Must Prevent It!: Poster caption. United States Navy Department Ordnance Bureau

Don't You Know There's a War On?: It would be impossible to locate the first use of this phrase, which appeared much more often in conversation than in print, but everyone must have heard it, and heard it oftener than he liked. It was a stock phrase of excuse, excuse for poor service, for reduction in quantity, for inferior quality, in fact for almost anything that went wrong and needed excuse

Doodlebugs: See Robot Bombs

Doorkey Children: Children left to fend for themselves (with a doorkey hanging on a string around their necks), most of them children of war workers. The phrase appeared during the course of World War II and was noted frequently in discussions of the rising tide of juvenile delinquency.—*Life. December 20, 1943. p. 105*

Dora: A defense line of fortifications built by the Nazis in Italy. Allied forces said the line had been known as the Adolf Hitler Line but captured German prisoners asserted it was called "Dora." Presumably, the imminent fall of the line led to its change in name.—*Newsweek. May 29, 1944. p. 22*

Dornier: Line of German warplanes. Included an open sea reconnaissance flying boat, three-engined monoplane, a seaplane, torpedo carrier and others.—*Democrat & Chronicle. Rochester, N.Y. September 8, 1940*

Double-V: Campaign for paper salvage launched by American Newspaper Publishers Association, March 8, 1945. "A V to speed victory and a V to aid veterans" was chosen as campaign slogan.—*Democrat & Chronicle. Rochester, N.Y. March 9, 1945. p. 10*

Doughboy's General: Nickname of General Omar Bradley because he won large victories in Africa with comparatively small loss of life.—*Reader's Digest. July 1944. p. 59*

Doughfoot: Nickname given to themselves by infantrymen. Its origin is strictly functional and it connotes to the infantryman the disagreeable, even miserable, conditions of his life caused by mud.

It is apt, too, because the infantryman's big four-buckle galoshes, worn over regular GI shoes, look more like oversized rolls of chocolate dough than feet after he has been a few hours in the fall and winter mud of the front lines. Some say the term started in Italy; others say in North Carolina, Georgia, and Louisiana; others in the campaign in France and Germany. . Who first coined or used it is uncertain.— *New York Times Magazine. December 10, 1944. p. 36*

Dovetails: Nickname for WAC 2nd Lieutenants.—*Democrat & Chronicle. Rochester, N.Y. October 9, 1943. p. 1*

DPC: Defense Plant Corporation. Subsidiary of RFC (Reconstruction Finance Corporation). DPC paid for the building of additions to privately owned plants and equipped them, and paid for building new defense plants which it leased to private operators.—*Newsweek. April 5, 1943. p. 58*

D Plus Ninety: See D-Day

DP's: Displaced Persons: General term applied to persons driven from their homes by the exigencies of war and cared for in refugee camps. There were many such camps in Europe.

Dracula: Code name for operation to seize Rangoon amphibiously from the south.—*General Marshall's Report. 1945. p. 60*

Draftee: One conscripted for military service.—*New York Times Magazine. December 2, 1945. p. 22*

Dragon: (American plane) Douglas B-23 medium bomber plane

Dragon Wagon: Tank recovery vehicle.—*Saturday Review of Literature. November 3, 1945. p. 7*

Dragon's Teeth: Concrete posts used as anti-tank barriers.—*American Notes and Queries. June 1944. p. 39*

Dragoon: Code name for invasion of southern France. First known as Anvil (q.v.), name was later changed to Dragoon.—*U.S. Army. ETO. CONAD History. p. 1*

D-Ration: A special chocolate bar, mixed with oat flour to raise the melting point (which for ordinary chocolate is 95°). This was for emergency use only and was not to be eaten except under orders, or in an extreme emergency. See also "Bail-out" Ration, C-Ration, K-Ration.—*Hoffmann. Feeding Our Armed Forces. p. 55*

"Drive the Enemy into the Sea": See "Forward to Tunis. . . ."

Drones: Pilotless, radio-controlled aircraft to be used in observing the effects of atomic bomb experiments. See also Beepers.— *American Notes and Queries. April 1946. p. 7*

Droop-snoot Bomber: New P-38 Lightning modified to lead standard P-38 formations in precision bombings; so called because a combined bombardier-navigator compartment was added in the nose of the plane, just ahead of the pilot's cockpit (AP dispatch from London, April 4, 1945).—*American Notes and Queries. April 1945. p. 7-8*

Drop It: Radar code message to British pilot not to attack.— *Newsweek. September 10, 1945. p. 92*

Dry Run: Something done for practice only, e.g., simulated bombings in which no bombs were actually dropped. The meaning later was expanded to include a rehearsal for any kind of event from a parade to an appointment with a superior officer.—*American Speech. October 1944. p. 224; December 1945. p. 261*

Duck: United States Army's amphibian truck. Nicknamed "Duck" after its official serial numbers DUKW.—*Collier's. July 31, 1943. p. 13; Newsweek. June 21, 1943. p. 42*

Duck Bills: Metal flanges welded to tank treads to give them wider grip, when tanks floundered in the greasy mud.—*Time. April 9, 1945. p. 34*

Duck Day: Slang term sometimes given to the day on which the GI received his discharge papers.—*American Speech. April 1946. p. 153*

Duff Gen: See Pukka Gen

Dugout Dug: Nickname of General Douglas MacArthur.— *Hersey. Into the Valley. p. 71*

DUKW: See Duck

Dulag: Abbreviation for German word Durchgangslager—a transit camp. See also Lager.—*Red Cross Courier. June 1943. p. 11*

Dulagluft: Abbreviation for German word Durchgangsluftwaffelager—a transit camp for airmen. See also Lager.—*Red Cross Courier. June 1943, p. 11*

Dumbo: See Black Cats

Dunkirk: Because of the retreat from Dunkirk of the British forces in June 1940 (one of the epic events of the war), the term "Dunkirk" came to mean any disastrous or forced retreat.—*American Speech. October 1942. p. 205*

Duration: Noun, which came to mean 'duration of the war.' Some government jobs were assigned with the understanding that they would last for the 'duration' plus six months. Other uses were noted in *American Speech. February 1941. p. 65*

Dust Bin: Name given to a British interrogation center near Frankfurt where top Nazi industrialists, financiers, and technical specialists were held (1945).—*American Notes and Queries. September 1945. p. 87*

Dynamite Meteors: See Robot Bombs

Dynamo: Nickname of Admiral Sir Bertram Home Ramsay, whose ships saved the British Army at Dunkirk. Dynamo was also the code name for the Dunkirk operation.—*Democrat & Chronicle. Rochester, N.Y. January 3, 1945. p. 5*

DZ: Designated area for paratroop landings.—*American Notes and Queries.—June 1944. p. 39*

"E": See Navy "E"

EAC: Engineer Amphibian Command. Part of United States Army's Services of Supply. EAC's task was to load, carry, and unload a complete infantry division in a shore-to-shore operation. Organized May 1942.—*Collier's. July 31, 1943. p. 13*

Eager Beavers: Underclassmen of the Army Air Force were called "Eager beavers" during their first thirty days of training. Meaning of the term was later expanded and it came into general use in the armed services to denote a soldier who was so anxious to impress his superiors that he would volunteer for every job that offered, or in other ways display unusual diligence.—*Flying. September 1943. p. 24; American Speech. April 1945. p. 148*

Eagle Day: Army slang term for pay day.—*Good Housekeeping. December 1942. p. 11*

EAM, ELAS, EDES: Greek political parties. EAM: Ethnikon Apeleutherotikon Metopon (National Liberation Front), a leftist political group dominated by Communists. ELAS: Ellinikos Laikos Apeleutheratikos Stratos (Hellenic Peoples Army of Liberation), the military arm of EAM.   EDES: Ellinikos Dimokratikos Ethnikos Stratos (Hellenic National Democratic Army), a rightist political group, also known as EAO.—*Buffalo Evening News. December 6, 1944; Spectator (London). February 2, 1945. p. 106; Britannica Book of the Year. 1945. p. 771*

Ear Wardens: Small nipple-shaped devices made of neoprene, inserted into the ear channel to prevent deafness or other injury resulting from noise shock; announced as an item to be adopted shortly by the Navy (AP dispatch from Washington, July 30, 1944).—*American Notes and Queries. August 1944. p. 70*

Earthquake Bomb: Six-ton bomb which penetrates into the earth so deeply that when its delayed-action fuse explodes, the result is 'earth quaking.'—*American Speech. April 1945. p. 144*

E-Boat: British name for Germany's mosquito launch-style torpedoboats. "E" stood for enemy.—*Nation. November 9, 1940. p. 447*

Echo: A radar wave reflected back from an object to the radar screen.—*Britannica Book of the Year. 1947. p. 840*

Eclipse: Code name for European operation—overrunning of Germany.—*American Notes and Queries. September 1945. p. 87*

EDB: Economic Defense Board. Started about June 1941.—*Newsweek. November 17, 1941. p. 20*

Edelweiss: An anti-Nazi youth movement inside Germany, particularly active in the Rhineland. An account of it was carried by the broadcasting station ABSIE.—*New York Times. December 31, 1944. p. 2E, 7E*

Eden's Army: As the Nazi drive surged on toward the Channel in May 1940, the danger of a paratroop invasion of England loomed larger. On May 14, 1940 Anthony Eden, the new British War Minister, broadcast an appeal for men between 17 and 65 to join a volunteer anti-parachute army. Within 24 hours 250,000 men had enrolled in "Eden's army." They were also nicknamed "Parashootists." —*Newsweek. May 27, 1940. p. 30*

EDES: See EAM

Egg: Lake Commacchio, near the Adriatic, is known to Allied troops as the "Egg."—*New York Times. January 14, 1945. p. 2E*

Eggs: AAF slang for bombs

Eight Ball: A soldier who got into trouble so much that he was a liability to his unit. See also Shell-Shock

Eisenhower Platz: Nickname for Grosvenor Square, London, because the Square was the heart of the American district. On it were located the American Embassy and several American headquarters. General Eisenhower's position as head of SHAEF made him so well known to Londoners that the nickname was a very natural choice. See also Little America.—*New York Times. November 24, 1946. p. 2E, 6E*

ELAS: See EAM

Electronic Raspberry: Term for process of jamming enemy radar by dispersing quantities of aluminum foil from planes. See also Radar countermeasures.—*New York Herald Tribune. November 11, 1945; American Notes and Queries. January 1946. p. 151*

Element C: Grill work of steel and cable forming anti-tank barrier.—*American Notes and Queries. June 1944. p. 39*

Emily: Nickname for Japanese plane

"Empires of the Future Are the Empires of the Mind": By Winston Churchill. Speech at Harvard University September 6, 1943. —*Vital Speeches. September 15, 1943. p. 715*

End of the Beginning: See "Beginning of the end"

Enemy Ann: Japanese radio propaganda mouthpiece, successor to Tokyo Rose (q.v.).—*New York Daily News. January 5, 1945*

Enemy Ears Are Listening: Poster caption. United States Office of War Information. Graphics Division

"The Enemy Must Be Hit, and Hit Hard, from So Many Directions That He Will Never Know Which Is His Bow and Which Is His Stern": By Franklin D. Roosevelt. At dinner of the White House Correspondents' Association, Washington, D.C., February 12, 1943, after his return from Africa.—*Vital Speeches. March 1, 1943. p. 293*

"Enemy on Island. Issue in Doubt": Final message sent from Wake Island by Major James P. S. Devereux, after a small band of Marines had held off a much larger Japanese force for fourteen days. —*Newsweek. July 30, 1945. p. 34*

Enlist in the Waves, Release a Man to Fight at Sea: Poster caption. United States Navy Recruiting Board

Enola Gay: Name of the Superfortress that dropped the first atomic bomb on Hiroshima, Japan.—*New York Times. April 7, 1946. p. 2E, 6E*

Entente: Monthly French magazine in exile, published in London.—*Saturday Review of Literature. July 17, 1943. p. 5*

Erk: British slang for aircraftsman and mechanic, and a beginner. In World War I and for some years afterwards, an erk meant an air mechanic. The word was probably a shortened pronunciation of air and ch from mechanic. In World War II, it came to mean a beginner in any field.—*Nineteenth Century. April 1944. p. 182*

Erpel Heart: The Ninth Armored Division seized the Remagen bridge over the Rhine in March 1945. Thousands of tons of supplies crossed it before it finally gave way. Supply trucks crossed it so often that many drivers held the order of the "Erpel Heart"—a pun on the Purple Heart medal and the little town of Erpel on the Rhine's east bank—for five trips daily.—*Newsweek. March 26, 1945. p. 34*

Ersatz: German for "substitute" or "synthetic"; widely used on the fighting and home fronts to signify materials of inferior quality; more recently applied to people, e.g., "The heroine called him an ersatz gentleman."—*New York Times Magazine. December 2, 1945. p. 22*

ETA: Estimated Time of Arrival

ETO: European Theater of Operations.—*New York Times Magazine. July 11, 1943. p. 16*

ETO Happy: GI expression (France and Italy) for "bored." See also Rock Happy.—*Yank. June 15, 1945. p. 2*

ETOUSA: European Theater of Operations United States Army. Headquarters of the American Army as distinct from SHAEF, Allied Headquarters. In 1942 it was pronounced "eetoosa." By 1944 the pronunciation had changed to "eetowza."—*Pyle. Brave Men. p. 302*

Eureka: See Rebecca Eureka

Evacué (m.) or **Evacuée** (f.): One who is forced as a safety measure to leave a war zone, e.g., many children were evacuées from London, being sent to the country which was considered safer during the heavy German bombing of London.—*Collier's. November 11, 1939. p. 12*

"Every Man in the Army Must Have the Light of Battle in His Eye": By Lieutenant General Sir Bernard Law Montgomery. —*Time. November 16, 1942. p. 28*

"Every Man Must Fight Like Ten": Marshal Gregory Zhukoff, Russian commander. "I am an exponent of the offensive. *Every man must fight like ten."—Newsweek. March 26, 1945. p. 38*

Every Minute Counts, Remember There's No Quitting Time on the Fighting Fronts: Poster caption. United States Coast Guard

EWB: In July 1941, President Roosevelt created a Board of Economic Defense, somewhat on the order of the Ministry of Economic Warfare(British). On December 17, 1941, the name was changed to Board of Economic Warfare, BEW or EWB. See also OEW.—*Newsweek. March 16, 1942. p. 31-2*

EWT: Eastern War Time. War time began February 9, 1942, when the entire United States set clocks ahead one hour for the duration of the war.—*World Almanac. 1943. p. 262*

Excalibur: (American plane) Vought-Sikorsky JR2S transport plane

Exhaustion: See Shell-shock

Expediter: An official charged with keeping uninterrupted the flow of materials or of routine work in industry and government. Some expediters were agents of the U.S. army and navy; others were in government bureaus such as WPB.—*Britannica Book of the Year. 1944. p. 770*

Expeditor: (American plane) Beech C-45 JRB transport plane

Expendable: From the verb expend, to consume by use in any way. In World War II, the term came into general use. It meant troops or equipment of any kind that for military purposes might be considered by the authorities worth consuming entirely to achieve an end. To quote from Mr. White's book: "Well, it's like this. Suppose you're a sergeant machine-gunner, and your army is retreating and the enemy advancing. The captain takes you to a machine gun covering the road. 'You're to stay here and hold this position,' he tells you. 'For how long?' you ask. 'Never mind,' he answers, 'just hold it.' Then you know you're expendable. In a war anything can be expendable—money or gasoline or equipment or most usually men. They are expending you and that machine gun to get time."—*White. They Were Expendable. p. 3*

Expert Infantryman Badge: (Approved November 11, 1943) Awarded for attaining the standards of proficiency established by the War Department, or by satisfactory performance of duty in action against the enemy. By the directive of October 17, 1944, eligibility for the Badge could be established only by attaining the standards of proficiency established by the War Department. See also Combat Infantryman Badge.—*Army and Navy Journal. October 28, 1944. p. 242*

"The Eyes of the World Are upon You. The Hopes and Prayers of Liberty-Loving People Everywhere March with You": By General Dwight Eisenhower. Words to the troops as the invasion of Europe started, June 6, 1944.—*Cue. June 10, 1944. p. 11*

Factory Buster: Bomb larger than a blockbuster.—*Saturday Review of Literature. March 10, 1945. p. 6*

Fairwing: U.S. fleet air wing, whose mission in the Pacific was primarily reconnaissance, to report enemy shipping to surface ships or bombers.—*American Notes and Queries. July 1945. p. 54*

Falange; Falangists: The Falangists are members of the Falange, a Spanish pro-Franco organization, with branches not only in Spain but also in Latin America. Literal meaning of the word Falange is Phalanx—the ancient Greek formation for heavy infantry

Falcon: (American plane) Curtiss SNC trainer plane

Fale (pronounced "folly"): Name usually given to small quarters for officers and men in certain areas of the Pacific, especially Samoa and Fiji. Word seems to derive from a Polynesian word meaning "house."

FALS: Foreign Area and Language Study.—*Library Journal. September 1, 1943. p. 645*

Family Fleet: See War Brides

F.A.N.Y.: Women's Transport Service (British). History of the corps is of interest; it has been in existence since 1909. Its members were the first women other than nurses to serve with the British Army. Originally it was called First Aid Nursing Yeomanry and it is still better known by the initials of this title.

The first F.A.N.Y.'s were recruited to do various forms of medical work; in 1916, however, they started the first ambulance convoy run by women for the British Army. From that time on they ceased to do purely medical transport work. When peace was signed in 1918, the F.A.N.Y. continued to recruit and train women transport drivers; they were called out during the General Strike of 1926. Although almost all of the original members of the F.A.N.Y. joined the A.T.S. (q.v.), the F.A.N.Y. has continued as an independent organization; their units are serving at home and abroad.—*Anderson. British Women at War. p. 19-20*

FAO: Food and Agricultural Organization of the United Nations.—*New York Times Magazine. May 19, 1946. p. 18*

Fat Boy: See Atomic Bomb nicknames

Father of the United Nations: Name applied by President Roosevelt to Cordell Hull.—*New York Times. October 28, 1945. p. 2E, 6E*

Fatherland War: See World War II

FBI's: Forgotten Boys of Iceland. United States soldiers in Iceland gave themselves this nickname.—*Newsweek. July 26, 1943. p. 32*

FBIS: Foreign Broadcast Intelligence Service. Plans for its organization were drawn up by Assistant Secretary Breckinridge Long, of the State Department. Financed by the President's special funds, it went into full operation in February 1941.—*Newsweek. October 8, 1945. p. 82*

FCC: Federal Communications Commission. Set up in 1934, it regulates interstate and foreign commerce in communications by wire and radio.—*World Almanac. 1943. p. 614*

FEAF: Far East Air Force.—*Air Force. June 1945. p. 37*

Fear: See "The only thing we have to fear. . . ."

Feather Merchant: Army-Navy expression meaning a lazy person. [Hillbilly dwarfs, etc., in the Barney Google comic strip were considered (prewar) "feather merchants" because they "pick up large feathers and fly off, waving them like wings."]—*American Notes and Queries. April 1945. p. 8.* Another account said the phrase originated with the Navy. It "comes from the crossed-feather device worn on the shoulder boards of ships' clerks, who are commissioned officers, and as a part of petty officers' rating badges to signify that they are yeomen. Hence a yeoman is a 'feather merchant.' The implication, of course, was that the yeoman took things easy on a swivel chair while the fighting men manned the guns. The term is now loosely applied to anyone with a 'soft berth.' "—*Letter from William B. Mellor, Jr. to Newsweek. April 23, 1945. p. 12, 16*

Femarines, Jungle Juliets, Leather-nectarines: Names given to themselves by the Women's Reserve of the Marine Corps.—*New York Times Magazine. September 17, 1944. p. 32*

FEPC: Fair Employment Practice Committee. On June 25, 1941, the President issued Executive Order no. 8802 declaring it to be the official policy of the United States "to encourage full participation in the national defense program by all citizens of the United States regardless of race, color, creed, or national origin." The order directed that all contracts between government and private firms should embody an anti-discrimination pledge. FEPC was set up to act as the enforcement agency; the committee included members of the public, of labor, of the Negro, and of industry.—*Nation. January 23, 1943. p. 121*

Ferret: Name given to a plane equipped with gear capable of spotting enemy radar. First developed for use in the North African campaign and later in the Pacific.—*Joint Board, OSRD, War Dept., Navy Dept. Electronics Warfare. 1945. p. 10, 32*

Festung Europa: See Fortress Europe

FFI: French Forces of the Interior. Patriot fighters who used guerilla tactics and fought many battles with Nazi garrisons as the Allied invasion forces closed in. The Allies had shipped armored vehicles to them and other heavy equipment had been captured from the Germans.—*New York Times. August 20, 1944. p. 1E*

F for Freddie: The most famous Mosquito bomber in the RAF, a veteran of 213 operational flights over France, Belgium and Germany. Stunt-flying in Canada to help sell war bonds, it crashed in Calgary and both pilots were killed.—*Newsweek. May 21, 1945. p. 74*

FIDO: Fog Investigation and Dispersal Operation, the system that kept fifteen British fields active even during the winter fogs. It consisted of an installation of horizontal pipes laid parallel to each side of a landing strip. Gasoline was forced through and out of the perforated pipes with tremendous force. When ignited (by men running alongside the pipes with torches) a wall of flame rose. The intense heat first vaporized the fuel in the upper (feeder) pipe, caused the smoke to subside, and burned off the fog, aiding planes to land safely. See also Go Fog.—*Time. June 11, 1945. p. 56*

Fifinella: Female gremlin, designed by Walt Disney as Wasp emblem, and which, because of the equanimity of its wearers, suggested the expression "Fifinellas don't cry."—*American Notes and Queries. December 1944. p. 134-5*

Fifth Column: Originally the Franco sympathizers within Madrid during the Spanish Civil War, 1936-39, so described in a radio address by General Emilio Mola when he was leading four columns of troops against the city. Hence secret sympathizers and supporters of the enemy engaged in espionage, sabotage and other subversive activities within defense lines. See also Sixth Column; Seventh Column. —*Webster's New International Dictionary. 1943. p. c; Hemingway. Fifth Column. p. v-vi*

Fifth Freedom: Freedom of the air. Britain and the United States signed an agreement in February 1946 guaranteeing observance of the Fifth Freedom by the two countries. Freedom of the air means, for example, freedom of aircraft of one nation to fly through the air space of another.—*New York Times. February 17, 1946. p. 2E, 6E*

52-20 Club: Name given to World War II veterans who, rather than take low-salaried jobs, were accepting the $20 a week unemployment compensation the government would pay for a year (i.e. 52 weeks).—*Britannica Book of the Year. 1947. p. 840*

Fighter-Bomber: The fighter-bomber was a regulation pursuit plane fitted with an under-fuselage mounting for carrying a 500-pound delayed-action bomb.—*American Speech. December 1945. p. 300*

Fighting Buffaloes: The 92nd Division of the U.S. 5th Army, Negro unit, led largely by Negro officers.—*Wilson Library Bulletin. April 1945. p. 536*

Fighting-hole Feet: Similar to trench feet in World War I. A disease contracted from life in foxholes.—*American Speech. February 1945. p. 77*

File 13: Army slang for waste basket.—*American Speech. October 1945. p. 226*

The Filthy Thirteen: A communiqué from the Ninth Air Force Troop Carrier Base, England, reported that American Indians in full war paint were among the first paratroop units to go into action in

France on June 6, 1944. They were members of an Engineer's Demolition Unit, the Braves. In training they had taken the name "The Filthy Thirteen." They were Yakis and Cherokees.—*Talks. July 1944. p. 2*

"Find 'Em, Fix 'Em, and Fight 'Em"—By Major General Terry Allen. In a directive to his division, General Allen wrote, "The successive steps of infantry combat are summarized by the expression 'Find 'em, fix 'em, and fight 'em.' "—*New Yorker. April 24, 1943. p. 22*

Fire Away—Buy Extra Bonds: Slogan for Fifth War Loan Drive. This caption appeared on a poster made from a painting by Georges Schreiber. It is a submarine picture, one of a series. The inspiration for the series came from experience on the submarine Dorado, which was later reported lost. In the corner of each poster is the dedication: In Memory of U.S.S. "Dorado."—*Newsweek. June 26, 1944. p. 100*

Fireball: A plane demonstrated by the Navy in October 1945. According to the builder, it was the first plane in the world to combine reciprocating and jet engines successfully. It could fly 320 miles an hour on the Wright cyclone engine in the nose or 300 miles an hour on the General Electric jet in the fuselage. When both engines were used, the Fireball could climb straight up at a mile a minute. When the war ended, Fireballs were just beginning to roll out of the plant of the Ryan Aeronautical Company.—*Newsweek. October 8, 1945. p. 76*

Fireball Express: The "Fireball Express," newest activity of the Air Transport Command, operated between the east coast of the United States and India and moved vital cargo to the Far East theater in ever-increasing quantities. These supplies moved on regular schedules with departures several times a week from Miami, Florida. The service was inaugurated on November 16, 1943.—*Air Transportation. October 1944. p. 27*

"The First Crack in the Axis Has Come": By Franklin D. Roosevelt. Radio broadcast July 28, 1943 following the successful invasion of Sicily.—*Vital Speeches. August 15, 1943. p. 642*

First Liberty Ship: "The Patrick Henry," the first unit of America's emergency fleet, was launched in Baltimore, September 27, 1941, and sponsored by Mrs. Henry A. Wallace.—*American Notes and Queries. December 1944. p. 135*

First to Land and Last to Leave: See We Build, We Fight

Fist Bazooka: Nazi weapon described by German captives as a "suicide gun" because it could be used only at very close range; loaded from the muzzle, cocked by hand, and fired by a pounding with the fist (AEF dispatch [AP] July 1, 1944).—*American Notes and Queries. August 1944. p. 71*

Flak: Derived from the German fliegerabwehrkanone—a gun to drive off aircraft. Sometimes given as abbreviation of flugzeugabwehrkanone. Also called AA or Ack Ack fire (anti-aircraft).—*American Speech. October 1942, p. 205; December 1944. p. 278*

Flak Happy: AAF slang for condition resulting from combat fatigue; a variation of the civilian expression "slap happy," which means slightly muddled mentally.—*New York Times Magazine.—June 4, 1944. p. 12*

Flak Shack: AAF slang for rest home where men who have had much battle strain go to relax and regain their composure. Both this term and "Flak Happy" seem to be strictly American in origin and use. See also Gremlin Grange.—*New York Times Magazine. June 4, 1944. p. 12*

Flakship: Battleship, because it shoots rapid-fire shells (flak) at aircraft.—*New York Times Magazine. December 2, 1945. p. 22*

Flaming Onion: British slang for a particular kind of German anti-aircraft projectile. In explosion it appeared onion-shaped.—*Democrat & Chronicle. Rochester, N.Y. September 8, 1940*

Flap: Slang term meaning a scare or alarm. Originated with the airforce and later came to mean any kind of row, enquiry or excitement.—*Reader's Digest. May 1940. p. 39; American Speech. February 1941. p. 76*

Flare-blitz: A shower of flares from enemy airplanes.—*American Speech. February 1944. p. 10*

Flash Gordon: Nickname of Major General George S. Patton, Jr. (United States Army).—*Current Biography. 1943. p. 571*

Flathatters: Navy nickname for careless pilots. See also Hedgehoppers.—*New York Times. September 24, 1944. p. 2E, 8E*

Flat-top: Name for a U.S. Navy airplane carrier.—*Word Study. April 1944. p. 3*

Flat-top Hill: On southern Okinawa; figured in the fighting there during the week of May 13-20, 1945. See also Chocolate Drop Hill, Conical Hill, Tombstone Ridge.—*New York Times. May 20, 1945. p. 2E, 6E*

Fleet Train: Auxiliary ships which, often in company with the Navy's Seabees, follow task forces in order to restore facilities and make supply replacements.—*American Notes and Queries. March 1944. p. 181*

Flight: See Air Force

Flintlock: Code name for operation for seizure of several atolls in the Marshall Islands.—*General Marshall's Report. 1945. p. 69*

Flitter: British term for one who slept away from home to escape air alarms.—*American Speech. February 1944. p. 10*

Flute: See Tuba

Fly-away: Air Force slang term for a plane which was flown to an overseas command instead of being shipped by vessel. Sometimes used of planes flown from factory to storage depots in the United States.—*American Speech. October 1945. p. 226*

Flying Blind: Flying by instrument

Flying Blow-torch: See Robot Bombs

Flying Box Car: Slang term for bomber.—*American Speech. October 1941. p. 165; December 1945. p. 300*

Flying Coffin: AAF slang for a dilapidated plane

Flying Cutter: Coast Guard's newest U-boat fighter in the western Atlantic (UP dispatch, April 1, 1944).—*American Notes and Queries. May 1944. p. 24*

Flying Dustpan: Device for dropping bombs in a concentric rather than a linear detonation pattern.—*American Notes and Queries. June 1946. p. 40*

Flying Fortress: (American plane) Boeing B-17 heavy bomber plane. The Joint Aircraft Committee, in considering names for planes, favored names of one word, so Flying Fortress was changed to Fortress

Flying Pencil: (German plane) Name commonly given by British pilots to the German plane Dornier Do. 17, because of its extremely long and thin fuselage

Flying Pig: British slang for aerial torpedo.—*Nation. November 9, 1940. p. 446*

Flying Stovepipe: A ram-jet engine originally designed to propel guided missiles. It was developed in the Navy's search for a supersonic missile to combat Japan's suicide planes and expected baka bomb attack. The war ended before it could be put to practical use. It was tested successfully on a flying model June 13, 1945, at Island Beach, N.J. It gets its name from the fact that it consists essentially of an open pipe. It can achieve a speed of 1400 miles per hour.— *Democrat & Chronicle. Rochester, N.Y. June 9, 1946. p. 9D*

Flying Stress: See Shell-shock

Flying Tigers: See AVG

FOB: Forward Observer. When landings were to be made and bad weather deterred the spotting planes, a "forward observer" was sent on shore ahead, to set up a wireless and direct the artillery fire from the ships.—*Newsweek. November 13, 1944. p. 39*

"The Folks Back Home Are Counting on Us. I Am Going to Get a Hit If I Have to Lay It on Their Flight Deck": By Lieutenant John James Powers. Said just before the flight when he dive-bombed a Japanese aircraft carrier in the Coral Sea, going so close that his plane was demolished by his own bomb. Awarded Medal of Honor.—*Newsweek. September 14, 1942. p. 31*

Food Is a Weapon, Don't Waste It! Buy Wisely—Cook Carefully—Eat It All: Poster caption. United States Office of War Information. Similar to slogan used in World War I, 1914-1918—"Food Will Win the War"

Foodaco: A new medium of exchange in surplus foods, invented by Allied prisoners of war. As a British prisoner wrote from Stalag Luft III, "We have an exchange system for surplus foods. It's called 'Foodaco' and works very well. Cigarettes are 40 points per hundred and chocolate 37 points per quarter pound. So those who require chocolate trade in their cigarettes and everyone is happy."— *American Red Cross. Prisoners of War Bulletin. August 1943. p. 9*

Foo-fighters or Balls of Fire: Mysterious balls of fire sent into the air by the Nazis. The balls traveled along at the same rate as the night flying planes on raids over Germany. They were apparently an electrical phenomenon related to lightning. They followed not only the speed of the plane, but changed speed and direction as the plane changed its speed and direction. Apparently designed by the Nazis as a psychological weapon, since the balls did not attack the planes.—*Democrat & Chronicle. Rochester, N.Y. January 2, 1945. p. 3; January 3, 1945. p. 5*

Footle or Footle Around: R.A.F. slang meaning to circle in search of a target, which to adventurous spirits seemed a waste of time.—*Nineteenth Century. April 1944. p. 183*

Forager: Code name for operation to capture the Marianas.—*General Marshall's Report. 1945. p. 71*

Forgotten Front: Name given by the GI's to the Italian Front. Original plan, as General Sir Harold R.L.G. Alexander explained to a press conference, was to knock Italy out of the war and the Germans out of Italy, but when this failed, the plan was to lure as many German divisions away from the western front as possible.—*Newsweek. November 13, 1944. p. 49*

Fortress: See Flying Fortress

Fortress Europe: (From German, *Festung Europa*) Armed Europe, especially middle Europe, as dominated by Hitler Germany.—*New York Times Magazine. December 2, 1945. p. 22; American Speech. October 1944. p. 225*

"Forward to Tunis! Drive the Enemy into the Sea": By General Sir Bernard Law Montgomery. In a message to his soldiers of the British Eighth Army on April 8, 1943, Montgomery ended with these words: "Let us make the enemy face up to and endure a first class Dunkerque on the beaches of Tunis. The triumphant cry now is: Forward to Tunis! Drive the enemy into the sea."—*Democrat & Chronicle. Rochester, N.Y. April 11, 1943*

"Forward—Unflinching, Unswerving, Indomitable": By Winston Churchill. Battle cry given to the British people in a radio broadcast on May 13, 1945, urging them on from VE-Day to VJ-Day. His address concluded with the words: "You did not shrink and I should be unworthy of your confidence and generosity if I did not still cry: *Forward—unflinching, unswerving, indomitable—till the whole task is done and the whole world is safe and clean.*"—*Democrat & Chronicle. Rochester, N.Y. May 14, 1945. p. 1*

Forwarder: (American plane) Fairchild C-61 GK transport plane

Foto Revy: Clandestine magazine sponsored by OWI and issued by the Underground in Denmark.—*Publishers' Weekly. December 15, 1945. p. 2616*

Four Freedoms: By Franklin Delano Roosevelt. At the conclusion of his message to Congress, January 6, 1941, Roosevelt said:

"The first is freedom of speech and expression—everywhere in the world. The second is freedom of every person to worship God in his own way—-everywhere in the world. The third is freedom from want — . . . everywhere in the world. The fourth is freedom from fear— . . . anywhere in the world."—*Baird. Representative American Speeches. 1940-41. p. 185*

Fox: Nickname of Brigadier General Claire L. Chennault (United States Army).—*Newsweek. July 6, 1942. p. 21*

The Fox: Nickname of Field Marshal Erwin Rommel (German Army). See also Desert Demon, Desert Fox.—*Newsweek. April 5, 1943. p. 17*; also nickname of General Sir Archibald Wavell (British Army).—*Current Biography. 1941. p. 902*

Foxhole: Temporary shelter or rifle pit, usually for a single soldier, and usually dug during combat. The word was also used during World War I.—*Times-Union. Rochester, N.Y. May 3, 1940; American Speech. February 1944. p. 74*

Foxhole Circuit: Overseas tour of USO Camp Shows. For circuits in U.S., see Blue Circuit, Hospital Circuit, Victory Circuit.—*Newsweek. July 31, 1944. p. 60*

Foxhole University: The United States Armed Forces Institute. Term coined by Stephen G. Thompson in *This Week Magazine (New York Herald Tribune). November 19, 1944*

"France Has Lost a Battle. But France Has Not Lost the War": By Charles de Gaulle. On June 17, 1940, General de Gaulle arrived in London. Early that afternoon he saw Churchill. In the course of the discussion he spoke the above words.—*Life. July 28, 1941. p. 73*

France-Amérique: Weekly. Published by the American segment of the Fighting French, it was started in June 1943. Editors were Henri Torres and Emile Buré; this French emigré press was located in New York City.—*Saturday Review of Literature. July 17, 1943. p. 4*

Frat Bait: Candy, chewing gum and cigarettes in the pockets of American and British soldiers in (European) occupied zones; one of the factors hastening the relaxation of the non-fraternization rule for allied troops in Germany and Austria.—*American Notes and Queries. June 1945. p. 40*

Fraterbait: Term used by American soldiers of the occupation forces to apply to attractive German girls. Term is coined from the non-fraternization order which was unpopular with the soldiers. From a UP dispatch by Lyle C. Wilson. July 2 [1945]. The term was used in an article in *Newsweek. July 30, 1945. p. 42*

Fraternize: To associate with enemy nationals. In Army slang, to have close relations, usually sexual, with a female enemy national. By extension, the word was used also with respect to the female population of allied countries and even American girls.— *American Speech. December 1946. p. 251*

Freddy's Freighters: See SSF

Free France: Fortnightly. French magazine in exile published by Free French Press and Information Service. Printed in English in New York City.—*Saturday Review of Literature. July 17, 1943. p. 4*

Free French: French patriots who were against the puppet government of Petain and Laval and were fighting under General de Gaulle for a France freed completely from Nazi domination

Freeze: To hold things where they are; e.g. prices were set or "frozen" at a certain limit, beyond which dealers could not raise them; foreign assets were "frozen" in American banks and could not be withdrawn, etc.—*American Speech. February 1944. p. 62*

"From This Day We Move Forward": By President Harry S. Truman. After the signing of the Japanese surrender documents on the S.S. "Missouri" on September 1, 1945 (U.S. time), President Truman proclaimed Sunday, September 2, as VJ-Day in a radio broadcast from Washington. The broadcast was heard on the "Missouri" and all the ships and shore stations of the Allied occupation forces in Japan as well as by the rest of the world. The President said, "From this day we move forward. We move toward a new era at home With the other United Nations, we move toward a new and better world of peace and international good will and cooperation. . . . This is a victory of more than arms alone. This is a victory of liberty over tyranny."—*Newsweek. September 10, 1945. p. 30*

Fruit Salad: Name given by servicemen to theater of operation ribbons, service ribbons and battle stars.—*Air Force. May 1945. p. 25*

FSA: Farm Security Administration. Created September 1, 1937, later placed on a war time footing. Gave aid to farmers to enable them to produce food needed to help win the war.—*World Almanac. 1943. p. 625*

FUBAR: Fouled Up Beyond All Recognition. Recently added armed services slang. See also JAAFU, JACFU, JANFU, SNAFU, SUSFU and TARFU.—*Newsweek. February 7, 1944. p. 61*

Führer: German term meaning chief or leader. Spelled with a capital it was the name given to Adolf Hitler, Chancellor of the Third German Reich

Führerprinzip: Literally, leader-principle. The Nazi system was based on the principle of personal leadership by which the aura surrounding the state was extended to its spokesman. This accounts in part for the rise of Hitler.—*Quarterly Review. January 1943. p. 77*

Fulmar: (British plane) Fairey fighter plane for service on aircraft carriers

G-5: New section of army set up to take over local government in lands occupied by our invasion forces. Other G sections are G-1 Personnel, G-2 Intelligence, G-3 Training and plans, G-4 Supply and evacuation.—*New York Times. May 21, 1944. p. 2E, 8E*

G Ivan: A Russian G.I.—*American Speech. February 1946. p. 74*

G-Suit: Also called Anti-G suit. G stands for gravity. Suits adopted by the Army Air Forces to prevent fighter pilots from "blacking out" in steep dives. The anti-gravity pneumatic pants applied pressure to the pilot's abdomen and legs, preventing the blood from pooling in the lower extremities.—*American Speech. April 1946. p. 142; Britannica Book of the Year. 1946. p. 832*

Gabelschwanzteufel: The Luftwaffe's name for the Lockheed P-38 Lightning (American) plane; i.e., "fork-tailed devil."—*PM. September 27, 1944*

Galvanic: Code name for operation for seizure of the Gilbert Islands.—*General Marshall's Report. 1945. p. 69*

Gas Hog: One who used too much gasoline during the gasoline shortage, and abused the gasoline-rationing privileges.—*American Speech. October 1942. p. 205*

Gate: See Buster

Gauleiter: Nazi term meaning leader of a district (Gau), a subdivision of the Third Reich. A Gauleiter was famous even in Germany for greed and profiteering ability. The word was used in the vernacular to describe an understudy of the Führer.—*New York Times Magazine. May 14, 1944. p. 2*

Gazelleburgers: See Hamburgers

GCA: Ground Control Approach. Radar device which permits blind landings of planes through overcast. Five radar operators inside a 2½ ton truck can "talk" a blind-flying plane to the airstrip and set it right down on the runway.—*Newsweek. August 20, 1945. p. 42*

G.E.A. War: Greater East Asia War, the Japanese term for World War, 1939-. Premier Tojo's address at opening of the 84th diet, January 21, 1944.—*Voices of History, 1944-1945. p. 45*

Geese: AAF slang for bombers in formation

General Bor: Recently identified as Lieutenant General Tadeusz Komorowski, a regular Polish Army Officer, who took his assumed name from the Polish word for forest.—*PM. September 27, 1944*

General Gee: Nickname of Major General Leonard Gerow.— *Democrat & Chronicle. Rochester, N.Y. July 17, 1943. p. 1*

General Mac: Nickname of Brigadier General Anthony C. McAuliffe, 101st Airborne Division, probably best remembered for his now historic answer to the German request for surrender—"Nuts" (q.v.).—*New York Times. December 31, 1944. p. 6*

General of the Army: New rank (5 star general) created during World War II. This title was made distinct from General John J. Pershing's title which remained as before, General of the Armies. See also Admiral of the Fleet.—*Saturday Review of Literature. March 10, 1945. p. 5*

General Patch Does a Tailoring Job: By Admiral William F. Halsey. The Admiral greeted the news of the conquest of Guadalcanal in the following words: "Having sent General Patch to do a tailoring job on Guadalcanal, I am surprised and pleased at the speed with which he removed the enemy's pants to accomplish it."—*Times-Union. Rochester, N.Y. February 10, 1943*

"General Pershing": (tank) Nickname of the American Army's latest (as of March 1945) tank, carrying a 90-mm. gun and heavier armor and called the "answer to the German Tiger."—*New York Times. March 11, 1945. p. 6E*

General "S. Bosy": Chief of the Czechoslovak military mission in Britain, self-identified, on June 4, 1945, as Bruno Sklenovsky, a former colonel on the Czechoslovak General Staff, who had been eagerly sought by the Germans throughout the war. He was the builder of the Czech defense fortifications, which included the Sudetan Line, made with French aid and regarded by the Nazis as a possible guide to the construction of the French Maginot Line.—*American Notes and Queries. June 1945. p. 39*

General Stubbornness: Nickname of Lieutenant General Vassili Ivanovitch Chuikov (Russian Army).—*Current Biography. 1943. p. 132*

Generalissimo: Commander of a large armed force. It is the title commonly given to Chiang Kai-shek, the Chinese leader, and also to Franco, the dictator of Spain, and Stalin of Russia

Genocide: A term invented by Professor Raphael Lemkin of Duke University. He compounded the word from the Greek "genos" (race, tribe) and the suffix "cide" (from the Latin, killing) to produce a term which means "the destruction of a nation or of an ethnic group."—*Pleasures of Publishing. November 20, 1944; New York Times. October 20, 1946. p. E 13; American Scholar. Spring 1946. p. 227-30*

Geopolitics: Political-geographical theory advanced by Professor Karl Haushofer and adopted by the Nazis. It deals with the dependence of a country's politics on physical environment, and was used by the Nazis to help persuade the German people that their course of aggression was the proper and divinely decreed course to take

"The German Has to Be Hit with Everything We've Got and Finally the Breaking Point Will Come": By General Dwight Eisenhower. Quoted in a picture caption.—*New York Times Magazine. December 24, 1944. p. 11*

"Germany Will Emerge Victorious from This Fight": By Adolf Hitler, Reichsfuehrer of Germany. In a speech to arms workers in Berlin, December 10, 1940, Hitler said: "Whatever may happen, Germany will emerge victorious from this fight."—*Vital Speeches. January 1, 1941. p. 177*

Geronimo: Battle cry of the paratroops in North Africa. Parachute troops have to be tough—"tough as the wily old Indian warrior Geronimo, that the Army fought in the Southwest in the 1880's and from whom the paratroopers got their battle cry." In frontier days of the West, "Geronimo" was shouted as an alarm to warn against an Indian attack.—*American Notes and Queries. November 1945. p. 125; Newsweek. November 30, 1942. p. 20*

Gestapaches: From a combining of the two words Gestapo and Apaches, this term was applied to French cutthroats who collaborated with the Germans. Led by an ex-convict, their job was to track down members of the French resistance movement and Allied officers dropped into France by parachute, and deliver them to the Gestapo. They were brought to trial in the Paris Court of Justice in December 1944.—*Newsweek. December 25, 1944. p. 50*

Gestapettes: Said to be the French designation for the women whom the Germans brought to France with them during the occupation.—*American Notes and Queries. September 1944. p. 85*

Gestapo: Geheime Staats Polizei, usually called the Gestapo, the secret police of Prussia. First under the control of Goering, later under the command of Heinrich Himmler. The official uniform was green, but the force usually operated as plainclothesmen. Numerically the organization was small and, like all such highly professional police groups, it was completely obedient to its commanders. Similar to the Gestapo was the Schupo, the former municipal police forces of Germany, later unified as a state organization of some 200,000 men.—*New Republic. July 18, 1934. p. 249*

Get Cracking on Something: R.A.F. slang meaning show action on a job.—*American Speech. February 1941. p. 76*

Ghost: Radar term for echoes which did not follow normal characteristics and for which definite targets could not be found.—*Army and Navy Journal. August 18, 1945. p. 1534*

Ghost Man: Name given by pilots to the aircraft carrier's signal officer on night duty. Dressed in a fluorescent-striped suit and with fluorescent paddles, he directs night fighters to safe landings on the carrier's deck.—*Newsweek. July 30, 1945. p. 36*

GHQ: General Headquarters, United States Department of War. First created on May 18, 1917; discontinued in August 1920. It was revived by order of the Secretary of War on July 26, 1940. It is located at the Army War College. Its duties are to assist the Chief of Staff by inspecting and supervising the training of the Regular, National Guard, and Selective Service units of the army.—*Ford. What the Citizen Should Know About the Army. p. 164-5*

GI: Government Issue—refers to articles carried by the Quartermaster. But so convenient a phrase as "GI" could not be allowed to rest with the Quartermaster's supplies. It was adopted into army slang in innumerable phrases. Among them can be found:

GI Ashcans: Heavy artillery shells

GI Bill of Rights: Four-point legislation setting up financial benefits for the U.S. veterans of World War II. Legislation covered (1) Speedy settlement of all disability claims, (2) Aid of a veteran's placement bureau in finding a job, and unemployment insurance for a maximum of one year, (3) Government guarantee of 50 per cent of any loan up to $4,000 to apply on home, farm or business property purchase or repair, (4) A free year of college, and more for longer service, if veteran was under 25 when he entered the service; and subsidy on apprenticeship for a vocation. The bill was signed by President Roosevelt in June 1944.—*Time. June 26, 1944. p. 63*

GI Brats: Officers' children

GI Cans: Ashcans or garbage cans. This term was in use in the army long before World War II; in this instance the GI stood for galvanized iron.—*American Speech. December 1946. p. 247*

GI Cocktail: Dose of salts

GI Haircut: Cut to one inch

GI Janes: Enlisted Wacs. Sometimes GI Jill, GI Josephine

GI Jim: Name for American veteran killed in World War II; coined by Representative Clare Boothe Luce (but term did not gain any wide use).—*American Notes and Queries. December 1944. p. 135*

GI Joe: Soldier. As to the origin of the term, Dave Breger (cartoonist), in a letter to *Time* magazine claimed to be the originator of the term. "GI Joe Trooper" was the name he gave to the cartoon hero whose exploits and misadventures he used in a series of cartoons for *Yank*. The first of these appeared in *Yank* June 17, 1942. He decided on the "GI" for its prevalence in army talk and "Joe" for the alliterative effect.—*Time. February 26, 1945. p. 7*

GI Krauts: Term used by army of occupation forces to refer to former privates in the German Army.—*New York Times Magazine. December 2, 1945. p. 22*

GI Liquor in the Pacific: "Kava"—made from roots of the kava tree, Polynesian and Melanesian islands; "Jungle juice"—made from dried fruits contained in J or K rations; "Night fighter"—fermented sap of nipa palm; "Plonk"—Australian vin ordinaire; "Sake"—Japanese wine or beer; "Tuba"—fermented sap from heart of coconut tree, Philippines.—*Esquire. January 1946. p. 209-210*

GI Moe: Army mule.—*New York Times Magazine. December 24, 1944. p. 32*

GI Round Table: An education program, sponsored by the War Department, planned for all the camps and theaters of war where American soldiers were. The program employed a series of illustrated booklets. Material for the booklets was prepared by the American Historical Association. The round table was a kind of discussion group. Participation was voluntary. Subjects covered included: What shall be done with the war criminals? Will the French republic live again? Do you want your wife to work after the war? What is propaganda? etc.—*New York Times Magazine. October 1, 1944. p. 10-11, 41*

GI Turkey: Corned beef and so on almost indefinitely. GI Joe for soldier is the GI term most universally known and accepted

Gibson Girl: Hand-cranked radio transmitter included in aircraft life rafts. So called from its "wasp-waist" shape

Gilda: Name given to the fourth atomic bomb, named after a film in which Rita Hayworth appeared.—*American Notes and Queries. July 1946. p. 53*

Gips: See World War II

"Give Us the Tools, and We Will Finish the Job": By Winston Churchill. Radio broadcast February 9, 1941.—*Churchill. Blood, Sweat and Tears. p. 462; Vital Speeches. February 15, 1941. p. 275*

Gizmo: Marine's word for anything or anyone he can't think of a word for. Similar to "whoosis."—*Time. July 19, 1943. p. 69*

Glacier Happy: See Shell-shock

Gladiator: (British plane) Gloster fighter plane

Glass house: Slang for power-operated turret in an airplane.—*Saturday Review of Literature. October 4, 1941. p. 9*

Glide Bombing: To bomb from a plane, by descending at an angle of less than 65° from the horizontal when releasing bombs. Steeper dives were called dive bombing (q.v.).—*Britannica Book of the Year. 1944. p. 770*

Glider Freights: Early in July 1943 the first glider "train" from the United States, surviving a towing of 3500 miles, arrived in

England. The single glider, which had an 84-foot wingspread, carried a ton and a half of freight.—*American Notes and Queries. August 1943. p. 70*

Globaloney: Term used by Clare Boothe Luce in a speech in the House of Representatives, Washington, D.C., February 9, 1943. In referring to Vice President Wallace, she said: "Much of what Mr. Wallace calls his global thinking is, no matter how you slice it, still 'Globaloney.' "—*Congressional Record. February 9, 1943. p. 800-1; Vital Speeches. March 15, 1943. p. 334*

Globerish: Word coined by commentator Clifford Evans to counter Representative Clare Boothe Luce's globaloney.—*PM. July 1, 1943*

Go Fog: A machine for blowing away fog from airfields. Invented by Ross Pleasants, a California man, it promises to be much cheaper than the wartime "FIDO" (q.v.) system. Though Mr. Pleasants worked on his invention before the war, he was unable to interest the Air Corps to the point of using it. "Go Fog" uses a simple coal burner with an electric blower. This throws up particles of calcium chloride which absorb the moisture of which fog is made.—*Newsweek. December 24, 1945. p. 66*

"Go Forward, Always Go Forward": By Lieutenant General George S. Patton, Jr. "Go forward, always go forward. You must not fail. Go until the last shots are fired and the last drop of gasoline is gone. Then go forward on foot."—*New York Times Magazine. April 4, 1943. p. 8*

Gobbledygook: Word invented by Maury Maverick to mean talk or writing which was long, pompous, vague or involved, usually with Latinized words.—*New York Times Magazine. May 21, 1944. p. 11*

God Bless America: Song title. Words and music by Irving Berlin. Introduced by Kate Smith, Armistice Day, 1938, in a radio broadcast

Goetterdaemmerung Plan: Unsuccessful Nazi blueprint for a fight to the death.—*American Notes and Queries. April 1945. p. 8*

Going Home Offensive: Name given by the GI's to the advance over the Roer River in Germany in February 1945. It was a major offensive and aimed at leading to a union of the American and Russian armies and completing the war in Germany.—*Newsweek. March 5, 1945. p. 27*

Going on the Stunt: British slang for going on maneuvers.— *American Speech. October 1941. p. 186*

Gold Brick Papas: An organization of "long-distance fathers who try to help their children by V-mail." Members must be stationed overseas, must never have seen their offspring, and must be known to have forwarded advice to their wives on the fundamental problems of baby care.—*American Notes and Queries. August 1944. p. 71*

Gold Fish Club: An organization founded by Lieutenant Colonel Baden-Powell Weil; membership limited to airmen who have crashed into the ocean.—*American Notes and Queries. November 1944. p. 117*

Gold Star Fathers, Inc.: Group of fathers of sons killed in World War II; organized December 9, 1945 by James M. Timmons, Caledonia, N.Y.—*New York Times. December 9, 1945*

Goldflake: Code name given to the movement of British and Canadian troops from Italy, through France and into Belgium in February 1945.—*U.S. Army. ETO. CONAD History. p. 376*

Good Show: R.A.F. slang. Term of praise. "Cracking good show" highest possible praise. "Bad show" adverse criticism, or comment on any regrettable happening.—*American Speech. 1941. p. 76*

Good-time Janes: See Victory Girl

Goof Off: Slang term for loafing, avoiding work in one way or another, making a mistake, etc.—a broad term. A person could "goof off" in any number of ways.—*American Speech. October 1945. p. 226; December 1945. p. 261*

Goofer: A British term (from the American goof) applied to people who ignored orders to seek shelter during air raids.—*American Speech. February 1944. p. 11*

Gooks: Term usually employed by enlisted men in referring to Melanesian and Polynesian natives on the Pacific islands

Goon Gun: Chemical Battalion's nickname (originating in July 1943) for the 4.2 mortar, put to long and hard use in Sicily and Italy; said to have functioned so effectively at Hill 715 (Mount Fratello), Sicily, on August 6, 1943, that the operation has since been popularly referred to as the battle of "Goon Gun Hill."—*Army and Navy Register. April 22, 1944*

Goop Bomb: A 500-pound incendiary bomb made of clusters of 6-pound bombs packed with jellied oil and magnesium, each of which spread flame over a radius of 30 yards. So called because the "fiery jellied oil contents" of the bomb suggested a sticky mass, which in laboratory slang is known as "goop." Used over Japan in March 1945.—*Army and Navy Register. April 22, 1944; Newsweek. March 19, 1945. p. 34*

Goose: (American plane) Grumman OA-9 JRF transport plane

Gooseberries: Name for breakwaters that formed the artificial harbor for landing British troops in France. See also Mulberry.—*Notes and Queries. January 12, 1946. p. 22*

Grand Slam: In radar code, "the enemy plane has been shot down."—*Newsweek. September 10, 1945. p. 92*

Grapeshot: Code name for spring (1945) drive in Italy by General Mark Clark's Fifteenth Army Group.—*General Marshall's Report. 1945. p. 24*

Grasshopper: Name given to high-winged cabin monoplanes of the tandem type.—*American Speech. October 1944. p. 225*

Graveyard Shift: Night shift in a factory, running from 12:00 midnight to 8:00 A.M., or from 11:00 P.M. to 7.00 A.M.—*Princeton University. Re-organization of Hour Schedules. p. 6*

The Greatest Mother in the World: Poster caption. War Fund 1943, American Red Cross

Green Diamond: See Com Z

Green Dragon: Nickname for LST.—*National Geographic. July 1944. p. 19*

Green Hornet: Nickname of Major General George S. Patton, Jr.—*Current Biography. 1943. p. 571; New York Times Magazine. June 20, 1943. p. 34*

Green Project: Combat veterans were flown to Casablanca by the Air Transport Command's streamlined "Green Project" to await passage home aboard ATC transport planes. Commanded by Brigadier General James S. Stowell, the Green Project derived its name from the fact that it had the "green light" (or go ahead signal) and highest priority ever granted an army movement of troops.—*Buffalo Evening News. July 11, 1945. p. 3*

Gremlin Grange: AAF slang for a rest home to which airmen suffering from battle fatigue went to rest up. Term stemmed from the RAF gremlin mythology. Anyone who began to see gremlins was ready for Gremlin Grange. See also Flak Shack.—*New York Times Magazine. June 4, 1944. p. 12*

Gremlins: Nickname given to the "Little People" who make things go wrong, particularly with airplanes. "The R.A.F. first learned about the little creatures in 1923 and called them gremlins—probably from the obsolete Old English transitive verb greme, meaning to vex. Yet it was not until World War II that the R.A.F. really got to know the gremlins."—*Time. September 14, 1942. p. 37.*

Another account, by John Moore, from the *Observer* of November 8, 1942, and quoted in *American Notes and Queries* on February 1943, p. 170, says that they were called Gremlins because "they were the goblins which came out of Fremlin beer bottles" which seems a very likely origin for such creatures.

Accounts differ, but *Newsweek*, September 7, 1942, quotes the following dispatch from Merrill Mueller, Chief of *Newsweek's* London Bureau: "The great-granddaddy of all 'bloody Gremlins' was born in 1923 in a beer bottle belonging to a Fleet Air Arm pilot whose catapult reconnaissance plane was cursed with perpetual engine trouble. This pilot was overloaded with beer the night before a practice maneuver, when his engine failed and he crashed into the waves. Rescued he said the engine failed because little people from a beer bottle had haunted him all night and had got into the plane's engine and controls during the flight . . . 'the bloody Gremlins did it.'" This article also says that the American Gremlins are called "Yehudis" because they are always "fiddling about." Another explanation of the American name Yehudi was that they were "the little man who wasn't there"— and his name was Yehudi.—*American Notes and Queries. April 1943. p. 16*

Expert "gremlinologists" recorded the characteristics of four new species: genus *Jockey*, that guided seagulls or pigeons into the windscreen of the approaching plane; genus *Incisor*, that teethed its young on the vital control wires of planes; genus *Optic*, that cast a kind of glow over the bomb sight just as it was being lined on a target; and genus *Cavity*, that riddled an airfield with troublesome little holes.— *American Notes and Queries. November 1942. p. 121-2*

Ground Crew: Mechanics and technicians who service a plane before and after flight, and keep it in proper condition

Ground-Gripper: AAF slang for non-flying personnel

Group: See Air Force

Grow More in '44: Slogan to encourage more Victory gardens in 1944.—*Publishers' Weekly. March 11, 1944. p. 1121*

Grow Your Own—Be Sure: Poster caption to encourage Victory gardens of vegetables.—*Publishers' Weekly. March 17, 1945. p. 1189*

Grumlins: Name given to "saboteurs of the spirit" on the home front, by Sam Rayburn, Speaker of the House. "The Grumlin," Rayburn declared, "does the same job of sabotage on the home front that the Gremlin (q.v.) does to the airplanes of our pilots fighting the Axis." Speech at East Texas State Teachers College.—*Democrat & Chronicle. Rochester, N.Y. August 6, 1943. p. 1*

Guerilla: (Sometimes spelled guerrilla) Small bands (not regular army) formed to harass the enemy. The word is used as a noun, also as an adjective, e.g. "guerilla warfare"

Guinea Pig Club: Composed of severely wounded RAF fliers who have undergone plastic surgery treatment, volunteered for experimental operations, and dedicated themselves to help one another in readjustment to civilian life.—*American Notes and Queries. March 1945. p. 185*

Guinea Pig Squadron: Ships sent out to locate the pressurized mines dropped by American planes in Japanese harbors and waterways. The crews worked on deck, with the engines operated by remote control from the bridge. These "pressurized" mines detonated when there was a pressure change in the water near them. Ordinary mine sweepers were so small, they did not set the mines off. Hence the "Guinea Pig Squadron" of larger ships.—*Newsweek. January 14, 1946. p. 56*

Gumbatsu: Japanese militarists; Zaibatsu—Japanese industrialists and financiers; Mombatsu—Japanese feudal, landed aristocracy. These ruling cliques in Japan were "liquidated" by General MacArthur.—*New York Times. July 22, 1945. p. 2E; November 18, 1945. p. 2E, 6E*

Gung Ho: Nickname for Lieutenant Colonel Evans F. Carlson. Gung Ho is a Chinese phrase meaning "work together." Gung Ho was also the name given to the Raider Camp on Espiritu Santo, in the New Hebrides.—*Lucas. Combat Correspondent. p. 98*

Gunner: (American plane) Fairchild AT-21 trainer plane

"Guns Will Make Us Powerful; Butter Will Only Make Us Fat": By Field Marshal Hermann Goering (Germany). Radio broadcast, Summer 1936.—*Oxford Dictionary of Quotations. p. 575b*

Gush (slang) : See entry under Kriegie

GWIBIT: Guild of Washington Incompetent Bureaucratic Idea Throatcutters. Originated by Representative Karl E. Mundt, Republican. After describing this new "Species Capitalensis," he goes on to say, "A gwibitzer is not to be confused with a kibitzer; the latter merely stands on the sidelines and watches while the former sits in the path of progress and trips those who would traverse it."—*Newsweek. December 27, 1943. p. 40*

Gyrenes: Slang term for Marines, used very generally throughout the Pacific theater of operations, said to have been applied to the Marines by the Chinese. Variously spelled gyrines and gyreens

Habbakuk Project: Two-million-ton ice and woodpulp "iceberg" carrier proposed as an anti-submarine plane base in the Atlantic; the two-year-old Allied government experiments were abandoned in 1943.—*American Notes and Queries. April 1946. p. 7*

Hais Pipeline: One of the pipelines under the English Channel which supplied the AEF with gasoline, named for Hartley, chief engineer of the Anglo-Iranian Oil Company, and Siemens, of the firm of Siemens and Henley. See also Hamel Pipeline.—*New York Times. May 24, 1945. p. 5*

Half-track: Vehicle with wheels in front and track assembly in the rear; often miscalled by civilians "armored car."—*New York Times Magazine. December 2, 1945. p. 22*

Hamburgers: Many variants of hamburgers appeared during World War II, among them gazelleburgers (made from gazelle meat in Northern Iran), caraburgers (made from carabao meat in the Philippines), beaverburgers, potatoburgers and many others. See also Buffaloburgers.—*American Speech. December 1944. p. 308-9; Yank. May 12, 1944. p. 7*

Hamel Pipeline: One of the pipelines under the English Channel which supplied the AEF with gasoline, named for Hammick, chief engineer of the Iraq Petroleum Company, and Ellis, chief oilfields engineer of the Burma Oil Company. See also Hais Pipeline.—*New York Times. May 24, 1945. p. 5*

Hampden: (British plane) Handley-Page medium bomber plane

Hand a Gong: Slang for the handing out of medals to flyers by the High Command

"The Hand That Held the Dagger Has Struck It into the Back of Its Neighbor": By Franklin D. Roosevelt. Address June 10, 1940. In reference to Italy's declaration of war against France and England.—*Vital Speeches. June 15, 1940. p. 515; Baird. Representative American Speeches. 1939-40. p. 82*

Handie-Talkie: A two-way radiotelephone system complete in a package weighing about five pounds. Built by Motorola for Army and Navy use. See also Walkie-Talkie.—*Life. April 16, 1945. p. 91* (advertisement); *Fortune. October 1943. p. 62*

Hang Out the Laundry: AAF slang for dropping paratroops

Hangar Flying: AAF slang for conversation about flying and kindred subjects

Hangar Geese: Airplanes stored in hangars and stripped down to provide spare parts for other planes.—*New York Times. August 11, 1943*

Hangar Pilot: AAF slang for one who does his best "flying" in conversation

Hangman: Nickname given to Reinhard Heydrick, former deputy director of the German State Secret Police.—*Current History. July 1942. p. 361*

"Hap" Arnold: Nickname of General Henry Harley Arnold, Commanding General of the United States Army Air Forces.—*Current Biography. 1942. p. 35; Time. June 22, 1942. p. 28*

Happy: Happy, used as a combining form meaning dizzy or exhilarated, turned up in many terms. According to an article by Dwight L. Bolinger, slap-happy was apparently the first, used as a synonym for punch-drunk. Later uses included Hitler-happy, power-happy, bar-happy, stripe-happy (Army), bomb-happy, trigger-happy, etc.—*American Speech. February 1944. p. 60*

Hardstand: Parking lot for one or more planes, built by Seabees. The surface must be "hard" enough to support the plane's weight, which is concentrated in the few square inches of wheel surface touching the ground.—*Huie. Can Do! p. 40 note*

Harvard: (American plane) North American AT-16 trainer plane

Hash Marks: Nickname for stripes on a soldier uniform that denote length of service. See also Hershey Bar. Also the title for a joke column in the soldier newspaper, *Stars and Stripes*, because, as the editor of the column (Captain J. C. Wilkinson) said, "All the jokes have served at least a three-year hitch."—*New York Times Magazine. April 29, 1945. p. 20*

Hatchet Day: "In the Low Countries, 'Hatchet Day' means the day of vengeance drawing near when the Axis will get it in the neck. So hatchet-conscious are the Nazis, they are arming their Dutch and Belgian stooges with pistols, rifles, and hand grenades. The higher-up German Nazis themselves dwell in houses converted into arsenals and stocked with food for a siege, and their passports are stamped for entry into Spain."—*New York Times Magazine. May 30, 1943. p. 2*

Hats Off to MacArthur: Song title. Words and music by Ira Schuster, Paul Cunningham, and Leonard Whitcup. Introduced in the spring of 1942.—*Considine. MacArthur the Magnificent. p. 117*

"Have Courage—Good Days Will Come Again. Long Live the Nation!": By George II, King of Greece. Words to his people as he was leaving the country.—*Time. June 22, 1942. p. 16*

"Have Our Country's Flag Unfurled and in Tokyo's Sun, Let It Wave in Its Full Glory as a Symbol of Hope for the Oppressed and as a Harbinger of Victory for the Right": By General of the Army MacArthur. In a simple ceremony on September 8, 1945, the American flag was raised in the compound of the U.S. Embassy in Tokyo, a symbol of the occupation of Japan by American troops.—*Newsweek. September 17, 1945. p. 39*

Havoc: (American plane) Douglas A-20 BD light bomber plane

He: See Plane Nicknames

He Conquers Who Gets There First: Motto of the First Troop Carrier Command, AAF.—*Life. September 4, 1944. p. 102*

"He Died Unquestioning and Uncomplaining, with Faith in His Heart and Victory His End": Citation on Colin Kelly in a dispatch writen by General Douglas MacArthur, December 1941.—*Considine. MacArthur the Magnificent. p. 16, 98*

Heads Up: In radar code language, "Heads up" meant "Nazi planes have torn through the coastal defense."—*Newsweek. September 10, 1945. p. 92*

Headspace: A serious term meaning the distance between the rear of a cartridge fully seated in the chamber of a weapon and the face of the bolt; soldiers gave it a comic twist by using it to refer to the 'headspace' of dumb fellow soldiers.—*American Speech. December 1945. p. 261*

Heavy: Short for heavy bomber.—*American Speech. December 1945. p. 301*

Hedgehog: Secret weapon used against submarines in the war. A bank of twenty-four rocket projectiles—each exploding on contact only—fired simultaneously to cover a large area.—*New York Times. November 18, 1945. p. 2E, 6E*

Hedgehogs: Name also given to small towns on the Eastern Front which the "Germans have transformed into strong points or 'hedgehogs.' "—*New York Times Magazine. October 29, 1944. p. 7*

Hedgehoppers: Army nickname for careless pilots. See also Flathatters.—*New York Times. September 24, 1944. p. 2E, 8E*

Heil: This word from the phrase "Heil Hitler" came to be used as a verb meaning 'to give the Nazi salute.'—*American Speech. February 1941. p. 65*

Heinkel: Trade name for a line of German planes, most often associated with a Heinkel 4-engined heavy bomber monoplane.—*Democrat & Chronicle. Rochester, N.Y. September 8, 1940*

Helicab: A flying automobile, designed by William B. Stout for Consolidated Vultee Aircraft Corporation.—*Business Week. August 7, 1943. p. 19*

Hell on Wheels Division: Nickname given to the U.S. Second Armored Division, which won fame in North Africa, Sicily, Normandy and across France. This Division also played an active part in the Battle of the Bulge (q.v.).—*Times-Union. Rochester, N.Y. January 9, 1945*

"Hell-on-Wings Chamber": In a small, blacked-out room at the Norfolk Naval Training Station, the illusion of aerial bombing and strafing was created by a new scientific device designed to make American anti-aircraft gunners the most deadly in the world. A projector and amplifier reproduced on a screen the sound and three-dimensional sight of speeding planes of all kinds. A machine gun which "fired" electrical tracers instead of bullets faced the screen. An automatic computer recorded hits and misses. Known by the navy men as the "Hell-on-wings chamber," the room's value in training gunners was proved at the Dam Neck Company anti-aircraft training and test station.—*Democrat & Chronicle. Rochester, N.Y. May 11, 1943*

"Hell, We Haven't Started to Fight. Our Artillery Hasn't Been Overrun Yet": By Major General Terry de la Mesa Allen (United States Army). Said at the invasion of Sicily, July 1943.—*Time. July 26, 1943. p. 29*

Hellcat: (American plane) Grumman F6F fighter plane

Helldiver: (American plane) Curtiss A-25 SB2C light bomber plane

Hell Hound: See Robot Bombs

"Hello, You Limey": By Sergeant Joseph A. Randall. "Hello, you limey!" was the affectionate hail given by Sergeant Joseph A. Randall of State Center, Iowa, to Sergeant A. W. Acland of Maida Vale, London, as reconnaissance patrols of the British Eighth Army and armored forces of the Second United States Army Corps met in an historic juncture on the hard-surfaced road amid desert wastes 42 miles from Gabes in Tunisia. "Very glad to see you," answered Acland, with typical British restraint. These two enlisted men stepped forward and shook hands for the first formal contact between British forces which had pursued Field Marshal Rommel 1500 miles and the Americans who pushed the Germans back 140 miles from Kasserine Pass in six weeks.—*Democrat & Chronicle. Rochester, N.Y. April 9, 1943*

Hell's Corner: Name given to Dover on the English Channel because it was so constantly under Nazi fire. See also Bing Bang Corner.—*New York Times. October 8, 1944. p. 2E, 7 E*

Hell's Pocket: A section on Saipan where the Japanese had dug themselves into deep limestone caves, impervious to bombs and naval fire. Sweating Americans dragged up big guns to shell the caves point blank.—*Newsweek. July 10, 1944. p. 34*

Help Him . . . Help Yourself . . . For Victory at Least 10% of Your Pay Every Payday: Poster caption. United States Treasury Department

Hermann: Nickname for unexploded two-ton Nazi bomb, buried for five years in South Croydon, England.—*American Notes and Queries. January 1946. p. 151*

Herrenvolk: (German, "master people") So used by Americans and English in disparagement of Nazi claims to superiority.—*American Speech. April 1942. p. 123*

Hershey Bar: Nickname for soldier's gold sleeve insignia denoting six months' overseas duty; named for Lewis B. Hershey, Director of Selective Service. See also Hash marks.—*American Notes and Queries. February 1946. p. 168*

He's a 'Fighting Fool'—Give Him the Best You've Got! Poster caption. United States War Production Board

H for V: Health for Victory Clubs. Started by Mrs. Julia Kiene in March 1942 in a Westinghouse plant in Mansfield, Ohio. Idea spread through the Westinghouse plants to other factories all over the country. Mrs. Kiene edits a monthly booklet which has recipes for every day for a month, menus for the three regular meals, charts to save time; she also writes a second monthly pamphlet which goes to the lecturers who conduct the H for V club meetings.—*Democrat & Chronicle Magazine. Rochester, N.Y. July 1, 1943. p. 5*

H-Hour: The hour of invasion. See also note under D-Day.—*New York Times Magazine. June 11, 1944. p. 14*

Highpockets: See Baka

"The History of Warfare Does Not Know Any Such Undertaking So Broad in Conception, So Grandiose in Scale, and So Masterly in Execution": By Premier Josef Stalin, in tribute to British and U.S. forces in effecting the Allied landing of troops in France.—*Newsweek. June 26, 1944. p. 28*

Hit Hard and Often with the Marines: Poster caption. United States Marine Corps

"Hit Hard, Hit Fast, Hit Often": By Admiral William Frederick Halsey. The Halsey battle cry.—*Time. November 30, 1942. p. 29*

"Hit the Enemy Twice: First, to find out what he's got; then, to take it away from him." By Lieutenant General Omar Bradley.—*Reader's Digest. July 1944. p. 58*

Hit the Sack: See Sack

Hit the Silk: Phrase used by pilots, meaning to parachute from their planes.—*Cosmopolitan. August 1943. p. 14*

"Hitler Can't Lick These People": By Harry L. Hopkins, President Roosevelt's personal envoy to London, on his return from thirty-two days of sharing the rigors of war in Britain.—*Newsweek. February 24, 1941. p. 20*

"Hitler Has Missed the Bus": By Sir Neville Chamberlain. Speech of April 4, 1940, London.—*Newsweek. April 15, 1940. p. 24*

"Hitler Has No Theme, Naught but Mania, Appetite and Exploitation": By Winston Churchill. Radio address, August 24, 1941.—*Vital Speeches. September 1, 1941. p. 677*

Hitler Weather: Bad weather capable of hindering Allied advances in Germany. (*New York Times* dispatch from London, September 23, 1944).—*American Notes and Queries. October 1944. p. 102*

Hitlerite: Noun (or adjective) signifying a sympathizer with, adherent of, or connected with Hitler. The word Hitlerite was recently added to the English language. It first appeared about July 1942 in translations of Russian communiqués.—*New York Times Magazine. October 3, 1943. p. 29*

H.M.S. Pepperpot; H.M.S. Porcupine; H.M.S. Rockgarden: Nicknames given to H.M.S. Penelope, a British ship, laid up in an eastern United States port for repairs in June 1942. "Pepperpot" for the thousand or so holes in her sides, and "Porcupine" for the wooden pegs driven into the holes. "Rockgarden" was given her after bomb hits on shore (when she was alongside a Malta dock) threw debris around her decks. She was finally sunk off Anzio in March 1944.—*Newsweek. June 15, 1942. p. 20; Time. March 20, 1944. p. 29*

Hobby Lobby: Slang term for the office of Colonel Oveta Culp Hobby, commander of the Women's Army Corps.—*New York Times Magazine. September 17, 1944. p. 32*

Hog-caller: Nickname for a portable loudspeaker.—*PM. September 17, 1944. p. 32*

"Hold the Line": By Franklin D. Roosevelt. Anti-inflationary order, April 8, 1943. "The Executive Order I have signed today is a hold-the-line order. To hold the line we cannot tolerate further increases in general wage or salary rates except where clearly necessary to correct sub-standard living conditions."—*New York Times. April 9, 1943. p. 1*

Hollywood Glider: Air Force slang for the B-17 Flying Fortress, so named because it appeared in numerous motion pictures.—*American Speech. December 1946. p. 310*

Homing Pigeon: See Ruptured Duck

"Homma May Have the Bottle—But I've Got the Cork": By General Douglas MacArthur. Homma, the Japanese commander (who later committed hara-kiri for his failure to overcome MacArthur) reported to Tokyo that he had got possession of the bottle and had MacArthur trapped in the bottleneck, and MacArthur commented as above.—*Miller. General Douglas MacArthur, Fighter for Freedom. p. 12*

Honest Bob: Nickname of Robert Gordon Menzies, former Prime Minister of Australia.—*Newsweek. September 1, 1941. p. 25*

Hoo Mana Wahui: (Hawaiian phrase meaning "Time will tell"). Used by Admiral Nimitz in taking command of the Pacific Fleet on December 31, 1941.—*New York Times Magazine. April 15, 1945. p. 38*

Hospital Circuit: Third and latest of the USO Camp Shows Circuits. This performed in hospitals in the U.S. and offered carefully selected entertainment for the sick and wounded, in close cooperation with medical officers. See also Blue Circuit, Victory Circuit, and Foxhole Circuit.—*Newsweek. July 31, 1944. p. 60*

Hot Rock: Code name given by Vice Admiral Richmond Kelly Turner to the operation of the invasion of Iwo Jima by the Marines.—*Newsweek. March 5, 1945. p. 34*

"However Hard the Road, Ultimate Victory Is Certain": By General Douglas MacArthur. On March 2, 1942, MacArthur received from the Moros in the province of Lanao on the Island of Mindanao, a pledge "to fight with all our strength against the Japanese and other enemies of the United States and Philippine government," and MacArthur replied as quoted above.—*Considine. MacArthur the Magnificent. p. 116*

Howlin' Mad: Nickname of Lieutenant General Holland M. Smith, commander of amphibious troops at Tarawa, Makin, Kwajalein.—*New York Times Magazine. January 21, 1945. p. 26*

Howling Horace: British term for air raid siren. See also Moaning Minnie.—*American Speech. February 1944. p. 11*

Hubba Hubba: A current equivalent of the street corner whistle; an exclamation of approbation, thrill, or enthusiasm. Origin claimed by U.S. Air Force, U.S. Navy, and the U.S. Marines. Its first use in World War II is uncertain but it became very prevalent, appeared on the radio, in the movies, in several popular songs, and in very general usage in conversation. Etymologically it might be traced back in English dialect to this: "Hubba—a cry given to warn fishermen of the approach of pilchards." (*English Dialect Dictionary v. 3, p. 263*). The same dictionary (v. 4, p. 501) lists "Pilchard—anything particularly good, ambitious or excessive." This dialectal meaning would accord very well with the way Hubba Hubba was used in the period of World War II.—*American Speech. February 1947. p. 34-9*

Hubby: Nickname of Admiral Husband E. Kimmel (United States Navy).—*Newsweek. December 15, 1941. p. 27*

Hudson: (American plane) Lockheed A-29 PBO light bomber plane (Patrol)

Huff Duff: High-frequency direction-finding device, with a range that makes it possible to detect and plot radio signals of as little as fifteen seconds' duration emitted halfway around the globe from plotting stations.—*New York Herald Tribune. January 16, 1946*

Human Barracudas: See UDT

Hump: The spur of the Himalayas that separates Assam and Yunnan and cuts through western China. See Over the Hump.—*New York Times. January 14, 1945. p. 6E*

Hurricane: (British plane) Hawker fighting plane. Companion fighter to Spitfire (q.v.)

Hurry: See Plane Nicknames

Hurry Them Back! Join the WAAC: WAAC recruiting slogan, 1942-43. Sometimes appeared as "Speed them back! Join the WAAC'"

Husky: Code name for operational plans of assault on Sicily. —*General Marshall's Report. 1945. p. 10*

"I Am Never Anxious when I Fight My Battles. If I Am Anxious I Don't Fight Them. I Wait until I Am Ready." Ascribed to Field Marshal Montgomery by J. Donald Adams in an article in *New York Times Book Review. January 28, 1945. p. 2*

"I Came Through and I Shall Return": By General Douglas MacArthur. His pledge after reaching Australia on March 17, 1942, after his escape from Bataan and Corregidor.—*Considine. MacArthur the Magnificent. p. 124*

"I Do Not Believe in a Real Danger of a 'New War'": By Premier Josef Stalin in September 1946, in a statement to the press.—*Vital Speeches. October 1, 1946. p. 742*

"I Have Not Become the King's First Minister in Order to Preside over the Liquidation of the British Empire": By Winston Churchill. Speech delivered at dinner for the Lord Mayor, London, November 10, 1942.—*Vital Speeches. November 15, 1942. p. 67*

"I Have Returned": By General MacArthur. On the morning of October 20, 1944, the American flag was planted on the shores of Leyte in the Philippines. MacArthur stood before a microphone on a Signal Corps truck on Leyte's beach and broadcast to the people of the Philippines, who had waited two and a half years for this: "This is the Voice of Freedom, General MacArthur speaking. People of the Philippines: I have returned! By the grace of Almighty God our forces stand again on Philippine soil. . . . The hour of your redemption is here. . . ."—*Miller. History of World War II. p. 661*

"I Predict a Great Empire Will Be Destroyed . . . I Know that It Will Be Britain": By Adolf Hitler. Speech to Reichstag, July 19, 1940.—*Vital Speeches. August 1, 1940. p. 625*

"I Report the Order to Defend Tunisia to the Last Cartridge Has Been Carried Out": By Colonel General Jurgen von Arnim, (German Army). Arnim, Axis Commander in Chief, was captured in the mountains south of Tunis after sending above message to Berlin. When taken to the headquarters of General Anderson, commander of the British First Army, he refused to sign an unconditional surrender. But his men had already stopped fighting.—*Newsweek. May 24, 1943. p. 22*

"I Shall Keep a Soldier's Faith": By General Douglas MacArthur. On his arrival in Melbourne, Australia, March 21, 1942.—*Democrat & Chronicle. Rochester, N. Y. May 25, 1942; Considine MacArthur the Magnificent. p. 126*

I Threw a Kiss in the Ocean: Song title. Words and music by Irving Berlin. Introduced by Kate Smith on the radio March 6, 1942

"I Was at Bataan and Then I Was at Corregidor": By General Jonathan Wainwright. In addressing eighty liberated prisoners of war in San Francisco, General Wainwright said: "In future years our greatest pride will be these words : *I was at Bataan and then I was at Corregidor.*"—*Charlotte (N.C.) Observer. September 26, 1945. p. 1*

"I Would Far Rather Die Fighting Hitler than Live under His Rule": By Frank Knox. Address at United States Conference of Mayors, St. Louis, Missouri, February 20, 1941. See also "It is better to die on your feet than to live on your knees."—*Vital Speeches. March 15, 1941. p. 325*

IADA: International Atomic-Development Authority. Bernard M. Baruch, American member of the United Nations Atomic Energy Commission, on June 14, 1946 announced the decision of the Commission concerning the atom bomb. The fourteen-point proposal included a setting up of an international atomic-development authority (IADA) created by treaties among the United Nations.—*Newsweek. June 24, 1946. p. 23*

IC: Inspected and Condemned. Similar to civilian NG (no good).—*House Beautiful. January 1945. p. 39*

I'd Rather Be with Them—than Waiting for Them: WAC recruiting slogan.—*Woman's Home Companion. September 1944. p. 77*

Idle Gossip Sinks Ships: Caption printed on envelopes furnished for soldier use by the USO (United Service Organization for National Defense). See also "Loose lips sink ships"

"If There Are Japs on This Island, They'll Not See an American Sailor Crawl. We'll Stand, and March, and Make Them Shoot Us Down, Like Men-O'-Warsmen": By Bomber Pilot Harold Dixon, (United States Navy).—*Trumbull. The Raft. p. 185*

"If We Fail, All Fails, and if We Fall, All Will Fall Together": By Winston Churchill. Speech to House of Commons July 29, 1941, on war production.—*Churchill. The Unrelenting Struggle. p. 221-2*

"If We're Good Enough, We Can Take It": By Elmer Davis. News broadcast February 16, 1942.—*Baird. Representative American Speeches. 1941-42. p. 117*

"If You Can Hold Out for 30 Days, We Will Send Help": American sense of humor comes to the fore! When word reached embattled Bataan of a Japanese submarine attack near Santa Barbara, California, it was suggested that the above message be sent by MacArthur to the commanding general of the Ninth Corps Area (California).—*Time. March 9, 1942. p. 21*

If You Can't Go Over, Come Across: Slogan for selling war bonds, widely used in 1942-43. This slogan is very similar to a poster used in World War I: "If you can't go across with a gun, come across with your part of the Red Cross War Fund"

If You Tell Where They're Going. . . They May Never Get There. Don't Talk about Troop Movements: Poster caption

IFF: Identification, Friend or Foe. A radar device. To tell our planes from the enemy a ground set sends a signal which "triggers" a set in a plane. This in turn sends back a coded signal. The same device is used between ships.—*Newsweek. August 20, 1945. p. 42*

IIIS: Interim International Information Service. See note under OWI

Ike: Nickname of General Dwight Eisenhower (United States Army).—*New York Times Magazine. June 20, 1943. p. 5*

Ilag: Abbreviation for Interniertenlager, a civilian internment camp. See also Lager.—*Red Cross Courier. June 1943. p. 11*

I'll Carry Mine Too! Trucks and Tires Must Last till Victory: Poster caption. To urge people to carry their own bundles, to save deliveries. United States Office of Defense Transportation

I'm Gonna Get Lit-Up when the Lights Go Up in London: Song popular in London in 1943.—*Newsweek. September 13, 1943. p. 102*

Immersion Foot: See Invasion foot

Imperative Books: In November 1942, the Council on Books in Wartime (q.v.) announced its intention of selecting certain new books which should be named "Imperatives." The basic idea was to single out for cooperative promotion by all branches of the industry books which were judged to represent important contributions to the country's war effort. No attempt was made to select an "Imperative" at regular intervals; the citation was given only when a deserving book came along. Books chosen were: 1) *They Were Expendable* by W. L. White; 2) *Into the Valley* by John Hersey; 3) *One World* by Wendell Willkie; 4) *U. S. Foreign Policy* by Walter Lippmann; 5) *A Bell for Adano* by John Hersey; 6) *People on Our Side* by Edgar Snow.—*Publishers' Weekly. December 25, 1943. p. 2308-10; March 25, 1944. p. 1287-8; Library Journal. October 15, 1944. p. 827*

Implement Our Ideals: See "It is necessary for us not only to have ideals. . . ."

The Impossible We Do At Once; the Miraculous Takes a Little Longer: Said to be the motto of the Army Service Forces. See also The Difficult We Do Immediately, etc.—*New York Times. November 4, 1945. p. 2E, 6E*

IMRO: Internal Macedonian Revolutionary Organization.— *Newsweek. August 13, 1945. p. 45*

"In Ashes They Must Lie": By Winston Churchill. Speech to Congress, Washington, D.C., May 19, 1943. "For in ashes they [the Japanese cities] must surely lie before peace comes back to the world." —*Vital Speeches. June 1, 1943. p. 484*

Incendiary: Originally a person who wilfully set fire to a building or other property. In World War II it came to mean an incendiary bomb. The phrase was shortened and the single word incendiary used. These bombs could not be extinguished with water but had to be smothered with chemicals, sand, or some other method to deprive them of oxygen.—*American Speech. February 1941. p. 66; Democrat & Chronicle. Rochester, N.Y. September 8, 1940*

"The Inescapable Price of Liberty Is an Ability to Preserve It from Destruction": By General Douglas MacArthur. In a letter to President Quezon of the Philippines.—*Miller. General Douglas MacArthur, Fighter for Freedom. p. 192*

Invasion Foot: Also called "Immersion foot." A tingling, burning sensation in the lower extremities followed within 48 hours by numbness and swelling; a peculiar form of frostbite that strikes feet and lower legs instead of ears and noses. Suffered by American soldiers on Attu.—*Newsweek. June 21, 1943. p. 31.* In the form known as Immersion Foot, it was more common among shipwrecked sailors, and was caused by immersion in salt water.—*Newsweek. January 29, 1945. p. 73*

Invest in Invasion: Slogan used in Third War Loan Drive, September 1943

I.P.: Initial Point. See Bomb Run

Iron Bottom Bay: Term applied to a bay off Tulagi in the Solomons, between Florida and Guadalcanal. It was there that four of the great surface actions of the Solomons campaign were fought. It was a name commonly used throughout the fleet and by the marines, largely because the map gave no name to that body of water. Later this same name was appropriated for St. George Harbor at Rabaul.— *American Notes and Queries. August 1944. p. 75; October 1944. p. 105; New York Times Magazine. May 20, 1945. p. 10*

Iron-Bottom Channel: Nickname for the Surigao Strait near Leyte in the Philippines, received this name after the Second Battle of the Philippine Sea.—*Newsweek. December 25, 1944. p. 18*

Iron Commander: Nickname of Marshal Gregory Zhukoff, commander of the Russian troops attacking Berlin.—*Newsweek. March 26, 1945. p. 38*

Iron Curtain: The supposed impenetrable censorship and secrecy dividing Soviet-dominated Europe from the rest of the world. Attributed variously to Winston Churchill and to William Joyce (Lord Haw Haw). See also Velvet Curtain.—*Britannica Book of the Year. 1947. p. 840*

Iron Mike: Nickname of Captain Edward J. Moran (U.S.S. Boise).—*New York Times Book Review. August 15, 1943. p. 5*

Iron Woman of the Fleet: Nickname given to the aircraft carrier "Cabot" for her run of 225,000 miles of operations in the Pacific.—*American Notes and Queries. June 1945. p. 40*

Island Hopping: Going from one island to another; especially military advance by seizing one island after another as a base. Used in the Pacific area.—*Britannica Book of the Year. 1946. p. 832*

Isolhash: Word coined by New York's Mayor LaGuardia (February 1943). He said that isolationist opponents of President Roosevelt's postwar program were trying to force on the American public a nauseating diet of "isolhash"—i.e. "Stale and discarded bigotry, narrow-mindedness, prejudice, hatred, greed and selfishness—all leftovers from the last war. . . . Spice this with witty phrases and catchwords and season with plenty of petty partisan politics."—*American Notes and Queries. March 1943. p. 181*

Issei: Japanese, born in Japan, who immigrated to the United States before the war.—*New York Times Magazine. December 2, 1945. p. 22*

"The Issue Is in Doubt": Message radioed from the Marines on Wake Island just before the Japanese overran the island.—*New York Times Magazine. January 14, 1945. p. 22.* See "Enemy on Island. . ."

"It Is a Sad Day for All of Us. . . . Everything I Had Worked for, Hoped for, and Believed in . . . Has Cracked into Ruins": By Neville Chamberlain, at outbreak of war, in a brief speech to the House after Britain's declaration of war against Germany.—*Time. September 11, 1939. p. 27*

"It Is Better to Die on Your Feet than to Live on Your Knees": There is some question as to who said this first. John Gunther in his book *Inside Latin America*, p. 63, attributes it to

Emiliano Zapata, but gives no source. Edgcumb Pinchon in his biography *Zapata the Unconquerable* quotes Zapata as saying, p. 44, "Better a fighting death than a slave's life," which is similar in idea though not in wording. Mr. Pilkington, editor of the magazine *American Notes and Queries*, says the original version occurred in a speech of "La Pasionaria" (Dolores Ibarruri) in Paris on September 3, 1936. See also *Chase. Falange. p. 23-4*

"It Is Evil Things We Shall Be Fighting against—Brute Force, Bad Faith, Injustice, Oppression and Persecution. And against Them I Am Certain the Right Will Prevail": By Neville Chamberlain, Prime Minister, at the conclusion of his radio announcement on Sunday morning, September 2, 1939, that England was at war with Germany.—*Time. September 11, 1939. p. 27*

"It Is Necessary for Us Not Only to Have Ideals . . . It Is Necessary that We Act to Implement Them": By Madame Chiang Kai-shek. Speech before the United States Senate, February 18, 1943. —*Vital Speeches. March 1, 1943. p. 303*

It Is the Better Part of Wisdom Not to Accept Failure Ignominiously, but to Risk It Gloriously": By Madame Chiang Kai-shek. Speech to House of Representatives at Washington, D.C., February 18, 1943.—*Vital Speeches. March 1, 1943. p. 303*

"It Must Not Be a Soft Occupation nor a Soft Peace": By General Jonathan M. Wainwright. General Wainwright, hero of Corregidor, was held for thirty-nine months in a Japanese prison camp. At a dinner given in his honor (as part of New York City's welcome) he said: "I have no desire for personal revenge, nor do I believe that others who suffered with me have that feeling. . . . But *it must not be a soft occupation nor a soft peace.*"—*Newsweek. September 24, 1945. p. 32*

"It Will Be a Long Campaign from Blitz to Obliteration": By Walter Winchell. In a radio broadcast June 5, 1943, warning against a feeling of over-optimism on the course of the war.

"It's a Long March from the Heel of Italy to the 'Heel' in Berlin": By Colonel Hans Adamson at a bond rally for the Third War Loan Drive. Reported by Walter Winchell on the radio September 26, 1943

Ivan the Terrible: Nickname of Lieutenant General Sir Iven Giffard Mackay, Commander in Chief of the Australian Army. Received this nickname during World War I.—*Current Biography. 1941. p. 548*

J-1, J-2, J-3: Symbols (from jeune) used by the French, during the occupation, in placing children in food-rationing units, covering, respectively, these three age groups—two to seven, seven to twelve, twelve to twenty-one.—*American Notes and Queries. January 1945. p. 149*

JAAFU: Joint Anglo-American Foul-Up. Recently added armed services slang. See also FUBAR, JACFU, JANFU, SNAFU, SUSFU and TARFU.—*Newsweek. February 7, 1944. p. 61*

JAC: Joint Aircraft Committee

JACFU: Joint American-Chinese Foul-Up. See also FUBAR, JAAFU, JANFU, SNAFU, SUSFU, and TARFU.—*American Notes and Queries. January 1946. p. 159*

Jakie: Nickname of Lieutenant General Jacob L. Devers, commander of the United States forces in the European theater.—*Saturday Evening Post. July 10, 1943. p. 15*

Jamming: Intentional introduction of spurious radiation into radio and radar frequencies to make the message unintelligible. See also Radar Countermeasures.—*Army and Navy Journal. August 18, 1945. p. 1534*

Jamoc: Slang term for coffee, contraction of Java-Mocha.—*Time. December 18, 1944. p. 9*

JANFU: Joint Army-Navy Foul-Up. See note under JAAFU. Same source

Jangos: Junior Army-Navy Guild Organization. Jangos are teen age (14-18) daughters of officers in all branches of the armed forces, who help out in war work in Washington, D.C. Most popular activity is the junior nurses' aide project which has been operating in Washington's Doctors Hospital for the past nine months. It has been so successful that the idea is now spreading to other cities and is being organized as a nationwide nursing unit.—*Life. April 26, 1943. p. 37*

JANIS: Joint Army Navy Intelligence Strategy.—*Time. April 22, 1946. p. 67*

Japanazi: Word coined from Japan and Nazi, used as an adjective pertaining to Japan and Nazi Germany, especially as military allies.—*American Speech. February 1943. p. 64*

Japes: Nickname given to the Japanese by the Marines in the Marianas Islands. The word is a combination of Jap and ape. Reported by Ernie Pyle.—*Democrat & Chronicle. Rochester, N.Y. March 12, 1945. p. 6*

Jaypees: Name sometimes given to jet-propelled planes. See also Jettie.—*Newsweek. October 9, 1944. p. 32*

JASCO: Joint Assault Signal Company. A comparatively small but important unit in Pacific amphibious warfare; its task was to guide and shape the direct support of ground forces before, during, and after a landing.—*American Notes and Queries. February 1945. p. 166*

JATO: Jet Assisted Take-Off. Plane with jet power unit attached to its wings, enabling it to take off rapidly.—*New York Times. October 8, 1944. p. 7E*

Je Suis Partout: A French weekly magazine, notoriously pro-Nazi.—*Newsweek. January 29, 1945. p. 54*

Jeep: A 1/4-ton, 4 x 4 truck, a small low khaki-colored army car in general use in the U.S. Army. Powerful, sturdy and versatile, it became known in all parts of the world wherever American soldiers penetrated. The car itself was not invented by any one person, but evolved gradually, a need for such a type of car being felt in World War I. The earliest experimental models (made by Willys-Overland, American Bantam, and Ford) were nicknamed Beep, Bug, Blitz Buggy, Chigger, Midget, Puddle Jumper, Peep, etc. The first Willys model was nicknamed Jeep and this name stuck. In February 1941, the Willys car was being put through some tests in Washington, with Katharine Hillyer, staff writer for the *Washington Daily News*, as a passenger. Someone asked the driver the "name of that thing, mister" and was told "It's a Jeep." A picture of the Jeep with its name in the caption appeared in the *Washington Daily News* on February 19, 1941. The term Jeep appeared in the Popeye comic strip as early as March 16, 1936, and may have been the genesis of the term as it was known in World War II (the little car that could do everything).—*American Speech. February 1943. p. 68-9; Wells. Hail to the Jeep. p. 31-2; Time. November 3, 1941. p. 31*

Jeepable: Describing rough roads impassable except by jeep.—*American Speech. December 1944. p. 310*

Jerrican: The German gas container which enabled Rommel to move with so much speed in the Libyan campaign; the cans could be stacked closely in trucks and then be thrown out along the road as the truck moved along at top speed. The Eighth Army used a copy of the Jerrican (hastily produced in England) when it started its march from El Alamein; and, until pipelines could be laid, Jerricans were shipped to Normandy during the liberation of France.—*Manchester Guardian. November 25, 1944*

Jerry: British nickname for a German fighter or his plane.— *Democrat & Chronicle. Rochester, N.Y. September 8, 1940.*

Jet Propulsion: See Rocket

Jettie: Jet-propelled airplane (AP dispatch. February 9, 1945. See also Jaypees.—*American Notes and Queries. March 1945. p. 182*

Jocko: Nickname of Rear Admiral Joseph James Clark. When a plebe at Annapolis, another plebe called him "The Right Reverend J. Jonathan Jockey Clark." The other boys called him Jock which later became "Jocko."—*Life. January 22, 1945. p. 41*

"Joe Blow" Biographies: Short personality pieces featuring fighting men and written for publication in hometown newspapers.— *American Notes and Queries. April 1945. p. 8; New York Times Magazine. October 21, 1945. p. 20*

Join the Navy and Free the World: Poster caption. United States Navy Department. Recruiting Bureau

Join the Wrens and Free a Man for the Fleet: Poster caption. Great Britain, recruiting poster. Women's Royal Naval Service

Jooms: Junior Observers of Meteorology. Being trained for government service to replace Weather Bureau men who have gone to war.—*Democrat & Chronicle. Rochester, N.Y. January 31, 1943. p. 8A*

Jumbo: Nickname of General Sir Henry Maitland Wilson.— *New York Times. August 20, 1944. p. 2E, 7E*

Jungle Juice: See GI Liquor in the Pacific

Jungle Juliets: See Femarines

Jungle Rot; New Guinea Crud; The Creeping Crud: GI names for any and every kind of skin disease.—*Time. August 13, 1945. p. 76*

"Jungle Warfare Is Like Fighting in the Inside of a Mattress, except One Can't See So Far": By Brigadier General Hanford MacNider.—*Democrat & Chronicle. Rochester, N.Y. February 3, 1943*

"Just Sight, Track, Shoot and Sink": By Lieutenant Commander Dudley W. Morton of U.S.S. Wahoo (submarine). "Last week the Wahoo returned to Pearl Harbor with a mop roped to the periscope and a record of having mopped up eight Japanese ships on a single patrol." To the skipper, it was just a routine matter of "sight, track, shoot and sink."—*Newsweek. May 3, 1943. p. 24.*   The Wahoo with Lieutenant Commander Morton on board was officially reported lost in the Pacific in December 1943.—*Democrat & Chronicle. Rochester, N.Y. December 3, 1943. p. 1*

Kaitens: Japanese human-steered torpedoes.—*American Notes and Queries. January 1946. p. 151*

Kamikaze: Japanese "suicide" aircraft squadrons.   Term is also applied to their defense strategy of suicidal resistance. The literal meaning of the word is "divine wind."—*New York Times. April 22, 1945. p. 6E; May 20, 1945. p. 1E, 2E, 6E*

Kamiseri: Nickname of General Hideki Tojo, premier of Japan. Given to him by his military colleagues. Translated it means "Razor blade."—*Current Biography. 1941. p. 863*

Kampfschwimmer: "Battle Swimmers."   Rubber-suited German soldiers wearing oxygen masks, and webbed flippers on their feet, who swam out into the Rhine to plant torpedoes to damage bridges in an attempt to prevent American armies from crossing.—*Newsweek. April 2, 1945. p. 32*

Kansan: (American plane) Beech AT-11 SNB1 trainer plane

Karigane: (Japanese plane) Mitsubishi MK-11 fighter plane

Katyusha: A Russian multiple rocket thrower, similar to the American bazooka rocket tank buster and the German Nebelwerfer.—*Newsweek. December 25, 1944. p. 24*

Kava: See GI Liquor in the Pacific

Kawanishi: (Japanese plane)

Keep 'Em Filing: Quip around red-taped government offices, Washington, D.C.; parody on poster caption "Keep 'em flying."—*Newsweek. June 15, 1942. p. 33*

Keep 'Em Flying: Poster caption. United States War Department

Keep the Flag Flying: See "Take every other normal precaution. . . ."

"Keep the Guns Firing": By Captain Lord Louis Mountbatten (British army). His command to his men after the destroyer Kelly had been hit by a half-ton bomb.—*Newsweek. September 8, 1941. p. 18*

Keep the War News Good by Buying War Stamps and Bonds: Motto used by Women's Division of New York State War Savings Committee.—*Democrat & Chronicle. Rochester, N.Y. September 8, 1942. p. 18*

"The Keystone of the Fascist Arch Has Crumbled": By Winston Churchill. Speech in House of Commons July 27, 1943 referring to the overthrow of Mussolini in Italy on July 25, 1943.—*Democrat & Chronicle. Rochester, N.Y. July 28, 1943. p. 1*

Khaki Wackies: See Victory Girls

Kibei: Japanese born in the United States and educated in Japan.—*New York Times Magazine. December 2, 1945. p. 22*

Kilroy: Folklore that grew up among the boys of the Air Transport Command. Wherever they flew they found that "Kilroy" had been there before them, though no one ever saw him. According to *Newsweek* (December 3, 1945) the real Kilroy was Sgt. Francis J. Kilroy Jr. One day in 1943 a notice appeared on the bulletin board at Boca Raton Field, Florida: "Kilroy will be here next week." It was written by Sgt. James Maloney as his friend Sgt. Kilroy lay ill with influenza. That started a campaign which made "Kilroy" the most famous man in the Army Air Forces. Transferred to another station, Maloney kept writing notices about Kilroy. Hundreds of others took it up. "Kilroy was here," "Kilroy ate here," "Kilroy slept here," and other items of information about "Kilroy" appeared at airfields all over the world. Imitators such as Corduroy and Clem also appeared but failed to attain the vogue of Kilroy.

According to *Time* (December 2, 1946) James J. Kilroy of Halifax, Massachusetts, says he first wrote "Kilroy was here" on the Lexington's hull in a shipyard. He won a contest for the best explanation of how the Kilroy thing started. He said he was a war worker at the Bethlehem Steel Company's Quincy (Massachusetts) shipyard. His job was to inspect tanks, double bottoms, etc., of warships under construction. In order to let his superiors know that he was doing what had been assigned to him, he followed the practice of scrawling "Kilroy was here" in yellow crayon on the work that had been inspected.

However it started, the name Kilroy became practically a household word on the home front, as well as with the armed forces.—*Newsweek. December 3, 1945. p. 64-5; Saturday Evening Post. October 20, 1945. p. 6; Esquire. April 1946. p. 70; Time. December 2, 1946. p. 46; American Notes and Queries. February 1947. p. 173*

Kimpai: Japanese military secret police organization.—*New York Times. September 16, 1945. p. 2E, 7E*

Kingfisher: (American plane) Vought-Sikorsky OS2U scouting observation seaplane

Kiwi: AAF slang for a non-flying officer

Knickerbocker Weekly: Dutch magazine in exile. Published in the United States of America.—*Saturday Review of Literature. July 17, 1943. p. 5*

K-9 Corps: Dogs in war. See DFD: Dogs For Defense

K-Ration: This ration, put out by the Army Subsistence Research Laboratory, started out under the name of Parachute Ration or Pararation. Its wide use by many different combat groups necessitated a more general name, and it was called Ration "K." It came in three boxes, breakfast, dinner and supper units, and contained over 3000 calories and all the proper vitamins. The ration included "Defense" Biscuits, made of molasses, whole wheat and soybean flour and flavored with spices. See also "Bail-out" Ration and C-Ration.—*Hoffmann. Feeding Our Armed Forces. p. 52*

K-Ration Tessie: Nickname given to baby Teresa Maria Russo, born in an American field hospital in Italy. Her mother was caught between the German and American lines, wounded and helpless several days before being picked up by an ambulance collection group. The baby's bassinet was an empty ration box. Hence the nickname.—*Democrat & Chronicle. Rochester, N.Y. September 25, 1943. p. 2*

Krauts: Nickname which the soldiers in this war used to designate Germans. "Boche" and "Heinie," common in the 1914-1918 war, were seldom heard in World War II.

Kriegie: Slang for Kriegsgefangener (Prisoner of War). Nickname was given to "old" American prisoners of war in German camps. Some of their slang was cited in an AP dispatch of May 27, 1944, London: Circuit—a walk; Purges—new arrivals; Bash—banquet; Gush—extra issue of anything; Cooler—punishment.—*American Notes and Queries. June 1944. p. 39*

KSMMP: Kin Seeking Missing Military Personnel. An organization made up of parents with sons missing in action, started by J. Rae Conway (Brooklyn), with the idea of supplementing the U.S. Government search for missing personnel, by contacts with missionary societies and natives of foreign lands and any other sources that might remain untapped by official investigation.—*Newsweek. May 6, 1946 p. 37*

L: "L" type ships (see also APA) were assault vessels, shallow and with a flat bow, enabling them to run up on beaches to unload. Among the most versatile of these was the LCI—Landing Craft, Infantry; others were LCC—Landing Craft, Control; LCIL—Landing Craft, Infantry, Large; LCK—Landing Craft, Kitchen; LCM—Landing Craft, Mechanized; LCP—Landing Craft, Personnel; LCRL—Landing Craft, Rubber, Large; LCRS—Landing Craft, Rubber, Small; LCT—Landing Craft, Tank; LCV—Landing Craft, Vehicles; LCVP—Landing Craft, Vehicle-Personnel; LSD—Landing Ship, Dock (ocean-going drydocks that carried and launched LCT's and LCM's); LSM—Landing Ship, Medium; LST—Landing Ship, Tank; LVT—Landing Vehicle, Tracked, a cargo and personnel carrier often called by armed personnel trac, amphtrac, water buffalo, alligator, and sometimes miscalled tank by civilians.—*New Yorker. August, 26, 1944. p. 16; New York Times Magazine. October 21, 1945. p. 49; March 4, 1945. p. 8; December 2, 1945. p. 22; Democrat & Chronicle. Rochester, N.Y. January 1, 1945. p. 32*

L Pilot: Liaison Pilot. Trained as a pilot and as an airplane mechanic, the candidate received rating as staff sergeant. He flew an unarmed, single-engine aircraft, usually the L-5 Stinson. He operated close behind the enemy lines and often flew over them evacuating casualties to rear bases and bringing supplies forward.—*Newsweek. June 25, 1945. p. 6*

LAB: Low Altitude Bombing.—*Army and Navy Journal. August 18, 1945. p. 1534*

Lager: German word for camp. German camps were divided into categories according to the type of prisoners of war they contained. See also Dulag, Dulagluft, Ilag, Luftlager, Marlag, Milag, Nebenlager, Oflag, Stalag, Zweilager.—*Red Cross Courier. June 1943. p. 11*

Lancaster: (British plane) Avro heavy bomber. This was one of the largest of the British heavy bombers and was equipped to carry the 8,000-pound "block-buster" bombs

Lancer: (American plane) Republic P-43 fighter plane

The **Last War:** See World War II

Lay On: R.A.F. slang. To provide or arrange.—*American Speech. February 1941. p. 76*

LCC, LCI, LCK, LCM, LCP, LCT, LCVP: See L

L.D.V.: Local Defense Volunteers (British); later called Home Guards.—*American Speech. February 1944. p. 11*

Leather-Nectarines: See Femarines

Lebensraum: German equivalent of the English "place in the sun." Literally "living room or space." This term came into use as a Hitlerian slogan of imperialism. It has been attributed to Professor Karl Haushofer, credited with being political adviser to Hitler. Origin of term goes back to the Swedish geographer Kjellen.—*New York Times Magazine. October 3, 1943. p. 29; January 7, 1945. p. 39; Quarterly Review. January 1943. p. 78*

Ledo Road: See Pick's Pike

LeMay Mission: Name given to attack on the Messerschmitt factory at Regensburg on August 17, 1943. This was the first shuttle bombing flight that was made by the Eighth Air Force from England to North Africa and back. It was led by Major General Curtis E. LeMay.—*Newsweek. August 28, 1944. p. 33*

Lend-Lease: An act passed in March 1941. The United States would supply munitions, food and other needed items to countries resisting the Nazis, in return for use of military bases or some other advantage. The Lend-Lease Administration was part of the OEM (q.v.)

Lerwick: (British plane) Saunders-Roe patrol bomber flying boat

"Let Me Save My Life and I Will Give You an Empire": Mussolini's words when he heard the death sentence pronounced by the Italian Partisan officers who tried him. His last words as they were about to shoot him, were "No! No!"—*Democrat & Chronicle. Rochester, N.Y. April 30, 1945. p. 1*

"Let Us Move Forward Steadfastly Together into the Storm and through the Storm": By Winston Churchill. An address broadcast February 15, 1942.—*Churchill. The End of the Beginning. p. 71*

Let's Finish the Job: Slogan for sale of war bonds in the 6th War Loan Drive, November-December 1944

Let's Get It Over with, with Bonds: Slogan used in Fourth War Loan Drive, January 1944

Let's Go—for the Knockout Blow: Slogan for Fifth War Loan Drive, starting June 12, 1944. $16,000,000,000 was the goal.—*New York Herald Tribune. News Week. June 4, 1944. p. 22*

Let's Pave the Road to Rome with War Bonds: Additional slogan for Third War Loan Drive, coined as a result of Secretary Morgenthau's suggestion that the closing days of the campaign be dedicated to General Mark Clark's Fifth Army in Italy.—*Democrat & Chronicle. Rochester, N.Y. September 25, 1943. p. 1*

La Lettre de La France Combattante: French magazine in exile; published in both French and English editions, London.—*Saturday Review of Literature. July 17, 1943. p. 5*

Liberate: Army slang. To scrounge, steal or loot.—*American Speech. December 1946. p. 251*

Liberation—Not Invasion: Phrase used by President Roosevelt in a press conference in May 1944, but later acknowledged by him to have been authored by Douglas S. Freeman, editor of the Richmond *News-Leader.* Dr. Freeman suggested that the term "liberation" should replace "invasion" in connection with the allied drive into German-occupied territories.—*New York Herald Tribune. June 4, 1944. p. 25*

Liberator: (American plane) Consolidated B-24 PB4Y heavy bomber plane

Liberator Express: (American plane) Consolidated C-87 transport plane

Liberty Ships: Name given to ships built during the war years, when the whole ship-building program was vastly enlarged

Liberty War: See World War II

Lichtenstein: See note under Tuba

"Lidice Lives" Committee: Formed in the summer of 1942 to persuade thirty-one towns, one for each United Nation, to adopt the name of the Czech village wiped out by the Nazis on June 10, 1942. A real estate development near Joliet, Illinois, became the first new Lidice on July 12, 1942; San Geronimo, Mexico, the second on August 30, 1942. The third Lidice was in Brazil, a locality near the Rio Claro close to the capital. It was proposed to change the name of Felighsburg, Quebec, to Lidice, but the inhabitants overruled the idea. However, it was planned to rename the Parc des Laurentides Lake in Quebec in honor of Lidice.—*New York Times. June 12, 1943. p. 2; Notes and Queries. December 30, 1944. p. 306; Newsweek. October 5, 1942. p. 48*

Lieutenant Super Grade: Fictitious rank created by senior-grade lieutenants in the Navy who envied the speedier Army promotions *(New York Times. July 8, 1945).—American Notes and Queries. July 1945. p. 54*

Lifebuoy: A flame thrower consisting of a ring-shaped tube and spherical container for compressed gas; carried by a foot soldier. See also Crocodile.—*American Notes and Queries. September 1944. p. 85*

Lightning: (American plane) Lockheed P-38 fighter plane

Lightning Joe: Nickname of Major General Joseph Lawton Collins.—*Newsweek. July 10, 1944. p. 26*

Lili Marlene: A German war song. Composed by Norbert Schultze in 1938, it became popular in 1941. In the early days of the war it was just another song number plugged in cafés, but in April 1941, the Nazis made their first broadcast from conquered Belgrade and signed off with a recording (by Lala Anderson, Swedish singer) of Lili Marlene. It became the favorite song of the German Afrika Corps, and when the British Eighth Army defeated the Germans in Africa, they felt that they had captured the song as well. It became a favorite of soldiers throughout the armed forces. In the U.S. it was shelved for some time because a music war committee thought it would hurt soldier morale. *Time* (May 3, 1943) reported that it had not yet been heard over the radio in America. (On November 24, 1944, I heard it on the radio, but how long before that it had been played, I don't know—Ed.) In 1944 the British Ministry of Information issued a documentary film, "The True Story of Lili Marlene," featuring the Swedish singer Lala Anderson. The song was often parodied (much as "Mademoiselle from Armentieres" was in World War I) and for a while seemed to be the smash song hit of World War II.—*Time. May 3, 1943. p. 40; Newsweek. June 26, 1944. p. 98; Life. June 5, 1944. p. 55*

Lily: Portable seadrome, consisting of a number of buoyancy cans with hexagonal surfaces so linked together as to give to the motion of the sea from any direction and yet remain sufficiently rigid to take the weight of heavy aircraft; invented by R. M. Hamilton of the Royal Navy; so called because of its resemblance to lily leaves or palms.—*American Notes and Queries. September 1945. p. 87*

Lily: Also nickname of a Japanese plane

Limping Annie: See Plane Nicknames

Li-pai: Pai Tsung-hsi (Chinese Chief of Staff of Military Training and Deputy Chief of Staff) and Li Tsung-jen (Commander of the Chinese 5th Army Group) are often spoken of as the same person under the name "Li-pai."—*Current Biography. 1942. p. 516*

Little America: Name given to Grosvenor Square (London) and the surrounding area, the site of apartment houses and public buildings occupied by United States troops. See also Eisenhower Platz. —*American Notes and Queries. August 1945. p. 70*

Little Big Inch: See Big Inch

Little Boy: See Atomic Bomb nicknames

Little Friends: AAF slang for fighter planes. See also Big Friends

Little Red Ball: See Com Z

Little Siegfried Line: Japanese line of defense across southern Okinawa.—*New York Times. May 27, 1945. p. 2E, 6E*

Little Steel Formula: Wage-stabilization plan which allowed an increase of 15 per cent in wages to match the rise in living costs between January 1, 1941, and May 1, 1942.—*Newsweek. February 8, 1943. p. 56*

Lizzie: See Plane Nicknames

Lodestar: (American plane) Lockheed C-56R50 transport plane

London: (British plane) Saunders-Roe reconnaissance flying boat

Lone Ranger: See Sea Ranger

Loony Joe: See Baka

Loose Lips Sink Ships: Poster caption. See also "Idle gossip sinks ships"

Loran: Long Range Navigation electronic equipment. An airplane equipped with this instrument can travel any pre-determined course regardless of weather, day or night, without depending on celestial navigation. Loran enables the navigator of an airplane to find his exact position at any instant accurately and rapidly.—*Philco Corporation. Radar on Wings. 1945*

Lord Haw Haw: Mike name of William Joyce, British citizen who gave radio broadcasts on short wave from Berlin, Germany. The name "Lord Haw Haw" was given to Joyce by William Hickey of the *Daily Express* (London) because of his imitation Mayfair accent and the fumbling humor in his ridicule of the British and American "plutocracies" and "mobocracies." A propaganda tool of the Nazis, he was labeled a traitor by the British. Captured in 1945, he was tried and found guilty and was sentenced to hang. Another British traitor, Norman Baillie Stewart, captured by U.S. troops in Austria, claimed that he was the original "Lord Haw Haw" being superseded after four months by William Joyce.—*Christian Science Monitor Magazine. July 18, 1942. p. 6; Democrat & Chronicle. Rochester, N.Y. May 20, 1945. p. 1A; Newsweek. June 11, 1945. p. 91; October 1, 1945. p. 47; American Speech. February 1944. p. 12*

Lord Hee Haw: Mike name of Fred W. Kaltenbach, an American citizen from Waterloo, Iowa. On short wave from Germany he broadcast crude lies and kept repeating that Roosevelt, Churchill, Stalin and the Jews were out to destroy civilization. He did not consider himself a traitor; he claimed that as the German element enabled Lincoln to save the Union, so now the same element must again save America. Indicted for treason July 26, 1943, by the District of Columbia Grand Jury. He was arrested by the Russians in Berlin, June 14, 1945.—*Christian Science Monitor Magazine. July 18, 1942. p. 6; Democrat & Chronicle. Rochester, N.Y. July 27, 1943; Newsweek. March 17, 1941. p. 64; July 16, 1945. p. 68*

"Lord, I'll Take Over Now; Thanks, Lord": Second Lieutenant Robert H. Knapp of Norwich, N.Y., on a mission over Germany in September 1943 began a vertical dive at 28,000 feet and both the controls and throttle froze. It is believed his speed exceeded 840 miles an hour. It wasn't until he had reached 5000 feet that the plane started to come out of the dive, and as its nose pointed back at the sky, the pilot used a phrase which he had heard his roommate use occasionally, "Lord, I'll take over now," and he added, "Thanks, Lord." When his plane was inspected for damage, it was found that the paint was literally peeled from the ailerons by the terrific wind his speed had created, but there was no structural strain.—*Democrat & Chronicle. Rochester, N.Y. September 29, 1943*

Louie the Louse: Marine slang for seaplanes.—*Newsweek. February 8, 1943. p. 52*

Love-Day: The conventional name of D-day at the invasion of Okinawa was changed to Love-Day. Ernie Pyle figured that the reason was possibly that the invasion was to take place on Easter Sunday.—*Democrat & Chronicle. Rochester, N.Y. April 6, 1945*

Loxygen: Term meaning liquid oxygen, used in connection with jet-propulsion.—*Newsweek. June 4, 1945. p. 90*

LSD, LSM, LST: See L

"Luce Thinking": See "The times call for clear, lucid thinking. . . ."

Lucky: Nickname of Marshal Rodolfo Graziani. Until March, 1941, Graziani was commander of all Italian troops in Africa. After the siege of Bardia it seemed unlikely that Graziani would ever use his nickname again.—*Current Biography. 1941. p. 342*

Luftlager: Abbreviation for Luftwaffelager, a prisoners-of-war camp for airmen. See also Lager.—*Red Cross Courier. June 1943. p. 11*

Luftwaffe: The air force of the Third German Reich.—*Webster's New International Dictionary. 1943. p. ci; American Speech. April 1941. p. 147*

Luger Luggin' Ludwig: A Canadian parody of the song Pistol Packin' Mama, turned up on D-day in Normandy.—*Newsweek. July 17, 1944. p. 65*

Luke the Spook: See Clem, Kilroy, etc.

Luxury of Hate: See "We can't have the luxury. . . ."

LVT: See L

Lysander: (British plane) Westland 2-seater all-purpose plane

---

"The MacArthurs Hope There Will Always Be Bullitts": William C. Bullitt, former ambassador to France and Russia, sent holiday greetings to General MacArthur. From the battlefield of Bataan, MacArthur replied as above.—*Newsweek. February 16, 1942. p. 30*

MACNIMAATZ: Name for the tripartite command in the Pacific (August 1945). To army and navy men, accustomed to command abbreviations, the word sounded logical enough—it told the story of the divided authority of General of the Army Douglas MacArthur, Fleet Admiral Chester W. Nimitz, and strategic air commander General Carl A. Spaatz.—*Newsweek. August 13, 1945. p. 33*

Mad Operator: Another war secret made public in June 1946. The term came from the initials of the name of the device—Magnetic Airborne Detector. It was a small magnetic finger on airplanes that pointed unerringly at submarines beneath the water. It could be attached to the extreme tail end of a plane or trailed from the end of a cable. In practice it was generally trailed from a cable to free it from the magnetic influences of the plane.—*Democrat & Chronicle.* *Rochester, N.Y. June 2, 1946. p. 1A*

Mae West: Name given by fliers in the RAF to designate an inflatable rubber life-belt which saved many an aviator's life after he had been forced to bail out over water. Miss West sent a letter to the RAF, on hearing that her name had been attached to a life-saving jacket. The last two paragraphs read: "If I do get in the dictionary— where you say you want to put me—how will they describe me? As a warm clinging life-saving garment worn by aviators? Or an aviator's jacket that supplies the woman's touch while the boys are flying around nights? I've been in *Who's Who* and I know what's what, but it'll be the first time I ever made the dictionary."—*American Speech. December 1944. p. 277*

Maggie: See Plane Nicknames

Maggie's Drawers: Slang term for the red flag which indicated a clean miss on the rifle range.—*Time. July 19, 1943. p. 69*

MAGIC: Name given to American Military Advisory Group in China, which was assisting the Chinese government in military matters. —*New York Times. October 6, 1946. p. 2E, 6E*

Magic Carpet: Term for carriers and other warships used to bring overseas veterans back to the United States. The Navy Department predicted that the "carpet" would finish its job by February 1946. —*New York Times. December 23, 1945. p. 2E, 6E*

Maginot-minded: Indicating a purely defensive attitude. So called from the Maginot line of defense which was believed by the French to be impregnable but which was effectively and quickly overrun by the Germans

"Makin Taken": By Major General Ralph Smith, 27th Division, United States Army. Message to Rear Admiral Richmond Turner in regard to amphibious operations in the Gilberts.—*Yank. December 24, 1943. p. 5*

The Man Who Missed Moscow: Field Marshal Gunther von Kluge, who replaced Field Marshal Karl von Rundstedt as leader of the Germans against the invasion in western Europe, was known as "The man who missed Moscow." His headquarters in Poland, France and Russia—in both victory and defeat—were so gloomy that he became known among fellow officers as the "Melancholy Baby."—*Newsweek. July 17, 1944. p. 18*

Manhattan Project: Name given to the atomic bomb research project. Three huge plants were built, one at Oak Ridge, Tennessee, one at Pasco, Washington, and one at Los Alamos, New Mexico.—*Time. August 13, 1945. p. 18*

Maquis: French underground organization. Their name came from the patois word for the underbrush in which they hid. Technically and in French usage, they were called Maquisards.—*Newsweek. July 10, 1944. p. 46*

Marauder: (American plane) Martin B-26 medium bomber plane

March of Death: Bataan fell on April 9, 1942. Major General Edward P. King, Jr. who made the actual surrender refused to give up Corregidor with Bataan. The Japanese captured, in addition to the troops, some 25,000 civilians. What happened to these men was not known until nearly three years later when the world was shocked by the revelation of the "March of death." Nothing like it had ever occurred in the history of modern warfare. When the march was over more than 5200 Americans and many times that number of Filipinos had been tortured to death. And this after General Yamashita had promised treatment befitting warriors and in accordance with the principles of international law.—*Miller. History of World War II. p. 459*

Mariner: (American plane) Martin PBM patrol bomber (Flying Boat) plane

Marines: Women's group of the United States Marine Corps The Marine Corps announced firmly that its new women's reserve would be called—not WAMS, not MARINETTES—but simply MARINES. The group was established February 13, 1943.—*Newsweek. February 22, 1943. p. 37; Time. February 22, 1943. p. 60*

Mark VI: German tank, the so-called Tiger tank. First tried out in Tunisia in comparatively small numbers, then introduced into Russia as one of Germany's new secret weapons. It was said to be the heaviest regular tank in use, weighing up to 60 tons.—*Newsweek. June 14, 1943. p. 23-4*

Marlag: Abbreviation for Marinelager, a prisoners-of-war camp for sailors. See also Lager.—*Red Cross Courier. June 1943. p. 11*

Mars: (American plane) Martin PB2M-1, a patrol bomber plane which could also carry cargo. When launched in 1940, it was probably the largest flying ship in the world

Marston Mat: Steel plank (pierced to make it lighter in weight) used to make emergency landing strips for airplanes. So called because it was first used at Marston, North Carolina.—*Huie. Can Do! p. 35 note, 41 note*

Martian: (American plane) Martin B-26 medium bomber. An extremely fast bomber, it was also equipped with a special gear to carry torpedoes and was used successfully against Japanese ships off the Aleutian islands

Mary of Arnhem: Helen Sensburg, propaganda broadcaster from Germany, was known as "Mary of Arnhem." She lived in England for ten years before the war. In her broadcasts she used to try to break down the morale of Allied troops in Holland. She was captured in Germany by the Allies in June 1945.—*Newsweek. June 4, 1945. p. 82*

Maryland: (American plane) Name given in Great Britain to the Martin 167W bomber and reconnaissance plane

"Massed Angered Forces of Common Humanity": By Franklin D. Roosevelt. Speech before a joint session of Congress, Washington, D.C., January 6, 1942. "The militarists of Berlin and Tokyo started this war, but the massed angered forces of common humanity will finish it."—*Vital Speeches. January 15, 1942. p. 195*

MAT: Military Air Transport.—*Air Transport. April 1945. p. 39*

Maytag Charlie: Slang for cruiser aircraft. Nickname for Japanese aerial scout, popularized by Allied naval forces in the Pacific area. See also Photo Joe.—*American Notes and Queries. June 1944. p. 39*

MCAA: Military Civil Affairs Administration. Of the various European governments-in-exile only the Netherlands Government in London maintained an independent organization similar to the Allied Military Government. The plan was for the Dutch officials to land with the first or second wave of troops. Thereafter the MCAA would work in close cooperation with Allied military leaders and govern Holland under a state of siege.—*Newsweek. January 31, 1944. p. 29*

M-Dogs: Army-trained dogs capable of detecting anti-personnel mines and booby traps laid by the enemy; called "the elite of the K-9 Corps." Involving an ability to spot metallic and non-metallic objects, the temperament of the dog was more important than the breed.—*American Notes and Queries. August 1944. p. 71*

Me: See Plane Nicknames

Meat Wagon: Slang term for Medical Corps ambulance.—*American Speech. February 1947. p. 55*

Meatlegger: Term coined by analogy to "bootlegger." One who sold meat contrary to rationing restrictions.—*American Speech. December 1943. p. 303*

Medal of Freedom: Civilian decoration created by President Truman for meritorious acts outside the United States since Pearl Harbor; to be awarded by the Secretaries of State, War, and Navy.—*American Notes and Queries. July 1945. p. 54*

The Mediterranean Magician: Nickname of Sir Archibald Wavell, British general.—*Current Biography. 1941. p. 902*

Melancholy Baby: See The Man Who Missed Moscow

Mellett's Madhouse: See Office of Government Reports

"Mellow Light of Victory": By Winston Churchill. Speech delivered to House of Commons, London, June 8, 1943.—*Vital Speeches. June 15, 1943. p. 515*

Men of Vichy: Name given to French collaborationists. Many had their headquarters in Paris, but all were known as "Men of Vichy."—*Newsweek. August 18, 1941. p. 22*

Merrill's Marauders: A group of fighters under Brigadier General Frank D. Merrill. He called for volunteers for a "dangerous and hazardous mission," welded them into a fighting group patterned after Wingate's Raiders. They went into action in Assam in 1944.—*Miller. History of World War II. p. 622; Time. March 20, 1944. p. 30*

Messerschmitt: Twin-engined German fighter monoplane, especially adapted to bomber escort work.—*Democrat & Chronicle. Rochester, N.Y. September 8, 1940*

Meteorskrieg: The speed and power of the first big German drive on France and Belgium in May 1940 exceeded by so much the speed of the famed Blitzkrieg that a new word seemed called for. *Meteorskrieg* was the word used in an article by Major General Stephen O. Fuqua.—*Newsweek. May 27, 1940. p. 23*

MIA: Official designation for armed services personnel "missing in action."—*Newsweek. May 6, 1946. p. 36*

Mickey: See BTO

Mickey Mouse Money: Filipinos' nickname for Japanese paper occupation currency (dispatch of May 12, 1945, Manila).—*American Notes and Queries. May 1945. p. 23*

Midget: See Jeep

MIDPAC: See AFMIDPAC; CPA

Milag: Abbreviation of militaerlager—a prisoners-of-war camp for soldiers. See also Lager.—*Red Cross Courier. June 1943. p. 11*

Militärwochenblatt: German army's weekly.—*Newsweek. September 14, 1942. p. 22*

"Milk for Hottentots": In Vice President Henry A. Wallace's speech "The Price of Free World Victory" (May 8, 1942), he quotes himself as saying: "The object of this war is to make sure that everybody in the world has the privilege of drinking a quart of milk a day." This statement soon became twisted into the slogan "Milk for Hottentots" and was referred to by Wallace in a speech at Detroit, Michigan as follows: "Those twisters of fact who shriek that your Vice President is a wild-eyed dreamer trying to . . . deliver a bottle of milk to every Hottentot every morning"—*Wallace. Price of Free World Victory. p. 19; Time. August 2, 1943. p. 20*

Milk-run: AAF slang for a routine mission flown daily. To some it connoted a mission completed without loss of either aircraft or personnel.—*Newsweek. June 12, 1944. p. 6*

Millimeter Pete: Marine slang for Jap artillery.—*Newsweek. February 8, 1943. p. 52*

Million-Dollar Battalion: The 716th Railway Operating Battalion, members of which were convicted of diverting cigarettes and other Army supplies into the French black market.—*American Notes and Queries. March 1945. p. 182*

Missimo: Nickname of Chiang Mei-ling (Madame Chiang Kai-shek).—*Newsweek. March 1, 1943. p. 38*

Mission: See Air Force

Mr. Bee: See Bee Ko

Mr. Guess-Who: See "B.B.B." program

Mister King: Haakon VII, King of Norway, so called by his loyal subjects.—*Newsweek. September 22, 1941. p. 22*

Mitchell: (American plane) North American B-25 PBJ medium bomber plane. Named after Brigadier General William E. ("Billy") Mitchell, it was the ship used by Lieutenant General James Doolittle on his historic raid over Tokyo

Mitscher Shampoo: Fliers' impression of and nickname for a large-scale and successful air attack under the command of Vice Admiral Marc Andrew Mitscher—e.g. the February 16, 1945, raid on Tokyo.—*Time. February 26, 1945. p. 25*

Mitsubishi OO Zeke: Mitsubishi Nate; Mitsubishi Rufe; Mitsubishi Betty; Mitsubishi Hap; Mitsubishi Nell; Mitsubishi Sally; Mitsubishi Topsy: Nicknames for Japanese planes

Moaning Minnie: London's air raid sirens, last heard on March 28, 1945, and officially discontinued on May 2, 1945; the alarm, first sounded on September 3, 1939, was heard 1,223 times thereafter. In Berkshire, England, the vicar of the parish referred to the air raid alarm as "Mona" and the all-clear signal as "Clara"—Mona was because the alarm was greeted with moans. Clara is self-explanatory.—*American Notes and Queries. May 1945. p. 23; June 1945. p. 43*

Moaning Minnie: This term is also sometimes applied to a German shell (see also Screaming Meemies), "the kind that scream at you and then curse voluble German on the way down."—*Time. October 9, 1944. p. 24; Nation. November 9, 1940. p. 446*

Mockups: Panels on which are flat-mounted, working models of aircraft parts. Used by the AAF to teach students actual workings of parts to supplement book work.—*Democrat & Chronicle. Rochester, N.Y. August 10, 1945*

The Modern Gordon: Nickname of Lieutenant General William George Shedden Dobbie (British army). He is called "The modern Gordon" because, like General Charles George Gordon of Khartoum, he is a constant student of Scripture.—*Newsweek. April 27, 1942. p. 23*

The Mole: Name given by the Danes to their underground humorous weekly. One of their proverbs says: "A very small mole-hill can upset a very big cart"—hence the name for their paper which they expected to be "upsetting" to the occupation forces.—*New York Times Magazine. February 11, 1945. p. 2*

Molotoff Bread Baskets: Big containers filled with small bombs which were released on the way to the ground from the bombing planes.—*Times-Union. Rochester, N.Y. September 10, 1940*

Molotoff Cocktail: Bottle of gasoline thrown at a tank to set it on fire; first used in Russo-Finnish war.—*New York Times Magazine. December 2, 1945. p. 22*

Mombatsu: See Gumbatsu

Mona: See Moaning Minnie

Monitoring: In December 1939 the British Broadcasting Company turned one of its departments into a vast listening post to hear not only what the German enemy was saying on the air, but also what neutrals were broadcasting. BBC men were on duty seven days a week, twenty-four hours a day. This listening-in was called monitoring.—*Times-Union. Rochester, N.Y. December 30, 1939*

Monsieur X: Designation (only recently disclosed) for the special commissioner in occupied France, who was appointed by General Charles de Gaulle and who for many months had been carrying out the function of delegate general of the French committee in occupied France.—*American Notes and Queries. August 1944. p. 71*

Monty of El Alamein: Nickname of General Sir Bernard Law Montgomery, Commander of the British Eighth Army in Egypt.—*Current Biography. 1942. p. 606.* A millinery hat style for women called the "Monty beret" was started, copied from a beret which Montgomery wore on duty in Africa

Moonlight Requisition: Slang for illegal requisition, unauthorized trade, or downright thievery of supplies.—*American Speech. February 1947. p. 55*

Moonlights: The low glimmer that replaced the "pin-points" of the complete blackout in London in 1944. It was said that by the new light, a pedestrian "with good sight and some straining," might be able to read a newspaper.—*New York Herald Tribune. November 22, 1944; American Notes and Queries. November 1944. p. 117*

Mopping Up: To clear an area won in attack by capturing or killing enemy soldiers remaining in it.—*Times-Union. Rochester, N.Y. May 3, 1940*

More Bombs on the Target: Motto of Major General Curtis E. LeMay. In August 1944, he was made commander of the Twentieth Bomber Command, operating over Japan.—*Newsweek. August 28, 1944. p. 33*

Mosquito (boat): American name for motor torpedo (PT) boats. The Germans call them *Schnellboote,* the Italians "Mas boats," the British "Hornets," and the Americans, "Mosquito boats" or "Mosquito fleet."—*New York Times Magazine. November 9, 1941. p. 16*

Mosquito (plane): British fighter bomber plane. A plywood airplane which British enthusiasts call "the world's fastest aircraft." Official designation of the plane is the De Havilland 98.—*Popular Science. December 1943. p. 100*

The Most I Can Sell, Is the Least I Can Do: Motto used by Women's Division of New York State War Savings Committee.—*Democrat & Chronicle. Rochester, N.Y. November 26, 1942. p. 2E*

Moth Ball Fleet: United States warships which (in January 1947) were undergoing preservative treatment which would enable them to be put back in use rapidly if needed.—*New York Times. January 26, 1947. p. 2E, 6E*

Mount Plasma: Nickname given by Marines to Mount Suribachi on Iwo Jima. The Japanese had set more than 115 guns in the volcano. The Mount was taken February 23, 1945. The campaign on Iwo was one of the toughest in Marine history.—*Newsweek. March 5, 1945. p. 36-7*

MTO: Mediterranean Theater of Operations

MTOUSA: (Pronounced EM-TOOS-uh) Mediterranean Theater of Operations United States Army. After NATOUSA moved up into Italy from North Africa it was renamed MTOUSA, sometimes shortened to MTO

Mugwump: GI name for opossum meat, which was eaten by the Japanese and the natives on Bougainville, but not eaten by the GI's.—*Newsweek. April 3, 1944. p. 33*

Mulberry: Secret name given to the artificial harbor which was carried across the Channel to assist the British landing in France. The breakwaters that formed the harbor were called Gooseberries (q.v.).

The word "Mulberry" was chosen, because it happened to come next in rotation on the Admiralty's List of Ships' Names then available for use in naval warfare.—*Notes and Queries. December 15, 1945. p. 263*

Multiple Mae West: See Quonset Hut

Munichism: A noun, meaning the spirit of the surrender at Munich (September 1938) ; appeasement.—*American Speech. February 1941. p. 66*

Mush: Nickname of Lieutenant Commander Dudley W. Morton of the U.S.S. Wahoo (submarine).—*Newsweek. May 3, 1943. p. 24*

Mustang: (American plane) North American P-51 fighter plane

Mystery Army: Name given by other units to the "Fighting Fifteenth."—*Newsweek. December 24, 1945. p. 54*

NAAFI: Navy Army Air Forces Institute. British equivalent of the American USO. Pronounced Naffy. The various NAAFI clubs were almost invariably called Naffies.—*American Speech. February 1944. p. 12*

NAAFW: National Association of Air Forces Women

Naffy: See NAAFI

Nakajima Oscar; Nakajima Kate; Nakajima Dave: Nicknames for Japanese planes

NAMRU: Navy Medical Research Unit. NAMRU 2 (Navy Medical Research Unit no. 2) was set up on Guam in January 1945. It was a 62-building research laboratory, with all facilities for the aid of medical men in the Pacific, and has now become the United States Naval Institute for Tropical Diseases.—*Newsweek. May 13, 1946. p. 58*

National Socialist Front Fighters: See Stahlhelm

NATOUSA: North African Theater of Operations United States Army.—*American Speech. December 1946. p. 285*

NATS: Naval Air Transport Service. Formed just after Pearl Harbor. Wherever the fleet goes, wherever the marines land, the NATS must be prepared to follow.—*New York Times Magazine. August 15, 1943. p. 14*

Navicert: Contraction of navigation certificate, paper issued by British government to merchant vessel, certifying that cargo was non-contraband, that is, not consigned to Germany. By letting ships through blockades, it did away with delay of search at contraband stations.—*Democrat & Chronicle. Rochester, N.Y. September 8, 1940*

Navigator: (American plane) Beech AT-7 SNB2 trainer plane

Navy "E": In 1906 the Navy instituted in the Fleet an award for excellence which has since been known as the Navy "E." First awarded for excellence in gunnery, this was later extended to include outstanding performance in engineering and communications. When the war in Europe placed a premium on the production of war equipment, the Navy "E" award was extended to embrace those plants and organizations which showed excellence in producing ships, weapons and equipment for the Navy. See also Army-Navy "E."—*Newsweek. February 2, 1942. p. 40; Eastman Kodak Co. Kodak Flies the Battle Flag of War Production (pam) no paging*

Navy League: U.S. Civilian organization—men and women—with national headquarters in Washington, D.C. Main task was to raise funds for auxiliary service to the personnel of the U.S. Navy, Merchant Marine and their families.

Navy League Service: Women's branch of the Navy League. Members are known as Nells

Nazi: A member of the National Socialist German Workers' Party; from German word Nationalsozialistische

NDMB: National Defense Mediation Board. Established by executive order of President Roosevelt, March 19, 1941. This board ceased to exist when the NWLB (q.v.) was established, and its duties were transferred to the NWLB.—*United States Government Manual. Summer 1943. p. 67*

NDRC: National Defense Research Council. An organization "to coordinate, supervise, and conduct scientific research on the problems underlying the development, production, and use of mechanisms and devices of warfare, except scientific research on the problems of flight." It was set up in 1940, with twelve members appointed by the President.—*Baxter. Scientists Against Time. p. 14*

Nebelwerfer: A German rocket thrower similar to the Russian Katyusha.—*Newsweek. December 25, 1944. p. 24*

Nebenlanger or N.L.: A branch camp (prisoners-of-war). See also Lager.—*Red Cross Courier. June 1943. p. 11*

Nells: See Navy League Service

Neptune: Code name for European operation—naval invasion of France.—*American Notes and Queries. September 1945. p. 87*

Netherlands News: Dutch magazine in exile; edited by Joseph W. F. Stolpleman.—*Saturday Review of Literature. July 17, 1943. p. 5*

Neue Zeitung: A German-language newspaper, issued by the American Twelfth Army Group for the German civilian population in the Aachen area.—*American Notes and Queries. January 1945. p. 160*

"Never above You—Never beneath You—Always beside You": By Walter Winchell. Toast at press banquet in Rio de Janeiro, Brazil, drunk in Brazilian coffee. Brazilian press adopted the toast as a slogan.—*Time. January 11, 1943. p. 41*

"Never Before Have We Had So Little Time in Which to Do So Much": By Franklin D. Roosevelt. Radio address February 23, 1942.—*Democrat & Chronicle. Rochester, N.Y. February 24, 1942. p. 2*

"Never Has So Much Been Withheld from So Many by So Few": Take-off on Churchill's famous statement, by a Yale professor fulminating over a decree of the Office of War Information. Quoted in Bennett Cerf's "Trade Winds" column in *Saturday Review of Literature. December 12, 1942. p. 14*

"Never in the Field of Human Conflict Was So Much Owed by So Many to So Few": By Winston Churchill. Speech before House of Commons, London, August 20, 1940, referring to the Royal Air Force.—*Churchill. Blood, Sweat and Tears. p. 348*

New Guinea Crud: See Jungle Rot

"A New Peace Which Will Give the Decent People Everywhere a Better Chance to Live and Prosper in Security and in Freedom and in Faith": By Franklin D. Roosevelt. Radio address to nation October 27, 1941.—*Democrat & Chronicle. Rochester, N.Y. October 28, 1941. p. 11*

NHA: National Housing Agency. Established by executive order of President Roosevelt, February 24, 1942. Administers the housing activities of the Federal Home Loan Bank Administration; stimulates private finance in providing housing in defense communities; provides necessary housing for persons engaged in war production.— *United States Government Manual. Summer 1943. p. 136*

Nickels: AAF code name for leaflets dropped over enemy territory.—*New York Times Magazine. August 11, 1946. p. 24*

Night Focus Cats: Night aerial photographers, who use flash bombs 8,000 times as bright as daytime news flash bulbs.—*New York Times. December 17, 1944. p. 2E, 7E*

Night Fighter: See GI Liquor in the Pacific

Night Fighters: Air Force slang for Maori girls. (Night fighter planes were painted black.)—*American Speech. October 1945. p. 227*

Nightingale: (American plane) Howard GH transport plane

Ninety-day Wonder: Nickname given to officers who received their commission after a three months course at an Officer Candidate School.—*American Speech. April 1945. p. 148; December 1946. p. 283.*

Ninth Army Navy: When the American Third and Ninth Armies struck across the Rhine in March 1945, khaki-clad men of the U.S. Navy ferried them over. Navy volunteers were assembled in England in October 1944 for intensive training with the army. To conceal their presence behind the American lines, they removed all Navy insignia and dressed in Army khaki. They were promptly dubbed the "Ninth Army Navy." Those working with Lieutenant General Patton's Third Army became members of the "U.S.S. Blood and Guts."—*Newsweek. April 2, 1945. p. 32*

Nip: Short for Nippon (Japanese). This term was used in broadcasts, journalistic dispatches and in conversation.—*American Speech. April 1943. p. 151*

Nisei: Americans of Japanese descent, born and educated in the United States.—*New York Times Magazine. December 2, 1945. p. 22*

Nissen Huts: The type of hut most used in British military camps was the Nissen hut, the same type that was known in the United States as the Quonset hut (q.v.). Nissen huts in general were of 16-foot or 24-foot span. When larger span huts were needed, a

Romney 35-foot span hut became standard. Nissen huts were also sent to Iceland for the use of United States personnel stationed there. —*Engineering News-Record. October 21, 1943. p. 98-9; Civil Engineering. September 1945. p. 425-7*

N.L.: See Nebenlanger

NMRDA: Navy Materiel Redistribution and Disposal Administration.—*New York Times Magazine. May 13, 1945. p. 38*

NMRI-448: A solution, more potent than DDT (q.v.), for killing bugs. It not only kills bugs already on the scene but repels others for a week or ten days. The liquid, named NMRI-448, was the 448th of 3000 compounds tested by the Naval Medical Research Institute.—*Newsweek. September 2, 1946. p. 53*

"No Atheists in Fox Holes": Attributed to Father William Thomas Cummings, Maryknoll Mission priest, in one of his field sermons on Bataan. The Reverend William T. Cummings was reported lost when a Japanese transport was sunk in December 1944. Later, word was received that he had survived the sinking of the ship, but died later of starvation and exposure aboard a Japanese prison ship.— *Romulo. I Saw the Fall of the Philippines. p. 263; American Notes and Queries. July 1945. p. 54; Times-Union. Rochester, N.Y. October 6, 1945*

No Boats, No Votes: See Repple Depples

"No Coasting to Victory": By Franklin D. Roosevelt. Address to the closing session of the New York Herald-Tribune forum, New York City, November 17, 1942. "There can be no coasting to victory." —*Vital Speeches. December 15, 1942. p. 131*

"No Hitlers, No Ruins, No Terrors": "Fibber" McGee signed off the air for the summer vacation (1943) with: "I hope that by the time I return in September, the score will read 'No Hitlers, no ruins, no terrors.' "—*Saturday Review of Literature. July 10, 1943. p. 14*

"No Liberty without Security": See "There is no liberty. . . ."

"No Other Means Is Left Me Than to Meet Force with Force": By Adolf Hitler. Excuse given by Hitler at the start of the war.— *New York Times. September 1, 1939. p. 1*

"No Runs, No Hits, No Errors": Baseball phrase used by Rear Admiral Oscar C. Badger, reporting to Admiral Halsey on the uneventful passage of fleet units into Tokyo Bay, after the Japanese surrender.—*New York Times. September 2, 1945. p. 2E*

Non-Fraternization: Pertaining to ban imposed on Allied occupation forces to prevent association with the enemy, especially women.—*New York Times Magazine. December 2, 1945. p. 22*

Norsk Tidend: Norwegian newspaper in exile. Published twice a week in London.—*Saturday Review of Literature. July 17, 1943. p. 5*

Nose-Bag: See Canary

"Nothing Became It More Than Its Last Hour of Trial and Agony": Tribute by General MacArthur from Australia to the valiant army on Bataan.—*Newsweek. April 20, 1942. p. 21*

Now . . . All Together: Slogan for the 7th War Loan Drive. Posters for the drive carried a reproduction of a painting copied from the famous photograph of the raising of the American flag on Mount Suribachi, Iwo Jima.—*New York Times Magazine. May 13, 1945. p. 12*

NRPB: National Resources Planning Board

"The Numbers They Brought Back Are the Measure of Their Devotion and Their Courage": By Winston Churchill. Tribute to Royal Navy, merchant seamen and volunteers who took part in the evacuation of Dunkirk. Speech before the House of Commons, London, June 4, 1940.—*Vital Speeches. June 15, 1940. p. 517*

"Nuts": Reply handed to Germans on December 22, 1944, by Brigadier General Anthony C. McAuliffe of the 101st Airborne Division, to their demand for the surrender of Bastogne before the siege was broken.—*Democrat & Chronicle. Rochester, N.Y. December 30, 1944.* A poem about this "The Word" by William Rose Benét appeared in *The Saturday Review of Literature. September 8, 1945. p. 36*

NWLB: National War Labor Board. Established within the Office of Emergency Management (OEM) by executive order of President Roosevelt, January 12, 1942; it replaced the National Defense Mediation Board. It was responsible for assuring uninterrupted production through its power to adjust labor disputes.—*United States Government Manual. Summer 1943. p. 67*

NW—NW: No work—No woo. Slogan adopted by women war workers at Albina shipyards in Portland, Oregon. They agreed not to date men who were absent from work.—*Reader's Digest. January 1944. p. 44*

NWSB: National Wage Stabilization Board appointed by President Truman in January 1946 to take the place of the NWLB (q.v.).—*New York Times. January 6, 1946. p. 2E, 6E*

OAP: Office of Aircraft Production

"Obey, but Think for Yourself": Slogan of Marshal Timoshenko (Russian Army).—*Mehring. Timoshenko, Marshal of the Red Army. p. 133*

Obliteration Bombing: Blotting out by concentrated bombing. —*American Speech. October 1944. p. 225*

OCCA: Officers in Charge of Civilian Affairs. Branch of United States Army. Will administer countries our fighting men occupy and will carry on until civilian governments can be reestablished.—*Newsweek. May 10, 1943. p. 67*

OCD: Office of Civilian Defense. Established within the Office of Emergency Management (OEM) by executive orders of June 20, 1941, July 16, 1941, and April 15, 1942. Function was to coordinate state and local civilian defense projects and be responsible for planning and executing programs for protection of civilian life and property in an emergency.—*United States Government Manual. Summer 1943. p. 71*

OCIAA: Office of Coordinator of Inter-American Affairs. Established within the OEM by executive order of President Roosevelt, July 30, 1941. To serve as the center for the coordination of the cultural and commercial relations of the nation affecting hemisphere defense.—*United States Government Manual. Summer 1943. p. 76*

O'clock: Term used largely by fliers in designating directions, e.g. "twelve o'clock" indicates straight ahead; "three o'clock" directly to the right, etc.—*American Notes and Queries. June 1944. p. 39*

OCR: Office of Civilian Requirements. A division under the War Production Board (WPB). The director of the OCR determined requirements for consumer goods and services. Also determined WPB policies for necessary rationing.—*United States Government Manual. Summer 1943. p. 120*

OCS: Office of Civilian Supply, worked as a division under the War Production Board.—*Newsweek. April 19, 1943. p. 41*

OCS: Officer Candidate School (United States Army): Officers' Chief Steward (United States Navy)

Octagon Conference: Conference at Quebec in September 1944. *—General Marshall's Report. 1945. p. 71*

ODB: Office of Dependency Benefits, Newark, New Jersey.— *New York Times Magazine. June 4, 1944. p. 42*

Odograph: A recording device on which distance and direction are integrated mechanically to produce a kind of road map of the route covered by a jeep, tank, or truck; developed by the Department of Terrestrial Magnetism, Carnegie Institution of Washington.— *American Notes and Queries. October 1944. p. 102*

ODT: Office of Defense Transportation. Established within the Office of Emergency Management by executive order of President Roosevelt, December 18, 1941. Coordinated transportation policies and activities of the federal agencies; had authority over all types of transportation.—*United States Government Manual. Summer 1943. p. 82*

OEM: Office of Emergency Management. Established by Administrative Order of President Roosevelt, May 25, 1940. Functions were—a) to assist the President in clearance of information with respect to measures necessitated by the emergency; b) to maintain liaison between the President and the emergency war agencies, and c) such other duties as the President might direct.—*United States Government Manual. Summer 1943. p. 62*

OES: Office of Economic Stabilization. Established within the Office of Emergency Management (OEM), by executive order of President Roosevelt, October 3, 1942. To control so far as possible inflationary tendencies.—*United States Government Manual. Summer 1943. p. 84-5*

OEW: Office of Economic Warfare. By executive order, July 15, 1943, President Roosevelt created the Office of Economic Warfare (OEW) and reposed in it the responsibilities of the Board of Economic Warfare (BEW), which he abolished, and all the foreign economic activities of the Reconstruction Finance Corporation (RFC). To administer the new agency, he selected Leo T. Crowley, head of the Federal Deposit Insurance Corporation, and Alien Property Custodian. Subject only to War Mobilization Director Byrnes and the State Department, Mr. Crowley was to conduct our economic warfare on the critical foreign front.—*America. July 24, 1943. p. 421*

"Of Course We Shall Take Burma Back, It's Part of the British Empire": By General Harold R. L. G. Alexander, in May 1942.— *Current Biography. 1942. p. 13*

OFEC: Office of Foreign Economic Coordination. Dean Acheson, Assistant Secretary of State, was appointed Director of the newly created OFEC on June 24, 1943, and took over for the State Department control of all U.S. economic work abroad.—*Newsweek. August 23, 1943. p. 46*

Off the Beam: See Beam

Office of Facts and Figures: Established in October 1941, under Archibald MacLeish, Librarian of Congress. To "facilitate the dissemination of factual information to the citizens of the country on the progress of the defense effort." Popularly, this soon turned into the "Office of Fuss and Feathers." See also OWI.—*Newsweek. June 22, 1942. p. 30*

Office of Government Reports: Set up in July 1939, "to distribute information concerning the purposes and activities of the executive departments and agencies." Headed by Lowell Mellett, former editor of the Washington *Daily News.* Housed in a $530,000 palace on Pennsylvania Avenue, it became known as "Mellett's Madhouse." See also OWI.—*Newsweek. June 22, 1942. p. 30*

Office of Lend-Lease Administration: Established by executive order of President Roosevelt, October 28, 1941. To administer the act of March 11, 1941, "an act to promote the defense of the United States."—*United States Government Manual. Summer 1943. p. 85-6*

Oflag: Abbreviation for Offizierslager; a permanent prisoners-of-war camp for officers. See also Lager.—*Red Cross Courier. June 1943. p. 11*

OFRR: Office of Foreign Relief and Rehabilitation. Directed by Herbert Lehman.—*Current Biography. 1943. p. 440*

Oh My Aching Back: Often contracted to Oh my back, or simply My back, this phrase in general use in the army meant several things—to express discontent, to express sardonic amusement, or used upon the receipt of bad news, etc. Genesis of the phrase is obscure, but may be connected with the fact that an aching back (which could not be expected to show visible symptoms) was often used as an excuse to avoid work.—*American Speech. December 1946. p. 242*

"O.K.": Mike name of Max Otto Koischivitz, a German native, one-time instructor at Hunter College, New York City. An American citizen, he was indicted for treason on July 26, 1943, for his activities in German propaganda short wave broadcasts.—*Democrat & Chronicle. Rochester, N.Y. July 27, 1943*

Okies: Name given by U.S. troops to the Okinawans.—*American Speech. April 1945. p. 151*

Old-Blood-and-Guts: Nickname of Major General George S Patton, Jr. (United States Army).—*Current Biography. 1943. p. 571*

Old Crock: Nickname of Brigadier General Anthony C. Mc-Auliffe—*New York Times. December 31, 1944. p. 6*

Old Dob Dob: Nickname of Lieutenant General Sir William George Shedden Dobbie (British general), for some time in charge of defense of Malta.—*Time. May 18, 1942. p. 24*

Old Faithful: See Plane Nicknames

Old Lady of the Pacific Fleet: Nickname given to aircraft carrier Enterprise—*New York Times. October 21, 1945. p. 2E, 6E*

The Old Man: Nickname of Major General George S. Patton, Jr. (United States Army).—*Current Biography. 1943. p. 571*

Old Maru: Nickname of the American battleship, Nevada.—*Newsweek. July 30, 1945. p. 34*

Olympic: Code name for an operation against Japan; this first phase was to have been a three-pronged assault on southern Kyushu in the fall of 1945. See also Coronet. The operation was made unnecessary by capitulation of Japan in August 1945.—*General Marshall's Report. 1945. p. 84*

Omaha Beach: Code name given to a stretch of beach from Grandcamp to Port-en-Bessin, hotly defended by the Germans against the Allies in the Normandy invasion on June 6, 1944. Other beach names used by the Americans were "Utah" and "Red."—*Life. October 30, 1944. p. 53; Newsweek. May 6, 1946. p. 34; U.S. General Staff. Omaha Beachhead*

OMGUS: Office of Military Government (United States). It replaced the United States Group Control Council for Germany.—*New York Times. October 14, 1945. p. 2E, 6E*

On the Beam: See Beam

"On to Tokyo": By General Douglas MacArthur, in Manila, after the conquest of the Philippine capital.—*New York Times. September 2, 1945. p. 2E, 7E*

"One by One—That Is His Plan": By Winston Churchill in referring to Hitler's method of conquest. Radio address August 24.

1941. See also "Divide and conquer."—*Vital Speeches. September 1, 1941. p. 677*

"One Continent Redeemed": By Winston Churchill. Comment after the Germans had been driven from Africa. Speech before Congress, Washington, D.C., May 19, 1943.—*Vital Speeches. June 1, 1943. p. 486*

$1.00 in War Stamps from Every American Will Build the Mystery Ship Shangri-La: Poster caption. United States Treasury Department. War stamp drive, July 1943, for purchase of a new airplane carrier to replace the Hornet (designated as Shangri-La by President Roosevelt in speaking of the base from which planes took off for the bombing of Tokyo)

One-Forty-Eight-and-a-Half: See Section 8

One Man Air Force: Nickname of Colonel Robert L. Scott, United States Army Air Forces. Commander of fighter-pilots in General Chennault's famous China Air Task Force.—*New York Times Book Review. August 1, 1943. p. 15.* In the Tunisian campaign this nickname was also given to Lieutenant Colonel Phil Cochrane.—*New York Times Magazine. February 13, 1944. p. 22*

One-Man Air Force: Nickname suggested by General Eisenhower for Captain Don Gentile, fighter pilot in the European theater of operations.—*New York Times Book Review. August 13, 1944. p. 1*

One-Man-Army: Nickname of Captain Arthur Wermuth. In action on the Philippine front, Captain Wermuth gained this nickname after it became known that he had killed 116 Japs and captured several hundred. He was captured by the Japanese just before the surrender of Bataan. Though starved and tortured through 41 months in prison, he was liberated in Manila in 1945.—*Miller. General Douglas MacArthur, Fighter for Freedom. p. 274; Newsweek. October 8, 1945. p. 62*

One Man Army of Anzio: Nickname of Private Alton W. Knappenberger who won the Congressional Medal of Honor for holding off two German companies and mowing down 60 Nazis on Anzio beachhead in Italy.—*Democrat & Chronicle. Rochester, N.Y. August 24, 1944. p. 5*

One of Our Cities Is Missing: "American airmen who have been bombing Germany are a little tired of the sameness of German communiqués. They've cooked up this one for Dr. Goebbels: 'A huge swarm of American and British bombers, intent on their usual mission of bombing hospitals and churches in the Reich, was intercepted and completely destroyed today by a small number of German fighter planes. Springing to the defense of helpless civilians, the Luftwaffe pilots shot down more than 300 of the giant attacking planes and left the remaining 50 so badly injured they were unable to return to their bases.

'None of our gallant German planes or pilots was injured.

'One of our cities is missing.' "—*Reader's Digest. January 1944. p. 4*

"One Symbol Only for Frenchmen—France Herself": By Franklin D. Roosevelt. In a statement given July 13, 1943 in honor of Bastille Day.—*Democrat & Chronicle. Rochester, N.Y. July 17, 1943. p. 3*

One World: Phrase popularized by Wendell Willkie. This same phrase with the same meaning was used in a speech given in Shanghai in October 1913 by Jabez Thomas Sunderland of the American Unitarian Association. But though the phrase was thus not a new one, it came into popular use only after being used by Wendell Willkie and helped, if not to clarify people's thinking, at least to point the way to a needed concept.—*American Notes and Queries. May 1945. p. 29*

"The Only Thing We Have to Fear Is Fear Itself": By Franklin D. Roosevelt. First inaugural address, March 4, 1933.—*Roosevelt. Looking Forward. p. 261; Roosevelt. Public Papers and Addresses. v. 2. p. 11*

"Only Those Are Fit to Live Who Are Not Afraid to Die": By General Douglas MacArthur. On July 26, 1941, MacArthur was made commander of the United States Army in the Far East. A few days later he inducted his Filipino air force into the U.S. Army. "It was during his address to the serious young brown pilots that he summed up his own clear outlook on life and death. His matchless summation of that outlook, '. . . only those are fit to live who are not afraid to die,' carried into the hearts of the men who stood stiffly before him."— *Considine. MacArthur the Magnificent. p. 9.* A phrase very similar to this was used by Theodore Roosevelt—"Only those are fit to live who do not fear to die" in *The Great Adventure. c1918. p. 1*

Op: R.A.F. slang for operator, hence Wop for wireless operator, from the abbreviation W. op., and therefore not to be confused with the American slang Wop, an Italian.—*Nineteenth Century. April 1944. p. 182*

OPA: Office of Price Administration and Civilian Supply. Established by executive order of President Roosevelt, April 11, 1941. Had two principal responsibilities: the prevention of inflation, and the protection of the consumer.—*United States Government Manual. Summer 1943. p. 152*

Open City: A city declared to be unfortified and undefended so that under international law, bombardment of it by the enemy would be illegal. Manila in the Philippines was so declared but was bombed by the Japanese who thus disregarded international law.—*American Speech. October 1944. p. 225*

Operation Annie: Name for a secret American radio station which broadcast nightly to German troops at the front. German confidence in it was so well built up that it finally led them into a disastrous trap.—*New York Times Magazine. February 17, 1946. p. 12-13*

Operation Berlin: British paratroopers besieged at Arnhem (see also Patch of Hell) received word that the British Second Army had worked up to the south bank of the Lek and that rescue was a possibility. To their break out and escape across the river they gave the term "Operation Berlin," typifying their unbroken spirit.—*Time. October 9, 1944. p. 24*

Operation Crossroads: Code name for atom bomb test at Bikini, which was planned for May 1946. The name was suggested by the commander of Joint Task Force 1, Vice Admiral W. H. P. Blandy, because, he said, the science of warfare and perhaps the future of civilization itself were at the crossroads. Posters displayed in the Pentagon, Washington, D.C., bore caption that humanity was at "its most fateful crossroads."—*Democrat & Chronicle. Rochester, N.Y. February 23, 1946; New York Times. June 30, 1946. p. 2E, 6E*

Operation Eclipse: Original plan for occupation of the Reich. —*Newsweek. December 24, 1945. p. 54*

Operation Eskimo; Operation Polar Bear: Two tactical exercises carried out by Canadian forces; the first, under conditions of dry cold, in the northern prairies of Saskatchewan, and the second in an area of wet cold, in the heavy snow of the mountains of British Columbia.—*American Notes and Queries. May 1946. p. 30*

Operation Exodus: Military code designation for trip of President Truman home from the conference at Potsdam with stopover in England to see King George VI.—*Time. August 13, 1945. p. 18*

Operation Hornblow: The Army's Chemical Warfare Service officers recorded the last round of an unhappy seven-week experience with a troublesome cargo of German mustard gas, in a report in August 1946 that 120 large bombs had been destroyed on Horn Island, off Pascagoula, Mississippi. The destruction, listed as Operation Hornblow, was accomplished by burning the bombs on the open beach. Lieutenant Colonel William J. Allen, Jr., directed the operation.— *Democrat & Chronicle. Rochester, N.Y. August 3, 1946. p. 1*

Operation Manhattan: Transfer of United Nations personnel from London to New York.—*New York Times. March 24, 1946. p. 2E, 8E*

Operation Mother-in-law: See War Brides

Operation Musk-Ox: Joint Canadian-American expedition for tactical research in Arctic territory. Also called "Exercise Musk-Ox." —*Newsweek. February 18, 1946. p. 50*

Operation Pluto: Pluto stands for Pipe Lines under the Ocean and refers to the twenty petroleum pipe lines laid under the English Channel from Britain to France after D-day in Normandy. The oil thus furnished played a large part in the success of operations in the war in Europe.—*New York Times. May 27, 1945. p. 2E, 6E; Democrat & Chronicle. Rochester, N.Y. May 24, 1945*

Operation Polar Bear: See Operation Eskimo

Operation Roll-up: Name given to task of caring for equipment which is declared surplus by the Navy.—*Democrat & Chronicle. Rochester, N.Y. March 29, 1946. p. 12*

Operation Selection Board: Name for round-up of Nazi plotters.—*New York Times. March 2, 1947. p. 2E, 8E*

Operation Stork: Name given to the sending of British war brides and babies to the United States to join their GI husbands. Mentioned by William Shirer in a broadcast Sunday February 10, 1946, over CBS. Also called "Operation War Brides."—*Newsweek. February 18, 1946. p. 61.* Name also given to evacuation by British officials of Berlin's children to the country to ease winter hardships.— *Newsweek. November 5, 1945. p. 47*

Operation War Brides: See Operation Stork

Operational Fatigue: See Shell-shock

OPM: Office of Production Management. Established by executive order of President Roosevelt, January 7, 1941. Later it was abolished and its duties taken over by the WPB (q.v.).—*United States Government Manual. Summer 1943. p. 117-18*

Oscar: Marine slang for submarine.—*Newsweek. February 8, 1943. p. 52*

OSRD: Office of Scientific Research and Development. Created within the Office of Emergency Management by executive order of President Roosevelt, June 28, 1941. To assure adequate provision for research on scientific and medical problems relating to the national defense.—*United States Government Manual. Summer 1943. p. 88*

OSS: Office of Strategic Services. By military order of June 13, 1942, the office of Coordinator of Information, exclusive of foreign information activities transferred to OWI, was designated Office of Strategic Services, and transferred to the jurisdiction of the Joint United States Chiefs of Staff. As modified by executive order of President Roosevelt, March 9, 1943, functions of the OSS were 1) to collect and analyze such strategic information as might be required by the Joint United States Chiefs of Staff, and 2) to plan and operate such special services as might be designated by the Joint Staff.—*United States Government Manual. Summer 1943. p. 164; New York Times Magazine. October 7, 1945. p. 12-13*

Our Carelessness Their Secret Weapon. Prevent Forest Fires: Poster caption. United States Department of Agriculture. Forest Service

"Our Defeats Are But Stepping-Stones to Victory, and His [Hitler's] Victories Are Only the Stepping-Stones to Ruin": By Winston Churchill. Speech in the Usher Hall, Edinburgh, when he received the freedom of the city, October 12, 1942.—*Churchill. The End of the Beginning. p. 239*

"Our Task Is Hard . . . The Time Is Short": By Franklin D. Roosevelt. Speech before joint session of Congress, Washington, D.C., January 6, 1942.—*Vital Speeches. January 15, 1942. p. 195*

Over the Hump: Designation of air route over the Himalyas from India to China. At the war's end, supplies were being flown over this route at a rate of two tons a minute.—*New York Times. September 2, 1945. p. 2E, 7E*

Overlord: Code name for operational plans to attack the Axis fortress in Europe—the Normandy invasion. This name replaced the earlier code name Roundup.—*General Marshall's Report. 1945. p. 11*

OWI: Office of War Information. Created by executive order of June 13, 1942. President Roosevelt merged the Office of Government Reports, Coordinator of Information, Office of Facts and Figures, and the Office of Emergency Management's Division of Information into a single Office of War Information and appointed Elmer Davis. newspaperman and radio news analyst as Director.—*Newsweek. June 22, 1942. p. 30; United States Government Manual. Summer 1943. p. 91.* The OWI was abolished August 31, 1945, by executive order of President Truman. All overseas information activities of the OWI were transferred, together with the activities of the Office of Inter-American Affairs, to the Department of State as a temporary entity to be known as the Interim International Information Service.—*Publishers' Weekly. September 8, 1945. p. 973*

Owl: (American plane) Curtis O-52 observation plane

OWM: Office of War Mobilization. Created by executive order of President Roosevelt, June 1943. Duties were "to develop unified programs and to establish policies for the maximum use of the nation's natural and industrial resources for military and civilian needs."— *Newsweek. June 7, 1943. p. 29*

OWMR: Office of War Mobilization and Reconversion.— *New York Times Magazine. September 23, 1945. p. 13*

P: "P" type ships (see also APA and L) are patrol boats. These vessels, ranging in length from 75 to 200 feet, played a major role in the successful anti-U-boat campaign in the Atlantic. Smallest of the group are the PT boats (patrol torpedo) which reached speeds of 70 miles per hour. Other "P" boats are PC—Patrol Craft; PCE— Patrol Craft Escort; PCS—Patrol Craft Sweeper. PT boats also played a dramatic role in the Pacific and it was in one of these that General MacArthur escaped from Corregidor.—*New York Times Magazine. October 21, 1945. p. 49; White. They Were Expendable* (about PT boats in the Philippines)

Padre X: A Canadian chaplain who chose to stay with the Canadians left on the beaches after the ill-fated raid on Dieppe. He helped the wounded, often exposing himself to unceasing enemy fire, and later shared their imprisonment. For some time known only as

"Padre X," he was later identified as Major John Weir Foote, Presbyterian Chaplain of the Royal Hamilton Light Infantry.   He was awarded the Victoria Cross.—*Newsweek.   February 25, 1946.   p. 54*

Pakistan: The word Pakistan was coined in 1933 by Chaudhrie Rahmat Ali, who explained that it was a symbol for the units that should make up the northwestern area.   The P stood for Punjab, A for the Afghan border states, K for Kashmir, S for Sind and TAN for Baluchistan.   The idea of Pakistan was the establishment of a separate Moslem state, strongly advocated by Mohammed Ali Jinnah, leader of the Moslem League.   The League proposed that areas with a predominantly Moslem population should be organized quite separately from the rest of India.   There was to be a Pakistan in northwestern India and another in the northeastern section.   These two, being predominantly Moslem in population, were to constitute a separate state to be ruled separately from the rest of India.   Thus India approached its freedom in 1947 as a divided country, Hindus against Moslems, but with some hope of working together through representation on a common Council.—*Smith. Divided India. p. 153-6, 240, 244; Shridharani. My India, My America. p. 574-6; Asia. October 1943. p. 567-70*

Pancake and Light: Radar code message meaning "land, refuel, and rearm."— *Newsweek. September 10, 1945. p. 92*

Pantiger: A new heavily armored German tank with six-inch plate; weighed more than sixty-five tons; so called by its British captors because it combined the best features of the Tiger and Panther tanks (AP dispatch, August 18, 1944).—*American Notes and Queries. September 1944. p. 85*

Panzer: Means armor but the term is not applied to armored cars, only to tanks. German Panzer units are tank units.—*New York Times Magazine. October 3, 1944. p. 29; American Speech. April 1941. p. 147*

Paper-Troopers' Salvage Program: An arrangement for boys and girls to collect waste paper from households in the community, to help keep the paper mills operating. The program was tested in Rochester, N.Y. under sponsorship of the *Democrat & Chronicle* and proved successful enough so that it was decided to set it up on a national basis. —*Democrat & Chronicle. Rochester, N.Y. August 26, 1944. p. 9*

Pappy: Nickname of Lieutenant Colonel Gregory Boyington, Marine flying ace (so called for his 32 years of age; old for a flyer). —*Newsweek. September 24, 1945. p. 33*

Parapooch: Dog dropped by parachute for military and combat purposes.—*New York Times Magazine. December 2, 1945. p. 22*

Parasaboteurs: Parachutists who land equipped to perform acts of sabotage.—*Newsweek. March 8, 1943. p. 48*

Parashooter or Parashot: A defense volunteer trained to deal with parachute troops of the enemy. Sometimes called Paraspotter.—*American Speech. February 1944. p. 12; Good Housekeeping. February 1941. p. 113*

Parashootists: See Eden's Army

Para-Ski: Descriptive of parachute troops equipped with skis. A member of the troop was called a para-skier.—*American Speech. February 1944. p. 63*

Paratroops: Soldiers who were flown to their objective and parachuted from the plane. The term is a blend of parachute and troops.—*American Speech. February 1943. p. 64*

Paravane: A torpedo-shaped underwater protective device with sawlike teeth in its forward end, for use by vessels in mined areas to sever the moorings of mines.—*Webster's New International Dictionary. 1944. p. 1775*

Pastorious: Nazi code name for a sabotage plan involving the blowing up of American aluminum factories.—*American Notes and Queries. January 1946. p. 152*

Patch of Hell: Name given to Arnhem by Alan Wood, a British correspondent who was with the airborne troops. The British airborne troops ran into stiff opposition. For most of the week the weather was so bad that even air-dropped supplies were scarce. After a week relief came, but casualties had been heavy.—*Time. October 2, 1944. p. 28*

Pathfinders: An R.A.F. force, trail-blazing bombers, with a specially trained crew and special fire-blazing balls. These planes went on ahead to mark by fires and flares the targets in enemy territory which the bombers were to hit.—*Democrat & Chronicle. Rochester, N.Y. January 31, 1944*

Patriotic War: See World War II

Patriotutes: See Victory Girl

Pattern Bombing: Concentrated bombing of an objective, such as took place before the surrender of Pantelleria, Italy (June 11, 1943). Bombardment began with a major target and then when that was erased, proceeded to another and another until, if the garrison held out, not a square inch of land was left untouched.—*Democrat & Chronicle. Rochester, N.Y. June 12, 1943. p. 2*

Paul Pry: British slang for giant searchlight. See also Bearded Lady.—*Nation. November 9, 1940. p. 446*

Paul Revere: Mike name of Douglas Chandler, one-time Baltimore columnist. Added to the Nazi propaganda program in April 1941, the Paul Revere program (like his famous predecessor) was supposed to incite his fellow countrymen to throw off the yoke of tryanny. "Paul Revere's" broadcasts were framed by the thud of galloping hoofs and by the Yankee Doodle march played by fifes. Invariably he closed by summoning "American patriots" to "ride again and to arouse the country against the President and the Jews." Indicted for treason on July 26, 1943, by the District of Columbia Grand Jury.—*Christian Science Monitor Magazine. July 18, 1942. p. 6; Democrat & Chronicle. Rochester, N.Y. July 27, 1943*

PAW: Petroleum Administrator for War. Established by executive order of President Roosevelt, December 2, 1942. The order abolished the Office of the Petroleum Coordinator for War and transferred to the new Administration all its records, personnel, property and funds.—*United States Government Manual. Summer 1943. p. 159*

PCAU: Philippine Civil Affairs Unit (pronounced "pee-cow"). After Manila was freed from Japanese dominance, it was the Army's PCAU which kept the city alive. It served hundreds of thousands of meals and set up water points to slake Manila's thirst.—*Time. March 5, 1945. p. 19; Newsweek. April 2, 1945. p. 55*

"Peace in Our Time": Phrase used by Prime Minister Neville Chamberlain on his return from Munich, September 30, 1938. This was his earnest hope and he thought that it might in some way be achieved.—*Hodgson. The Man Who Made the Peace: Neville Chamberlain. p. 110*

"Peace without Vengeance Has Been Achieved": By Winston Churchill, referring to the settlement of the civil war in Greece, in his speech to the House of Commons on the Yalta Conference.—*New York Times. March 4, 1945. p. 2E, 6E*

Peaceful America: See "There is not sufficient room. . . ."

Pearl Harbor: The name of the U.S. Naval base in the Hawaiian Islands which was treacherously attacked by the Japanese December 7, 1941, at the same time that their emissaries were in Washington conferring on peace. During World War II, "Pearl Harbor" ceased to be just the name of a place and came to mean instead the attack itself, e.g. in the phrase "Remember Pearl Harbor." Some interesting reactions and quotations on Pearl Harbor were: President Roosevelt—"December 7, 1941, a date which will live in infamy." Winston Churchill—"It only remains for two great democracies to face their task with whatever strength God may give them." Senator Burton K. Wheeler (Democrat, Montana)—"The only thing now is to . . . lick hell out of them." President Manuel Quezon of the Philippines— "The flag of the United States will be defended until the last round of ammunition has been fired." Emperor Hirohito of Japan—"The hallowed spirits of our imperial ancestors . . . give us confidence." Adolf Hitler—"That Japan took this step must fill all decent people with profound satisfaction." Attaché at New York Japanese consulate, clearing out his belongings—"This is a special Sunday." Cordell Hull, Secretary of State—"Japan has been infamously false and fraudulent." General John J. Pershing, commander of the AEF in World War I— "All Americans today are united in one ambition—to take whatever share they can in the defense of their country."—*Times-Union. Rochester, N.Y. August 14, 1945*

Pee-cow: See PCAU

Peel Off: Aviation term. To "peel off" is to curve away from another aircraft. The movement as one machine comes up close to another and then slants away is supposed to resemble the act of peeling off the skin of a banana.—*American Speech. April 1943. p. 151*

Peep: See Jeep

Pencil Pusher: AAF slang for the navigator on a plane

Pentagon Feet: War building ailment complained of by workers in the Pentagon Building, mammoth new home of the War Department and center of its vast activities. Located across the Potomac from Washington, the building occupies 43 acres of a 300-acre plot.—*Democrat & Chronicle Magazine. Rochester, N.Y. July 11, 1943. p. 2*

Pentolite: A new explosive, more powerful than TNT, though not as potent as RDX (q.v.).—*Newsweek. December 8, 1941. p. 43*

"The People of Germany Are Just as Responsible for Hitler as the People of Chicago Are for the Chicago Tribune": By Alexander Woollcott. Last words before the microphone before his collapse, January 23, 1943. He was participating in a "People's Platform" program on the subject, "Is Germany incurable?"—*Saturday Review of Literature. February 13, 1943. p. 15*

People's War: See World War II

Pep Tires: Nickname for doughnuts, so called by American Red Cross workers in England

Period One: Name given to the time expected to elapse between the downfall of Germany and the end of the war with Japan.— *Wall Street Journal. March 31, 1945. p. 1*

PGC: Persian Gulf Command. Over a single-track railroad, through mountain passes, unbroken deserts, and the vilest climate on earth, the men of the PGC supplied the Russians with the materials that saved Stalingrad and pushed back the Nazi tide.—*New Yorker. January 13, February 17, March 24, April 7, 1945*

Philippines Pledge: Made by General Douglas MacArthur to President Quezon of the Philippines: "We'll go back to the Philippines, Mr. President, and if necessary I'll put you back in Malacanan on the points of my bayonets."—*Romulo. I Saw the Fall of the Philippines. p. 165*

Phony War: Phrase attributed to Senator Borah to refer to the period of apparent inactivity of the warring nations in western Europe from September 1939 to the spring of 1940. See also Sitzkrieg.—*Welles. The Time for Decision. p. 75*

Photo Joe: German aerial scouts; nickname popularized by Allied naval forces in the Channel area. See also Maytag Charlie.— *American Notes and Queries. June 1944. p. 39*

P.I.A.T.: Projector, Infantry, Anti-tank, a mortar-type weapon often erroneously likened to the U.S. rocket-firing bazooka.—*Time. October 9, 1944. p. 24*

Piccolo: See Tuba

"Pick Out the Biggest One and Fire": By Captain Edward J. Moran. "It was a dark night, with long swells running. The U.S.S. Boise, knifing along at 25 knots, was part of a cruiser column, screened by destroyers, sent to head off a Jap landing force in the Solomons. Suddenly there were enemy ships to starboard. . . 'How many ships have you spotted?' 'I have five in sight, sir.' 'Pick out the biggest one and fire.' " See also "We'll take the big ones first."—*Time. November 30, 1942. p. 18*

Pick's Pike: Nickname for the Ledo Road (a section of the Stilwell Road) from Ledo in Assam, India, to Wanting on the Burma

Road in Yunnan Province, China. Built to take supplies into China. General (at that time Col.) Lewis A. Pick took command of the Ledo Road project in October 1943. In fifteen months he pushed the road from the forty-five mile mark to a junction with the Burma Road 420 miles away. The route passed through 102 miles of mountains and over two 4,000 foot mountain passes.—*New York Times Magazine. February 11, 1945. p. 12; Yank. March 30, 1945. p. 5*

Piggy-back: Nickname for a large plane that carries a smaller one.—*New York Times Magazine. December 2, 1945. p. 22*

Pilot-less Planes: See Robot bombs

Pin-up: A picture for a soldier to pin up on the wall of his quarters. According to an editorial in *Newsweek* (July 16, 1945. p. 19), the idea of "pin ups" is not new with this war. "The demand for decorative damsels existed among the troops of Spanish-American war times and it increased considerably when the Yanks started 'over there' in 1917. But the GI's of today have boomed pin-ups into big business, with one firm alone having sold more than 60,000,000 pictures since Pearl Harbor." But even though the idea is an old one, the term pin-up (or pinup, as it is sometimes written) seems to have first come into general usage in this war. Pin-up girls were mentioned on the back cover of *Yank* (the Army weekly) March 12, 1943, and later issues published pictures of photogenic Hollywood stars and models for GI use as pin-ups. At the outset of the war Walter Thornton, recalling the enthusiasm of soldiers in World War I for pinning up photographs, offered General Powell (of Fort Dix) some 5000 photographs from his files. General Powell's letter of acceptance was the beginning of the Thornton Pin-ups, which soon became a familiar sight in all parts of the world. The Thornton pictures typified the wholesome girl-back-home type, rather than the glamorous show-girl type. According to a survey made by editors and photographers of *Life* magazine in 1941, Dorothy Lamour outnumbered all others as the soldiers' favorite pin-up girl. This mention of "pin-up" is the earliest noted in print.—*Life. July 7, 1941. p. 34-7; American Speech. April 1944. p. 149-50; Newsweek. July 16, 1945. p. 19; American Notes and Queries. July 1946. p. 56; Britannia Book of the Year. 1944. p. 770*

Pipers: See Vipers

Pipeline Time: Army phrase designating the period of time elapsing between the time when a requisition left a depot and the time the requested supplies arrived there. Also called Turnaround

Time.—*American Speech. October 1945. p. 227.* The phrase Turn-around Time was contributed to this book by a former War Department officer

Plain Mister Bee: See Bee Ko

Plane Nicknames: The plane itself was usually referred to as a kite. Individual makes of planes had special nicknames as follows: Blenburgher—Blenheim; Cat—Catalina; Daffy—Defiant; Hurry—Hurricane; Limping Annie—Anson (from the unevenness of its engine-note); Lizzie—Lysander; Maggie—Miles Magister; Old Faithful—Ausan; Spit—Spitfire; He—German Heinkle; Me—German Messerschmidt; You—German Junkers ('you' from the pronunciation of German ju).—*Nineteenth Century. April 1944. p. 183; Saturday Review of Literature. October 4, 1941. p. 9*

Planes, Not Predictions: See "We Need Decisions. . . ."

Plonk: See GI Liquor in the Pacific

Pluto: See Operation Pluto

POA: Pacific Ocean Areas

POE: Port of Embarkation

Pogled: Word used by British and American soldiers to describe the condition of Germans taken prisoner in the Salerno region, meaning "slap-happy in its most acute and superlative degree."—*American Notes and Queries. November 1943. p. 119*

Point Rationing: A rationing method announced by the Office of Price Administration (OPA), establishing a secondary currency of points alongside the dollar currency. Essential articles of which the supply was at all limited were listed and given a price in points. Every person in the country was given a book of stamps representing a certain number of points. His purchase of articles on the controlled list was limited by the number of points in his possession.—*Business Week. May 9, 1942. p. 15-16*

Pointie-Talkie: A linguistic manual issued during the war, mainly for the use of airmen grounded in strange territory. If they met natives, they could point to certain phrases in the book in the native's language and thus give out information or ask questions. It worked satisfactorily when the natives could read!—*Word Study. May 1946. p. 2*

P.O.L.: Petroleum, oil, and lubricants, known as P.O.L. in army talk.—*New Yorker. September 23, 1944. p. 16*

Police Boxes: Reinforced brick shelters built at street inter-sections, London, to protect London "Bobbies" on duty during air raids.—*Newsweek. October 13, 1941. p. 29*

Polly Plane: Aircraft fitted with loudspeaker to announce messages to ground forces.—*New York Times Magazine. December 2, 1945. p. 22*

Polo Players' Unit: A term applied to G-2 in certain army circles; said to have come from the fact that early in the war there was "quite a rush out of society and moneyed strata into military intelligence."—*PM. December 28, 1944*

POM: Preparation for Overseas Movement

Pom-pom: Vickers-Maxim automatic machine-cannon firing one-pound shells from looped belt; or any similar weapon. Name came from the drumming sound of its fast fire.—*Democrat & Chronicle. Rochester, N.Y. September 8, 1940*

Popski's Private Army: A picked lot of fearless fighters combed from about a half-dozen European countries, led by the legendary "Major Popski," whose real identity was not revealed. The activities of this group had much to do with the rapid advance of the British Eighth Army after its landings in Italy.—*New York Times. December 12, 1943. p. 37*

Porcupine: Nickname given to B-29's, equipped to put enemy radar out of action. They carried in place of a bomb load as many as 18 jammers (see Radar Countermeasures) as well as the necessary receivers and operators. So many spinelike antennas projected from the fuselage that the planes were called Porcupines.—*Joint Board, OSRD, War Dept., Navy Dept. Electronics Warfare. 1945. p. 30*

Portal Houses: Proposed prefabricated houses for England, so called after Lord Portal, whose ministry was in charge of housing. Punch played up the name in jokes about "crossing one's portal."—*Saturday Review of Literature. March 10, 1945. p. 6*

Potatoburgers: See Hamburgers

Pour La Victoire: Weekly. Newspaper of French emigré press. Started in January 1942; edited by Geneviève Tabouis in New York City.—*Saturday Review of Literature. July 17, 1943. p. 4*

POW: Prisoner of War

Pow-Wows: American Prisoners of War Club; recently organized by Paul A. Kovacs as the national organization for American soldiers taken prisoner in World War II by the German armies. The new "club" has a potential membership of 125,000.—*American Notes and Queries. July 1946. p. 60*

Pozit: See VT Fuse

PPI: Plan Position Indicator, a radar navigational aid. See also Loran and IFF.—*Newsweek. May 20, 1946. p. 66*

P-Planes: See Robot Bombs

"Praise the Lord and Pass the Ammunition": Attributed to a minister at Pearl Harbor. First attributed to Chaplain William Maguire (and so quoted in *Life.* November 2, 1942. p. 43), but he is reported as claiming that he didn't remember saying it and "positively didn't man a gun" at Pearl Harbor. Real author of the phrase seems to have been Naval Lieutenant Howell Forgy, Presbyterian chaplain. The phrase is also the title of a popular song. Words and music by Frank Loesser. Song came out in September 1942. Famous Music Corporation. c1942.—*Democrat & Chronicle. Rochester, N.Y. November 1, 1942*

Praise the Lord and Pass the New Editions: Slogan coined by American Red Cross for second Victory Book Drive (q.v.) held January 5 through March 5, 1943.—*New York Times Book Review. January 3, 1943. p. 8*

Prang: R.A.F. slang meaning to bomb a place, especially to bomb it heavily. Term may be a blend of paste and bang. It also came to mean crash.—*Nineteenth Century. April 1944. p. 184; Time. March 22, 1943. p. 51*

Prayer Wing: Army fliers and civilians who offered a daily prayer for early victory; originated with the ferrying division of the Air Transport Command.—*American Notes and Queries. March 1945. p. 183*

Praying Mantis: A Spitfire (British plane) which folds its wings, thus giving the British Royal Navy a big increase in fighter strength of carrier-based aircraft.—*New York Times. October 8, 1944. p. 7E*

Precision Bombing: Pattern bombing of a single group of related objects, with the most important object pinpoint bombed.—*American Speech. December 1945. p. 301*

Preco: Preparatory Commission of the United Nations Organization. It held its first regular meeting in November 1945.—*Newsweek. December 10, 1945. p. 55*

"Preparation—Liberation—Assault": By Winston Churchill. The three phases of the struggle ahead were summed up in the above words, in a speech to the Canadian Senate and House of Commons at Ottawa, Canada, and broadcast to the world, December 30, 1941.— *Churchill. The Unrelenting Struggle. p. 370*

A Present with a Future: Slogan for sale of war bonds, used at Christmas time, 1942. Noted especially in advertising of E. W. Edwards & Son, (Rochester, N.Y.) department store, suggesting war bonds as Christmas presents.—*Democrat & Chronicle. Rochester, N.Y. December 24, 1942. p. 13*

Preserve Your Freedom, Too: See A Bond in Every Kitchen

"The President of the United States . . . Is the Author of This Mighty Undertaking and in All of It I Have Been His Active and Ardent Lieutenant": By Winston Churchill in reference to launching of North African counter offensive against the Axis forces. Speech at dinner for the Lord Mayor, London, November 10, 1942.—*Vital Speeches. November 15, 1942. p. 67*

PRF: Pulse Recurrence Frequency. Radar term for the frequency at which a radar transmitter was pulsed.—*Army and Navy Journal. August 18, 1945. p. 1534*

Priority: Being at the top of the list for getting scarce commodities. For example, war plants engaged in vital production were given top priority (or first chance) to get the scarce metals and materials needed for their work

Privateer: (American plane). Early in the war the Navy recognized the need for long range patrol aircraft capable of carrying out both radar and radar intercept searches. The first plane expressly designed for this purpose was the PB4Y2. Known as the Consolidated "Privateer," it had so many plastic-dome-covered antennas, it soon received the nickname "Warthog."—*Joint Board, OSRD, War Dept., Navy Dept. Electronics Warfare. 1945. p. 24*

"The Problems of Victory Are More Agreeable than Those of Defeat, but They Are No Less Difficult": By Winston Churchill. Speech before Parliament, November 11, 1942, on the victory in Egypt and African campaign.—*Vital Speeches. December 1, 1942. p. 104*

Project Transcom: See Transcom Project

Prop Wash: AAF slang for gossip. Prop wash means the wind stream from the propeller, so gossip is an easy derivative to understand

"Providence Has Called on Me to Restore to My People Their Freedom and Honor": By Adolf Hitler, Chancellor of Germany. Speech to Reichstag, July 19, 1940.—*Vital Speeches. August 1, 1940. p. 625*

Proximity Fuse: See VT fuse

PRP: See Purp

PT Boat: See Mosquito (boat); also P: "P" type ships

Puddle Jumper: Observation plane, sometimes with bazookas on its wings. Also a nickname for Jeep (q.v.).—*Newsweek. October 2, 1944. p. 31*

Pukka Gen: R.A.F. slang for absolutely authoritative information. "Duff gen" meant a wrong steer, or false information. "Gen" undoubtedly came from the phrase "for the general information of all ranks," "pukka" from Hindustani and "duff" from the English underworld, "duff goods" being trashy or inferior.—*Nineteenth Century. April 1944. p. 184*

Pulpit: Slang term for the cockpit of an airplane.—*Saturday Review of Literature. October 4, 1941. p. 9*

Pulsojet: See Ramjet

Purges: See note on Kriegie

Purp: Nickname of War Production Board's Production Requirements Plan, or PRP. It was the rating under which the WPB determined the amount of raw materials available and allotted them on basis of a manufacturer's importance to the war effort. See also CMP.—*Newsweek. October 12, 1942. p. 69*

Purple Heart Corner: AAF slang for outside plane in lowest flying element of bomber formation

Purple Heart Valley: Valley in Italy—under such constant German fire that "if a man came back alive and in one piece without the Purple Heart (U.S. decoration for wounds in action) the return was considered a gift from the gods."—*New York Times Book Review.* November 26, 1944. p. 7, in a review of Margaret Bourke-White's book *They Called It Purple Heart Valley*

Put 'Em Across: Motto of EAC, Engineer Amphibian Command (q.v.).—*Collier's. July 3, 1943. p. 13*

"Put Your Confidence in Us": By Winston Churchill. Radio address February 9, 1941. "Here is the answer which I will give to President Roosevelt: Put your confidence in us."—*Churchill. Blood, Sweat and Tears. p. 462*

PWD: The Army's Psychological Warfare Division.—*American Speech. February 1946. p. 74*

Quacks: Nickname given to C.W.A.C.S. (q.v.), Canadian Women's Army Corps.—*Newsweek. September 28, 1942. p. 11*

Quadrant Conference: President Roosevelt, Prime Minister Churchill and Combined Chiefs of Staff met in Quebec in August 1943 after King Victor Emmanuel of Italy proclaimed the resignation of Mussolini.—*General Marshall's Report. 1945. p. 17-18*

Queen Day: Practice test for the Bikini bombing, June 24, 1946.—*Newsweek. July 1, 1946. p. 20*

Quickies: Undeclared strikes in the form of work stoppages for a few hours or a day or two.—*Newsweek. February 8, 1943. p. 56*

Quiet Mason Mac: Nickname of Lieutenant General F. N. Mason MacFarlane (British Army).—*Current Biography. 1943. p. 478*

Quisling: A traitor, after Major Vidkun Quisling, head of Norwegian Nazi party, who on the German invasion of Norway (April 1940) accepted chief place in a Nazi-sponsored government.—*Webster's New International Dictionary. 1943. p. ciii; American Speech. April 1941. p. 147*

Quonset Huts: Developed by the Navy at Quonset Point, Rhode Island, and used as barracks, garages, schools, machine shops, apartments and many other things. In shape they resemble a long cylinder, cut in half lengthwise, with the flat side on the ground. The Navy began investigation of prefabricated housing in 1941 and by June of that year, huts were being sent to England under lend-lease. By the end of 1942, having made more than 34,000 huts, the Navy handed the job to the Stran-Steel Division of the Great Lakes Steel Corporation. The huts come in different sizes—20' x 48' and 40' x 100' being the most usual. Several can be joined together. The greatest single collection of "40's" was a warehouse on Guam. It covered 54,000 square feet and was nicknamed the Multiple Mae West — *New Yorker. March 16, 1946. p. 21-2*

Racon: Radar Beacons. Stations which served as the radar equivalents of lighthouses.—*Army and Navy Journal. August 18, 1945. p. 1534*

Radar: Navy code word meaning Radio-Detection-and-Ranging. An instrument called a radiolocator, developed to detect approaching enemy planes, was revealed by Britain in June 1941 as having been widely and successfully used since the war begun. It was developed in 1935 by Robert Alexander Watson Watt, a Scot, Air Ministry adviser on telecommunications. According to *Time* magazine, quoting the Navy, the man who coined the word Radar was Commander (now Captain) S. M. Tucker.

The word Radar was kept under close military secrecy for some time but news of it was released to the public by the United States War and Navy Departments in the spring of 1943. Among other things the official Army-Navy statement said: "Radar has stood guard at many danger points along United Nations frontiers and at sea, warning of the coming of aerial and sea-borne enemy forces, and contributing toward victory in combat."

A radar instrument not only can detect the presence of an enemy plane or ship but can also determine its direction and distance. And since it operates through the medium of radio it can accomplish these things with the speed of light, in total darkness, through fog, and in all weather conditions.—*Newsweek. June 30, 1941. p. 20-1; New York Times Magazine. May 23, 1943. p. 14-15; Time. August 20, 1945. p. 78; Dunlap. Radar. p. 2*

Radar Altimeter: Radar device which gives the pilot his height over land (not height above sea level) and which thus made possible low-altitude bombing and strafing of Japanese ships and German lines. Up to 4000 feet, it is accurate within 6 feet.—*Newsweek. August 20, 1945. p. 42*

Radar Code Phrases: British radar personnel had a series of code phrases which were understandable to all British pilots, but which were never fathomed by the Germans. For some of the phrases and their meanings, see Bandit at Four Angels; Bogey; Buster; Chickens; Drop It; Grand Slam; Heads Up; Pancake and Light; Sweet (or Sour) Oranges; Tallyho

Radar Countermeasures: Measures developed by the United States to thwart enemy radar. These measures were developed early in the war and involved the use of aluminum foil (that same foil that we missed from cigarette packages and candy bars). This foil in strips, dropped by planes during the Normandy invasion was known by the code name "Window." This term was chosen probably because the foil was originally cut in squares. Rolls of long foil streamers that were used later against the Japanese radar were known as "Rope." In October 1943 another radar jammer (device for upsetting enemy radar calculations) was tried by the AAF. This was known as "Carpet" and was a small transmitter which sent out continuous waves to confuse the Wurzburgs (q.v.). It was carried by the heavy bombers, and the combination of Carpet and Window jamming proved far more effective than either type alone. In all, some 10,000,000 pounds of aluminum foil in the form of Window strips were dropped over Europe by our British-based bombers. See also Tuba.—*Popular Science. January 1946. p. 82; Joint Board, OSRD, War Dept., Navy Dept. Electronics Warfare. 1945. p. 14; Time. December 3, 1945. p. 52.. Baxter. Scientists Against Time. p. 158-69.* See also Electronic Raspberry

R.A.F.: Royal Air Force, Britain

Raff: British term—to shell, bomb or otherwise maul. From R.A.F., Royal Air Force.—*American Speech. February 1944. p. 13*

Les Rafs: French nickname for British air force pilots.—*Nation. November 9, 1940. p. 447*

Railroad Tracks: Army slang for a captain's bars.—*American Speech. February 1947. p. 55*

Ramjet; Pulsojet; Turbojet: Different types of war-developed jet-propulsion power for aircraft.—*New York Times. November 18, 1945. p. 2E, 6E*

RAMPS: Repatriated American Military Personnel—patients, dischargees and former prisoners of war, all of whom had priority in being returned from overseas to America.—*Newsweek. June 11, 1945. p. 33*

Rangers (U.S.): Worked in cooperation with the British Commandos (q.v.). They were named after Rogers's Rangers, the rough, colonial Indian fighters of Major Robert Rogers. The first mention of the Rangers was the report that they had taken part in the Dieppe raid. All Rangers were volunteers.—*Newsweek. August 31, 1942. p. 21-2*

Rank—To Pull Rank: Phrase meaning to use one's superior rank to obtain unfair advantage, extra service, etc.—*American Speech. December 1945. p. 261; December 1946. p. 284*

Raobs: Radiosonde Observations; to determine temperature, humidity and pressure at altitudes of fifteen miles or more. See also Rawin.—*Newsweek. November 27, 1944. p. 78*

Rata: (Russian plane) Standard fighting plane

Ration: This word was derived from the French military term "ration," and started its career in English as a military term. Members of the armed services were allotted rations (a certain amount of food) normally and regularly, but civilians met the word in abnormal times (as in World War II) when food had to be restricted. The general pronunciation of the word in military circles was with a short a, and this pronunciation was quite generally taken over by civilians, though the long a pronunciation was also heard. See also Point Rationing.—*American Speech. April 1943. p. 128-30*

Rationing Means a Fair Share for All of Us: Poster caption. United States Office of Price Administration

Rawin: A new technique (combination of radio and electronic devices) which enables weather men to chart wind velocity and direction at various altitudes. See also Raobs.—*Newsweek. November 27, 1944. p. 78*

The Razor: Nickname of General Hideki Tojo, Premier of Japan in December 1941.—*New York Times. September 16, 1945. p. 2E, 7E*

R.C.A.F. (W.D.) C.W.A.A.F. was the original designation of the Canadian Women's Auxiliary Air Force under an organization order of September 5, 1941. But when all ranks were made subject to the Air Force Act, an Order-In-Council, February 3, 1942 wiped out any possible discrimination by designating the women's force the "Women's Division" as an integral part of the Royal Canadian Air Force. Now referred to as R.C.A.F. (W.D.).—*Whitton. Canadian Women in the War Effort. p. 11-12*

R-Day: May 12, 1945—Redeployment Day, day when armed services in European Theater of Operations would begin to be moved from Europe.—*Democrat & Chronicle. Rochester, N.Y. May 12, 1945. p. 1.* It was announced on the radio May 11, 1945

RDX: A new explosive developed in cooperation with the British. It gets its name from Research Department Formula X.

RDX was the name given to it by the British (the Germans called it 'hexogen,' the Italians 'T4') but the Americans took over the British designation RDX. It was credited with 40 per cent more bursting power than TNT.—*Newsweek. December 8, 1941. p. 43; May 20, 1946. p. 66*

Reaction Motor: See Rocket

Rebecca Eureka: Radar device, an adaptation of IFF for paratroop operations. The Rebecca set in the troop carrier triggers the Eureka set strapped to the leg of a paratrooper on the ground. This permits exact spotting and the parachuting of additional troops or supplies.—*Newsweek. August 20, 1945. p. 42*

Rebilletable: British term—eligible for assignment to a new evacuation billet.—*American Speech. February 1944. p. 13*

Reconnaissance: Broadly, scouting. In the war, it usually meant aerial scouting, in which photographs might be taken to show results of bombardment or to construct maps for future attack.—*Democrat & Chronicle. Rochester, N.Y. September 8, 1940*

Recruit: (American plane) Ryan PT-32NR trainer plane

Red Ball Express (or **Red Ball Highway**): A new Army branch or service carrying high priority freight to the front. Organized after the break-through at St. Lo, the truck convoys kept pace with General Patton's advance. The term Red Ball came from an old American railroading technique whereby priority cars were marked with a red dot. See also Com Z.—*New York Times. October 8, 1944. Sect. iv. p. 5; American Notes and Queries. October 1944. p. 102*

Red Devils: Name given to the British airborne troops "holding a tiny bridgehead on the north bank of the Lek," near Arnhem, so called because of their scarlet berets.—*PM. September 25, 1944*

Red Market: Point-free meats sold as better cuts for which points were required.—*New York Times. December 10, 1944. p. 7E*

Red Patch Devils: Name given by the Germans to the Canadian Army First Division; divisional insignia a red patch.—*Newsweek. October 15, 1945. p. 68*

Red Points: In rationing of food, "red points" (paper coupons first, later small red fiber discs called tokens) were necessary when buying meat, butter, oils and fats. During part of the rationing period, markets were allowing extra red tokens in exchange for pounds of saved fats, since fats were badly needed for the war effort. See also Blue Points

Red, White and Blue Circuit: Name applied to a program of stage presentations covering the nation's army camps, given by Camp Shows, Inc.—*Newsweek. December 8, 1941. p. 43*

Reefer Cargoes: Perishable foods. The word "Reefer" refers to refrigeration equipment.—*New York Times. February 24, 1946. p. 2E, 6E*

Reefs: Rochester Emergency Enlistment Forces. The first group of its kind to come into existence in America, the Reefs who formed the crew of the S.S. Rochester were organized shortly after the formation of the Waves in 1942. Made up entirely of civilian volunteers, members manned the ship (a down-town office in Rochester, N.Y.) in nautical fashion in three watches a day. The purpose was three-fold: 1) give out information regarding women's branches of the naval services; 2) enlist applicants for the services; 3) through informal parties enable new recruits to become acquainted with each other before leaving for boot training.—*Democrat & Chronicle. Rochester, N.Y. July 2, 1944. p. 1D*

Das **Reich:** Weekly publication of German Propaganda Ministry.—*Newsweek. July 12, 1943. p. 20*

Reichswehr: Standing army (German) serving under long-term enlistments, under the control of the Reich's Minister of War.—*New Republic. July 18, 1934. p. 249*

Reliant: (American plane) Vultee AT-19 trainer plane

The **Reluctant Dragon:** This designation was applied to several ships of the Pacific Fleet because for various reasons they saw little action over a certain period; two of these were the "Boise" and the "Saratoga."—*American Notes and Queries. October 1944. p. 105*

Remember Pearl Harbor: In Office of Production Management press releases from Washington, December 10, 1941, three words, in spaced capitals, appeared above OPM heading: "Remember Pearl Harbor."—*New York Times. December 11, 1941. p. 20*

Repple Depples: Replacement depots.—*American Speech. December 1946. p. 254*

Resting Horse: The Chinese at first referred to General of the Army Marshall as "Resting Horse," the true meaning of their phonetic approximation of his name "Ma Shieh Erh."—*Newsweek. January 28, 1946. p. 36*

Resurrection March: March back to safety of 510 Allied captives (mostly American) after being freed from Cabanatuan prison camp, Luzon, Philippine Islands. The rescue was undertaken by a group of American Rangers and Filipino guerillas.—*Democrat & Chronicle. Rochester, N.Y. February 2, 1945. p. 1*

Revenge Troops: Reported to be Field Marshal Erwin Rommel's term for men who manned the German west wall defenses, since most of the men were natives of cities badly bombed by the Allies; the troops wore arm bands with slogans such as "Revenge for Hamburg," etc.—*American Notes and Queries. June 1944. p. 39*

Revetments: Walls of earth piled up on three sides of the hardstand (q.v.) to protect the plane from flying shrapnel.—*Huie. Can Do! p. 40 note*

"A Revolutionary Moment in the World's History Is a Time for Revolutions, Not for Patching": By Sir William Beveridge.—*Beveridge. Social Insurance and Allied Services. p. 6*

RFOFM: Records For Our Fighting Men. With the help of the American Legion RFOFM conducted a drive in 1942 to collect old records. These were sold by the pound to the manufacturers for credit toward the purchase of new records. The selection of the records to be purchased was done by the Subcommittee on Music of the Joint Army and Navy Committee on Welfare and Recreation. See also AFMR.—*Newsweek. June 14, 1943. p. 86*

Rhino Tank: Used in Normandy campaign to break through hedgerows; four pieces of angle iron sharpened at one end and welded to a steel plate at the other (attached to front of tank giving it an appearance resembling a rhinoceros); invented by Sergeant Curtis G. Culin, 102d Cavalry Reconnaissance Squadron, of Cranford, New Jersey.—*New York Herald Tribune. October 17, 1944*

Rhubarb: R.A.F. slang meaning "a target of opportunity." When a flyer was "on a rhubarb" it meant he was flying low, strafing whatever he found—trains, troops, airdromes, etc.—*Time. March 22, 1943. p. 51*

Rice Paddy Navy: See SACO

Rick: Nickname of Captain Eddie Rickenbacker.—*Newsweek. July 5, 1943. p. 28*

"Right to Bomb Rome": By Anthony Eden, British Foreign Secretary. Speech in House of Commons, January 20, 1943. "I think that the Prime Minister made it plain last September that we have as much right to bomb Rome as the Italians had to bomb London, and we should not hesitate to do so to the best of our ability and as heavily as possible if the course of the war should render such action convenient and helpful."—*Newsweek. February 1, 1943. p. 23*

Rising Sun Magnetron: A radar tube so called because its hollow core resembled the Rising Sun emblem of the Japanese flag. Shortly before V-E Day, Allied radar equipment produced finer and clearer pictures than ever before. Observers in planes high over Germany could detect individual ships, remote buildings and concealed installations. The power behind these pictures was the "Rising Sun Magnetron," invented in the Pupin Physics Laboratories at Columbia University.—*Newsweek. June 3, 1946. p. 52*

R.N.V.S.R.: The Royal Naval Volunteer Supplementary Reserve (British). The full title was so cumbersome, the initials were used almost entirely.—*American Speech. February 1944. p. 13*

"The Road to Berlin Is Long and Hard but It Is Very Sure": By Franklin D. Roosevelt. Message to American troops in North Ireland. Major General Russell P. Hartle, who commanded the first American forces in the British Isles, read the President's message at ceremonies commemorating the first anniversary of the arrival of United States troops.—*Democrat & Chronicle. Rochester, N.Y. January 27, 1943. p. 1*

Roads to Tokyo: See "There are many roads. . . ."

Roblitz: Severe bombardment by robot bombs; a combination of robot and blitz.—*New York Times Magazine. December 2, 1945. p. 22*

Robomb: Newspaper headlines shortened the name of Robot bombs (q.v.) to Robomb.—*Democrat & Chronicle. Rochester, N.Y. August 24, 1944. p. 13*

Robot Bombs: One-ton jet-propelled bombs launched against England by the Germans in the summer of 1944. They were aimed chiefly at London. This bombardment began soon after the invasion of the continent by the Allied forces June 6, 1944. While officially known as Robot bombs, they soon acquired nicknames, such as Buzz-bombs, Doodlebugs and Whizzbangs. Other names for the bombs included Pilot-less planes (this was official British designation, shortened to P-planes) ; Bumble bombs; "the things" (this was a commonly used designation among British people as a whole along the line of their customary reference to Hitler as "he") ; dynamitmeteore (dynamite meteors)—Nazi name for them, though the German public continued to refer to them as Wuwa, short for Wunderwaffe, or Wonder Weapon; V-1 for Vergeltungswaffe Ein (reprisal weapon no. 1) ; Hell hound (German radio version) ; Winged comet; Robot raider; Flying blowtorch; Whirley; Bastards (so called in certain Army circles) ; Blastard (name given by Pierre Dupong, Prime Minister of Luxembourg).—*American Notes and Queries. June 1944. p. 38; July 1944. p. 54; Life. July 24, 1944. p. 19-20; Newsweek. June 26, 1944. p. 24; July 10, 1944. p. 30; July 24, 1944. p. 33; June 4, 1945. p. 90*

Robot Raider: See Robot Bombs

Roc: (British plane) Blackburn fighter plane

Rock Happy: GI slang (Pacific area) for "bored."—*Yank. June 15, 1945. p. 2*

Rocket: Rocket power principle (jet propulsion) was discovered in China in 1232 A.D. Its modern application is seen in the robot, the bazooka and the jet-propelled plane. All of these work on the same principle: a motor that thrusts, or pushes, instead of building up rotary motion in a shaft or wheel. This motor is called a re-action motor; it produces its thrust by jetting out a stream of gas or other material at high velocity. The response that follows provides the push—and the name, "jet propulsion." See also U.P.—*Newsweek. June 4, 1945. p. 90*

Rocket (Foreign names for): Chinese: Huo-chien, "arrow of flying fire"; Italian: Ruchetta; German: Rakete; French: Fusée; **Spanish: Cohete;** Dutch: Vuurpijl, "fire arrow."—*Newsweek. June 4, 1945. p. 90*

Roger: In aviation "Roger" means that a pilot's radio message to his operational base has been received satisfactorily. "Roger" is always used in aviation parlance, instead of "O.K." or "all right."—*Times-Union. Rochester, N.Y. July 31, 1943.* Roger, though it started in the Air Corps, became the standard affirmative for all branches of the service. Also taken over to a certain extent by civilians

Rodger Young: (Song) Words and music by Private First Class Frank Loesser. The song celebrates the heroic act of an infantry private (Rodger Young) who was killed in action at Munda on New Georgia Island in the South Pacific on July 31, 1943.—*Life. March 5, 1945. p. 117*

Roll-back, Rollback: A forcible return (of prices) to a former, and lower, level. Term appeared in *Time* magazine in May 1942.— *American Speech. February 1944. p. 63-4*

Rommel, Count Yo' Men!: Negro artillerymen provided a battle cry for Americans on one sector of the Tunisian front. With each fire order, the boys kissed the projectile, and as it went on its way chanted in rhythm "Rommel, count yo' men."—*Times-Union. Rochester, N.Y. June 25, 1943. p. 13*

Romney Huts: See Nissen Huts

RON: In the Army Air Forces it means "remain over night"; in the Navy, used as a suffix, it means squadron. For example "Comdesron" stands for "Commander destroyer squadron."—*American Notes and Queries. May 1945. p. 23*

Ronchie: Air Force slang term meaning slipshod, careless.— *Reader's Digest. September 1944. p. 76*

Roof-Spotter: British term. A look-out for enemy aircraft.— *American Speech. February 1944. p. 13*

Rope: See Radar Countermeasures

Rota: (British) A tour of duty, as of a fire-watcher. In general, rota applied to tours of duty which were taken in rotation by different persons.—*American Speech. February 1944. p. 13; December 1944. p. 294*

Roundup: Designated code name for tentative cross-Channel operations. See also Sledgehammer and Overlord.—*General Marshall's Report. 1945. p. 8*

Royal Order of Whale Bangers: An "exclusive" club open only to airmen who have mistakenly dropped depth charges on whales, supposing them to be enemy submarines.—*American Notes and Queries. July 1946. p. 60*

RPPA: Republican Postwar Policy Association. Started by Deneen A. Watson in May 1943. Aim was that the Republican party drop its isolationist viewpoint and take a stand for an American share in international collaboration after the war.—*Newsweek. July 19, 1943. p. 42*

RSOP: (Pronounced Arsop) Operation of Reconnoitering, Surveying, and Occupying a Position.—*Word Study. April 1944. p. 3*

"The Rubber You Saved May Be the Rubber That Saved Rickenbacker": By Walter Winchell. Radio broadcast Sunday, November 15, 1942, following the rescue of Captain Eddie Rickenbacker who was found alive on a rubber raft in the Pacific

Rudolfs: To avoid issuing faulty parachutes to airmen, the army tested them by the use of heavy dummy figures. These dummies were nicknamed Rudolfs, after Rudolf Hess.—*Newsweek. December 1, 1941. p. 41*

Rugged: Wonderful, terrific, awful, difficult. A slang word in very general use among members of the armed services; the particular meaning has to be gathered from the context

Ruptured Duck: GI nickname for the discharge button which honorably discharged veterans wear in their lapels. Also nicknamed Screaming Eagle. The emblem was copied from a design in Meyer, *Handbook of Ornament* (p. 82), which in turn was copied from a bas-relief originally in Trajan's Forum in Rome. The Navy calls the emblem Homing Pigeon.—*Time. October 29, 1945. p. 11; November 19, 1945. p. 10; Newsweek. March 18, 1946. p. 34*

Russian Flu: A disease that hit large portions of many (bombed) urban areas within Germany; so called because it was supposedly of eastern origin (dispatch from Stockholm, November 2, 1944).—*American Notes and Queries. November 1944. p. 117*

SAARF Teams: Special Allied Airborne Reconnaissance Force teams parachuted into POW areas to take supplies to prisoners or to help them get out.—*New York Times. May 22, 1945. p. 5*

SAC: Supreme Allied Command. Headquarters in London.—*New York Times Magazine. March 5, 1944. p. 5*

Sack: Name for bed. "Hit the sack" means to go to bed; Sack Time means just lying on your cot doing nothing.—*House Beautiful. January 1945. p. 39; Democrat & Chronicle. Rochester, N.Y. February 27, 1945. p. 4*

SACO: Sino-American Cooperative Organization; a secret organization that helped win the war in the Pacific. Calling themselves members of "The Rice Paddy Navy," American naval personnel—disguised as Chinese—set up more than fifty weather stations in unoccupied China, spied on Jap shipping, and radioed their information through Chungking to Fleet Admiral Nimitz. Starting directly after Pearl Harbor, they trained and armed some 25,000 Chinese guerillas to protect the project.—*Newsweek. September 24, 1945. p. 50*

Sacred Cow: Nickname given to the plane especially designed by Douglas Aircraft for the use of President Roosevelt.—*Newsweek. June 11, 1945. p. 40*

Sad Sack: A cartoon character made immortal by the *"Yank"* cartoonist Sergeant George Baker. His Private Sad Sack symbolizes all the poor bemused civilians who blundered their way through the mazes of army life.—*Saturday Review of Literature. November 3, 1945. p. 7*

Sake: See GI Liquor in the Pacific

Sandy: Nickname of Major General Alexander M. Patch (United States Army).—*Newsweek. February 1, 1943. p. 24*

Sans Origine: A French term, literal meaning "without origin." It was a term used on Army, Navy, or Air Force cables to indicate that the name of the originating point was deleted by censorship regulations lest it be of use to the enemy.—*Ontario Library Review. February 1942. p. 50*

Saturation Bombing: Bombing a complete area, as contrasted with precision bombing, aimed at a definite objective.—*American Speech. December 1945. p. 301*

"Save Freedom with Pitchforks": By Franklin D. Roosevelt. In a Fourth of July broadcast, 1941, the President said "We cannot save freedom with pitchforks and muskets alone after a dictator combination has gained control of the rest of the world."—*Vital Speeches. July 15, 1941. p. 589*

Say "Yes" to Your Carrier Boy: Slogan used in Rochester, N.Y. during the July 1943, war stamp drive for the new airplane carrier "Shangri-La." Part of a nationwide drive. Newspaper carrier boys in Rochester participated in the drive by taking orders for and delivering stamps.—*Democrat & Chronicle. Rochester, N.Y. July 16, 1943. p. 16*

Scalded Cat: Term used to describe the hit-and-run forays of Nazi airmen during their recently renewed attacks on London.—*Time. March 12, 1945. p. 30*

SCAP: Supreme Commander Allied Powers. General Douglas MacArthur in his capacity as commander of the allied armies occupying Japan; also the combined headquarters which carried out his directions

SCAT: South Pacific Combat Air Transport.—*Air Transport. January 1945. p. 28-32*

Schnorkel: See Snorts

Schupo: See Gestapo

Scope: Radar term for the cathode ray tube indicator.— *Army and Navy Journal. August 18, 1945. p. 1534*

Scorched Earth: In the undeclared war of Japan against China (begun in 1937), the retreating Chinese adopted a defensive policy of burning cities, utility plants, food stores, field crops, etc. leaving nothing of value for the invaders. This became known as the "scorched earth" policy, and has been generally adopted in World War II.—*Webster's New International Dictionary. 1943. p. ciii*

"Scorched earth policy" can be traced back to 512 B.C., when the Persian armies under Darius the Great invaded the Pontic steppes. "The Scythians decided not to meet the Persians in regular battle, but to retreat inland, driving away their cattle, burning the grass and wrecking the wells." Quoted from George Vernadsky's *Ancient Russia,* in a review of the book by Bertram D. Wolfe, in the *New York Herald Tribune Book Review. September 12, 1943. p. 16*

Scrambled Eggs: Gold braid on the caps of high naval officers —and hence applied to the officers themselves.—*American Notes and Queries. February 1946. p. 175*

Scrappy: Nickname of Major General Russell P. Hartle (United States Army).—*Newsweek. July 26, 1943. p. 25*

"Scratch One Flat-Top!": Lieutenant Commander Robert E. Dixon sent the above message to his carrier after sinking a Japanese carrier at the Coral Sea battle, off Misima Island May 7, 1942.— *Johnston. Queen of the Flat-Tops. p. 181*

Screaming Eagle: See Ruptured Duck

Screaming Meemie: A German multi-barreled rocket-mortar (so named for the sound it made when fired).—*Saturday Review of Literature. November 3, 1945. p. 7*

Screening: Army term. Salvaging good parts, junking bad parts of damaged war material. "Screening requisitions" meant checking accuracy, quantity and quality. "Screening personnel" meant examining the records for an applicant's qualifications.—*American Speech. October 1945. p. 227*

Scrounge: A slang term which dated back to World War I, but became more prevalent in World War II, especially during the blackouts in London. It really meant stealing or larceny. See also Liberate.—*Reader's Digest. May 1940. p. 39*

Scuttlebutt: Navy slang for gossip or overactive imagination; rumors and stories not based on fact.—*American Notes and Queries. May 1945. p. 23*

S-Day: Day set for the landing on Luzon in the Philippines. See also A-Day, D-Day.—*New York Times. January 21, 1945. p. 6E*

Sea Fox: (British plane) Fairey reconnaissance catapult seaplane for cruiser and battleship use

Sea-going Bellhops: Nickname for marines.—*Fox. Blind Adventure. p. 163*

Sea Mule: A new pushing and towing craft for use in invasion operations; more maneuverable and more economical in construction than a tug; two-engined, with a two-foot draft and a five-man crew. —*American Notes and Queries. June 1944. p. 39*

Sea Otter: A new type cargo ship announced by the United States Navy in September 1941, as an answer to the threat of German submarine sinkings. Called "Sea Otter" because of its resemblance to the animal. First ideas for it were evolved by Commander Hamilton Bryan and Warren Noble; final plans were designed by W. Starling Burgess.—*Newsweek. September 29, 1941. p. 40*

Sea Ranger: (American plane) Boeing XPBB-1 bomber plane. Sometimes referred to as the Lone Ranger because the Navy ceased to be interested in large flying boats for patrol-bomber purposes

Sea Squatters: Aviators forced down at sea, successful in inflating their rubber rafts and rescued alive.—*New York World Telegram. April 3, 1944*

Seabees: Construction Battalions, United States Navy. Work of the Seabees was formerly done by civilians, but experience at Guam, Wake and Cavite led to the Navy decision to put their construction men in uniform. Supposed to land at the same time or just after the

Marines. Their work was to make a landing field, hospital, fortifications, docks, barracks—in short to build secret naval bases.—*Collier's. September 19, 1942. p. 21*

"The Seabees Are Always Happy to Welcome the Marines": By Lieutenant Bob Ryan of Ventura, California. At Segi, New Georgia, the Seabees were on hand to greet the Marines, much to the surprise of the Marines, since they usually were first to land.—*New York Times. September 12, 1943. p. 43* (not in late city edition)

Seagull: (American plane)   Curtiss SO3C scouting observation seaplane

Seamew: (American plane)   Curtiss SO3C observation plane

"Seared and Scarred and Blackened from One End to the Other": By Winston Churchill. Speech in House of Commons July 27, 1943 in which he offered Italy choice of surrendering unconditionally, trusting in Allied justice, or being "seared and scarred . . ." as above.—*Democrat & Chronicle. Rochester, N.Y. July 28, 1943. p. 1*

Seavacuation: This term, meaning evacuation overseas, appeared in the British press in 1940.—*American Speech. February 1944. p. 13*

The Second Phase of the World War: See World War II

Section 8: Discharge due to inability to adapt oneself to army life. Formerly called one-forty-eight-and-a-half, but changed to Section 8 when the revision of Army regulations changed the numerical designation of the part which dealt with such a discharge.—*American Speech. December 1945. p. 261*

See the Chaplain: Army slang phrase meaning to resign oneself to the continuance of an unpleasant situation. "See the Chaplain" was the standard advice to one with a grievance about which nothing could be done. Phrase probably stemmed from the fact that the Chaplain was one person who was always ready to listen with sympathy.—*American Speech. December 1946. p. 252*

"See You in Tokyo": From December 7, 1941 on, that was the stock parting phrase of men throughout the Pacific. For months it seemed an empty boast but in September 1945, it became a promise.—*Newsweek. September 3, 1945. p. 19*

Seep: Navy's name for a seagoing jeep, especially developed for the use of the marines.—*Word Study. April 1944. p. 4*

Selectee: Men inducted into the army through the selective service program were known as selectees.—*American Speech. December 1941. p. 306*

Semper Paratus—Always Ready, Serve with the Spars: Poster caption. Recruiting poster for United States Coast Guard Women's Reserve

"Send Us More Japs": United States Marines on Wake Island. "From the little band of professionals on Wake Island came an impudently defiant message phrased for history. Wake's Marines were asked by radio what they needed. The answer made old Marines' chests grow under their campaign bars: 'Send us more Japs.'"—*Time. December 29, 1941. p. 14.* This story was denied by Lieutenant Colonel James P. S. Devereux. As commander of Wake's garrison, he would have been the ostensible author of the message. When found at a prison camp in Japan, he told newsmen the first thing he wanted to get on record was a denial of ever having radioed: Send us more Japs. On the other hand, Commander Campbell Keene, veteran of the fall of Wake and four years of Japanese imprisonment, says that the message was sent, by an "exuberant young Navy communications officer, Ensign Bernard J. Lauff, who on the night of December 11, 1941, tacked the never-to-be-forgotten phrase on to the tail of an official message he had filed to Pearl Harbor." Ensign Lauff, when questioned, said it was possible he might have sent it, although he couldn't recall. In any case, whether the message was sent or not, the spirit of the words reflects the spirit of the Marines.—*Newsweek. September 24, 1945. p. 87-8; Democrat & Chronicle. Rochester, N.Y. September 28, 1945; Times-Union. Rochester, N.Y. September 28, 1945*

Sentinel: (American plane) Vultee L-5(O-62) OY liaison plane

Separatee: Army-coined term for a man awaiting discharge at a separation center.—*American Notes and Queries. October 1944. p. 102*

Seventh Column: Phrase coined by the Promotion Department of the Liberty Mutual Insurance Company in July 1942. Meant "carelessness" especially as applied to industry. Widely spread advertisements described the importance of this menace to American life. See also Fifth column; Sixth column

Sextant Conference: Name given to meeting in Cairo in late 1943 of President Roosevelt and Prime Minister Churchill.—*General Marshall's Report. 1945. p. 27*

SHAEF: Supreme Headquarters Allied Expeditionary Force (Europe). Disbanded in July 1945. General of the Army Eisenhower saluted his Allied forces in a last order of the day: "No praise is too high for the manner in which you have surmounted every obstacle." See also USFET.—*Pyle. Brave Men. p. 302; Newsweek. July 23, 1945. p. 40.* Some Parisian wits, irked by American requisitioning of Paris hotels, claimed that the initials SHAEF stood for Société des Hôteliers Américains en France (Society of American Hotelkeepers in France).—*Newsweek. April 9, 1945. p. 30; American Speech. December 1944. p. 307*

Shangri-La: This term (the setting of James Hilton's book *Lost Horizon*) came to mean an imaginary, or secret, military (especially air) base. President Roosevelt announced in 1942 that the American planes which bombed Tokyo took off from a secret base in Shangri-la. (This was later revealed to be the airplane carrier Hornet.) Spelling of the term differed—Shangri-La, Shangri La or Shangri-la.—*American Speech. February 1944. p. 64*

Shell-Shock: In World War I, shell-shock was a popular or slang term indicating psychoneuroses; in World War II some of the popular terms used to indicate this same condition were: Eight Ball, Barracks Wacky, Bomb Happy, Glacier Happy, Zeroitis, Convoy Jitters. All of these terms were used for men in camp. Exhaustion and War Fatigue were used interchangeably for nervous and mental disorders. Operational Fatigue and Flying Stress usually indicated a neurotic condition. War Nerves described any general group of symptoms. War Weariness meant abnormal indifference.—*American Mercury. September 1944. p. 343*

Shiggy: Nickname given by United States newspapermen to Mamoru Shigemitsu. He was made Foreign Minister of Japan by Premier Tojo in April 1943.—*Newsweek. May 3, 1943. p. 38*

SHINGLE: Code name to denote the amphibious assaults of elements of the U. S. Fifth Army at Anzio, Italy, in January 1944. —*U.S. Army. ETO. CONAD History. p. 378*

Shingle Stowing: Air Force term for setting planes at an angle with the deck so that they would overlap each other like shingles.—*American Speech. October 1945. p. 227*

"A Ship Not Sunk Is Better than a New Ship Built": By Winston Churchill. Speech to House of Commons London, February 11, 1943, after his return from Casablanca.—*Vital Speeches. March 1, 1943. p. 295*

Shipyard Orphans: Name given in Portland, Oregon, to the neglected children of mothers who worked in the shipyards. See also Doorkey Children.—*Life. December 20, 1943. p. 102*

Shoot Down in Flames. Tear Off a Strip: R.A.F. slang phrases meaning to give someone a bawling out.—*American Speech. February 1941. p. 76*

Shooting Star: In a race to catch up with German jet-propelled aircraft, the United States Army Air Forces developed a combat jet plane, the P-80 or Shooting Star. An Air Forces announcement said the P-80 was "the fastest fighter in existence."—*Newsweek. March 12, 1945. p. 72*

Shooting the Breeze: Talking it over. Sometimes appears as Batting the breeze. Slang phrase in quite general usage in the armed services.—*House Beautiful. January 1945. p. 39*

Shoran: Short range radar device which could measure long distances on the earth's surface within a few feet of perfect accuracy. This meant that the world's maps could be checked, and unmapped areas mapped, with greatly increased ease.—*Time. May 13, 1946. p. 95; Business Week. May 4, 1946. p. 36*

Short Snorter: A club for fliers who have done an impressive amount of flying. The club began as far back as 1925 and its official name was Grand Order of Unbenevolent, Purely Mercenary, Short Snorters. It was kept alive largely in Alaska but became particularly prevalent during World War II. Any person who qualifies by amount of flight travel may be taken into membership by two other Short Snorters, to each of whom he pays $1 and gets their signatures on another bill which he keeps. If challenged at any time when he is not carrying his signed bill, he has to forfeit more dollars.—*Flying. February 1944. p. 57*

Short Timer: Slang for soldier nearing the end of his enlistment period

Shuttle Raiders: American bombers striking enemy territory by way of the new half-way U.S. bases in Russia.—*American Notes and Queries. June 1944. p. 39*

"Sighted Aircraft Carrier. Am Trailing Same. Please Notify Next of Kin": Last message radioed by a PBY pilot in the Battle of Midway.—*Newsweek. June 7, 1943. p. 22*

"Sighted Sub, Sank Same": By Donald Francis Mason, United States Navy. Report February 1942.—*New York Times. April 2, 1942. p. 1*

Singapore: (British plane) Short patrol flying boat

The **Singing Frog:** Nickname of Japanese Prime Minister General Kuniaki Koiso. His nickname derives from the fact that when sake loosens his voice he croaks into song.—*Newsweek. March 19, 1945. p. 65*

"Sink or Swim with the United States": "Philippine independence . . . is now being determined on the battle-fields of Russia and in the Atlantic Ocean. . . . We will sink or swim with the United States." Statement of platform by Manuel Quezon as he accepted in August 1941 the nomination to succeed himself as president of the Philippine Islands.—*Newsweek. August 25, 1941. p. 15*

Sireen: The hooters sounded to warn of approaching enemy aircraft in Britain were named sirens. In conversation they were often called "sireens," possibly because the word siren sounded too clipped.—*American Speech. February 1944. p. 14*

Situation Test: A wartime technique developed by the Army to select men for the OSS. The candidate would be placed in a situation similar to an actual one which he might encounter as an agent. By watching his emotional reactions, the testers could judge his ability to face real-life situations.—*Newsweek. July 8, 1946. p. 52*

Sitzkrieg: A term meaning "sitting-war" used to designate the inactivity of the warring nations (Germany and England) during the winter of 1939-1940. Also referred to as "Phony war" regardless of the constantly accumulating evidence of Hitler's military strength. *Words. April 1940. p. 59; American Speech. April 1941. p. 148*

Sixth Column: A term devised for gossipers and rumor mongers by Colonel Richard C. Patterson, Jr., New York State Chairman of the Defense Savings Staff. On March 24, 1942, President Roosevelt took up the cry against the "sixth column." See also Fifth column; Seventh column.—*Newsweek. April 6, 1942. p. 27*

Skinny: Nickname of Lieutenant General Jonathan M. Wainwright.—*Considine. MacArthur the Magnificent. p. 122; Current Biography. 1942. p. 862*

Skip-Bombing: Low-level bombing with delayed-action bombs which ricochet into the target.—*American Speech. December 1945. p. 302*

Skua: (British plane) Blackburn fighter and dive bomber

Skyhook: Aerial cargo container, developed by Materiel Command, Wright Field. Released from an airplane, it floats to earth without forward motion. It has a capacity of about seventeen gallons.—*American Notes and Queries. December 1944. p. 135*

Skymarker Bomb: Bomb dropped to locate targets hard to find. It left a trail of coloured smoke which lasted five minutes and which could be seen by a plane five miles away.—*Britannica Book of the Year. 1946. p. 833*

Skymaster: (American plane) Douglas C-54 R5D transport plane

Sky-Prodders: Slang term for U.S. anti-aircraft guns.—*American Speech. February 1943. p. 76*

Skytrain: (American plane) Douglas C-47 R4D1 transport plane

Skytrooper: (American plane) Douglas C-54 R4D3 transport plane

Sledgehammer: Code name for the emergency plan for cross-Channel operations. See also Roundup.—*General Marshall's Report. 1945. p. 8*

Slig: Word formed from the initial letters of sucker, lowbrow, idiot and goodwill-buster. Quoted by an Algiers correspondent early in February 1944; defined as an "act of discourtesy or stupid criticism" which, among the armed forces, becomes an "added shell for the guns of Axis propaganda."—*American Notes and Queries. March 1944. p. 181*

Slim: Nickname of Vice-Admiral Sir James F. Somerville (British naval officer).—*Current Biography. 1943. p. 723*

The **Slot:** Term given by Navy men to the narrow stretch of water between New Georgia Island and Choiseul and Santa Isabel Islands, in the Solomons.—*National Geographic. October 1944. p. 449*

Smatchet: A weapon introduced into commando warfare. "It is a powerful knife, which, if applied by a well-trained commando fighter to the proper parts of an opponent's body, may cause considerable disorganization." The term itself may be a blend of smash and hatchet, or it may derive from the Spanish machete.—*American Speech. December 1944. p. 279*

Smiling Albert: Nickname of Field Marshal Albert Kesselring (Nazi general), so named because of his accustomed toothy grin.—*Newsweek. May 21, 1945. p. 56*

SMOE: Origin of term—A Navy man says "Our explanation of Smoe's origin is as follows: the electrical term OHMS which appears on drawings of radio circuits, when held up backward to the light reads SMHO. This little gentleman who knew what was going on behind the circuit changed his name to SMOE." See also Clem, Kilroy, etc.—*Newsweek. December 31, 1945. p. 6*

Smoke-jumpers: Forest-fire-fighting parachutists, recruited largely from conscientious-objector groups.—*New York Herald Tribune. March 1, 1944*

Smoky Joes: Planes which dropped smoke bombs to mark a target, a technique perfected by the Royal New Zealand Air Force to strengthen its attacks in jungle areas.—*New York Times. April 7, 1945. p. 6*

SNAFU: Military slang. Pronounced snaffoo. Means the situation is normal, all fouled up and completely confused. The word comes from the initial letters of "Situation Normal. All Fouled Up." See also FUBAR, JAAFU, JACFU, JANFU, SUSFU and TARFU. —*Times-Union. Rochester, N.Y. October 14, 1944. p. 7; American Speech. February 1946. p. 70-2*

Sniperscope; Snooperscope: Instruments developed during the war to enable soldiers to see enemy movements in the dark. The sniperscope is mounted on a rifle, the snooperscope on the helmet. They both use infra-red rays to aid night vision. The snooperscope is a more complex instrument.—*New York Times. April 21, 1946. p. 6E; Newsweek. April 29, 1946. p. 58*

Snorts: Periscope-like airshafts that allow German submarines to "breathe" by permitting the recharging of batteries beneath the water and enabling the sub to remain under water twenty to thirty days, according to German claims; called Schnörkel Spiral by the Nazis.—*New York Herald Tribune. December 12, 1944*

Snowdrops: London nickname for white-helmeted American military police.—*New York Times. April 9, 1944; American Notes and Queries. April 1944. p. 9*

Snowmobile: Power-driven sleigh, designed in Canada for a once-considered invasion of occupied Norway.—*American Notes and Queries. April 1946. p. 8; American Speech. October 1945. p. 165*

Social Offensive: See "We must move on to a great social offensive. . . ."

Society of Goldbrick Papas: Described in an AP dispatch, July 14, 1944, as an organization of "long-distance fathers who try to help their children by V-mail"; the society's by-laws state that members (it numbered about 100 in 1944) must never have seen their offspring, and must be known to have forwarded advice to their wives on the fundamental problems of baby care.—*American Notes and Queries. August 1944. p. 71*

SOFAR: Sound Fixing And Ranging; underground sound system developed by the U.S. Navy, enabling air and ship survivors to be located far at sea.—*Newsweek. May 27, 1946. p. 58*

Soldier Shows: Stage presentations produced, directed and performed by soldiers for soldier audiences. The Special Services Division of the Army sent traveling soldier show units to most overseas areas and to Army hospitals in this country. In the last year of the war CATs (q.v.) were employed to play the feminine parts in the overseas Soldier Show Units.—*Information furnished by a former War Department officer*

SONAR: Sound, Navigation And Ranging. A secret weapon, used by the Navy to ferret out completely submerged U-boats which could not be located by radar (q.v.).—*Democrat & Chronicle. Rochester, N.Y. April 7, 1946*

"Soon We and Not Our Enemies, Will Have the Offensive; We, Not They, Will Win the Final Battles; and We, Not They, Will Make the Final Peace": By Franklin D. Roosevelt. Radio address February 23, 1942.—*Democrat & Chronicle. Rochester, N.Y. February 24, 1942. p. 2*

SOP: Standard Operating Procedure; any prescribed, preferable or habitual method of doing a thing.—*American Speech. December 1946. p. 250*

Sophomore: (American plane) Fleetwing BT-12 trainer plane

Sortie: See Air Force

S.O.S. (Services of Supply): See A.S.F.

"The Soul of France Can Never Die": By Winston Churchill. Message to General de Gaulle, leader of the Free French Forces, July 14, 1941.—*Churchill. The Unrelenting Struggle. p. 189*

Sour Oranges: See Sweet (or Sour) Oranges

Soyokaze: (Japanese plane) Mitsubishi long-range bomber plane

SPA: South Pacific Area

SPAB: Supply Priorities and Allocations Board. Established by executive order of President Roosevelt, August 28, 1941. When the War Production Board was created, the SPAB was abolished and its personnel, records, and property were transferred to the WPB (q.v.).—*United States Government Manual. Summer 1943. p. 117*

Spam Can: U.S. Marine term for the handie-talkie, a smaller version of the walkie-talkie.—*New York Times Magazine. June 30, 1946. p. 17*

Spam Fleet: Nickname for LCT's and other utilitarian, slow-moving craft (*New York Herald Tribune*, in release from Baie de la Seine, June 16, 1944).—*American Notes and Queries. June 1944. p. 39*

The Spanish Laval: Nickname of Ramón Serrano Suñer, brother-in-law of Francisco Franco, Head of State and President of Spain.—*Newsweek. September 14, 1942. p. 46*

Spars: Women's Reserve of the United States Coast Guard Reserve. Bill creating it was signed on November 22, 1942. The title was taken from the motto of the Coast Guard: "Semper Paratus."—*Education for Victory. January 15, 1943. p. 27*

Speed Them Back! Join the WAAC: See Hurry Them Back

Spiders: Term applied to Nazi steel-rail work buried in Normandy beaches to hamper Allied landings.—*American Notes and Queries. June 1944. p. 39*

Spike: Nickname of Rear Admiral William H. P. Blandy, Chief of Ordnance, United States Navy.—*Current Biography. 1942. p. 86*

Spinning Your Wheels: AAF slang for wasting time or energy and accomplishing nothing

Spit: See Plane Nicknames

Spitfire: (British plane) Supermarine fighter plane. England's most famous fighter plane. This and the Hurricane were the backbone of the RAF Fighter Command

A Spitfire a Day Keeps Hitler Away: Favorite wall slogan in the Netherlands Indies, which have sent Britain the money for forty Spitfires and eighteen bombers and raised funds for twenty-seven more Spitfires.—*Newsweek. March 10, 1941. p. 31*

Spoiler: Cartoon character. See Dilbert

Sprog: R.A.F. slang for new recruit, from the transposed letters of frog spawn, which like the recruit is very very green. Sprog was also used as an adjective meaning new or inexperienced.—*Nineteenth Century. April 1944. p. 182*

Squadron: See Air Force

Squawk Sheet: A pilot's report of any defects discovered in flying a plane from factory to an air service command.—*American Speech. October 1945. p. 227*

SS: Schutzstaffel or Elite Guard. The SS was the innermost circle in the Nazi system of concentric elites. Its purpose, as defined by Heinrich Himmler, who was in charge of it, was "to find out, to fight, and to destroy all open and secret enemies of the Fuehrer, the National Socialist movement, and our racial resurrection." The Elite Guard traced its origin back to the original Hitler headquarters guard, organized in 1923. In the early days of the party, the Nazis were in constant fear of attack by their enemies, and a bodyguard was built up. This was the Sturm Abteilung (SA) of which the SS was then a part. In 1926 the SS, numbering only 250, was relegated to the background and the brown-shirted SA troopers became dominant. In 1929 Himmler took over the task of organizing the SS and of building it up along racial ideals—only men of pure Aryan stock could become members of the SS. In 1933 the rapidly growing Schutzstaffel was divided into three major groups: the SS-Allgemeine, nonspecialized troopers; the SS-Verfügungstruppe (SS-VT), troops at the disposal of party chiefs; and the SS-Wachverbände, men for guard duty. The SS-VT gave birth to the Waffen-SS, Elite Guard troops organized as army units and fully equipped. At first the SS served with the regular army (the Wehrmacht) but were disliked because they felt themselves superior and showed it plainly. Meanwhile the Waffen-SS began an intensive campaign to get the best recruits for itself. To quell civil disturbances Himmler formed thirty Death's Head Special SS-Sturmbanne. These Death's Head Units among other duties had exclusive control over all German concentration camps. The SA ("Brown Shirts") were reduced in power at the time of the Nazi purge, when their leader, Ernst Rohm, was executed, and the power of the SS (black uniform) increased.—*Science Digest. February 1943. p. 44; New Republic. July 18, 1934. p. 249; Newsweek. August 7, 1944. p. 44*

SSF: Special Service Force. Canadian and American troops fighting together under a single command. The First SSF arrived in

Italy in 1943 but their activities were kept secret for a year. Their commander was Brigadier General Robert T. Frederick and the men referred to themselves as "Freddy's Freighters," because of the loads they could carry, due to the physical stamina stressed by General Frederick.—*Reader's Digest. November 1944. p. 99, 100*

Stahlhelm: The Steel Helmets (German); a voluntary organization of khaki-uniformed veterans, originally a private association, but tending to be brought more and more into semi-official relationship with the Nazi party. The membership was conservative and partially monarchist. The organization was rechristened the National Socialist Front Fighters.—*New Republic. July 18, 1934. p. 249*

Stalag: Abbreviation for Stammlager, a permanent camp for noncoms or privates, or a base camp from which labor detachments were sent out. See also Lager.—*Red Cross Courier. June 1943. p. 11*

Stand-ups: Pictures of girls who failed to wait for the men to come home, and married someone else. Instead of being "Pin-ups," they were called Stand-ups. See also "Dear Lootenant" Letters.—*Newsweek. April 2, 1945. p. 46*

Stanraer: (British plane) Supermarine flying boat for bombing and patrol

STAR: Specialized Training and Reassignment.—*Library Journal. September 1, 1943. p. 645*

"The State of This Nation Is Good—the Heart of This Nation Is Sound—the Spirit of This Nation Is Strong—the Faith of This Nation Is Eternal": By Franklin D. Roosevelt. Annual message to Congress, Washington, D.C., January 7, 1943.—*Vital Speeches. January 15, 1943. p. 198*

Stateside: American soldiers abroad used the adjective Stateside to refer to things back in America. For example, "There was a genuine Stateside flavor to the celebration." The word Stateside antedates World War II, having been long used in Hawaii and the Philippines, but it was picked up and popularized by service personnel overseas.—*Yank. December 1, 1944. p. 4c; American Notes and Queries. March 1947. p. 188*

Stick: British term. A number of bombs arranged for release from a bombing plane in a spaced series across a target.—*Webster's New International Dictionary. 1943. p. civ*

Stilwell Road: New name given to the Ledo-Burma Road by Generalissimo Chiang Kai-shek in honor of General Joseph W. Stilwell. See also Pick's Pike.—*New York Times. February 4, 1945. p. 2E, 6E*

Stilwell Stride: 105 steps per minute. Pace at which General Joseph W. Stilwell led the group of soldiers and civilians from Burma to India.—*Time. June 1, 1942. p. 21*

Stinky: See BTO

Stirling: (British plane) Short heavy bomber plane

Strafe: A German term which came into use in World War I in the phrase "Gott strafe England," meaning "God punish England." Strafe is now used to describe the operation in which troops are machine-gunned from low-flying planes.—*New York Times. April 28, 1946. p. 2E, 8E*

Strategic Bombing: Strategy, in a military sense, is the art of directing the larger movements and operations of a campaign. Strategic bombing meant bombing in accordance with a large overall plan, such as destroying an enemy's industries to cripple his power.—*American Speech. April 1946. p. 144*

Stuka: Word coined by the Germans to identify the dive bombers. The word is derived from the German combined word for "dive battle bomber"—sturzkampf-bomber.—*Democrat & Chronicle. Rochester, N.Y. May 7, 1940*

"Sturgeon No Longer Virgin": Message sent by Lieutenant Commander W. L. Wright. Wright, commander of the submarine Sturgeon, sent the above message after his ship sank her first Japanese vessel after Pearl Harbor.—*American Notes and Queries. February 1946. p. 168*

Submerge and Sweat: Lieutenant Commander Philip H. Ross' comment on submarine crew's reaction to attack: "You just sweat when you're depth charged. You submerge, sit there and sweat. What else can you do?"—*Times-Union. Rochester, N.Y. June 25, 1943. p. 14*

Subversive: The adjective subversive, "having a tendency to upset or overthrow," came into general usage in World War II with the meaning, activities inimical to the war effort

Sunderland: (British plane) Short long-range patrol flying boat, used for service in Atlantic patrol

Sunny Jim: Nickname of Major General Alexander A. Vande-grift.—*Current Biography. 1943. p. 779*

Super-Dumbo: Name given to a B-29 which accompanied an air raid over enemy territory in the role of observer and rescuer to any Superfort which might meet trouble.—*American Speech. April 1946. p. 144*

Super Lieutenants: See Lieutenant Super Grade

Superfortress: (American plane)   Boeing B-29 bomber plane

SUSFU: Situation Unchanged, Still Fouled Up.   See also FUBAR, JAAFU, JACFU, JANFU, SNAFU, and TARFU

Swab (or Swab-jockies): Nickname for sailors.   In World War I it was "Gobs" but in World War II, "Swabs."—*American Mercury. November 1943. p. 552*

Swaddy: Nickname of a buck private in Australia.—*Cosmopolitan. August 1943. p. 16, 85*

Sweat; Sweat Out: A term meaning to wait helplessly, nervously, anxiously for something over which you have absolutely no control; that is, waiting for the return of war planes carrying your pals, or waiting for promotion, or waiting for an overdue letter from home. All branches of the services used the phrase "sweating it out" but the Air Forces claim that they started it.—*New York Times Magazine. June 4, 1944. p. 12*

Sweet (or Sour) Oranges: Radar code for good (or bad) weather.—*Newsweek. September 10, 1945. p. 92*

"Swift Off the Mark": Joseph H. Mears, British Navy, said of the American Rangers, whom he had seen in action in Sicily, they're "pretty swift off the mark."—*Democrat & Chronicle. Rochester, N.Y. August 18, 1943. p. 13*

Swimmie-Talkie: Through the lipometer, a "microphone fitted with a special gland that passes air but excludes water," a soldier who ducks in a beachhead landing still can talk to shore from under 10 inches of sea water.—*Newsweek. July 23, 1945. p. 87*

Swing Shift: Factory workers who work during the week on different hours but do not work Saturday or Sunday. This name is sometimes given to the shift working from 4 P.M. to midnight.—*Princeton University. Hours Administration as Influenced by the Defense Program. p. 9; American Speech. December 1943. p. 305*

Swish: Thermal-jet engine, an air-stream affair in which air is delivered into the combustion chamber by means of a rotary compressor.—*Newsweek. June 4, 1945. p. 90*

Swordfish: (British plane) Fairey torpedo carrier or reconnaissance plane

SWPA: Surplus War Property Administrator. William L. Clayton was named SWPA and had the job of working out and trying out methods and policies for disposing of $50,000,000,000 worth of goods and plants created for war by American industry and acquired by the government.—*Newsweek. April 17, 1944. p. 66*

SWPA: Southwest Pacific Area

SWPC: Smaller War Plants Corporation. Started in August, 1942, with the purpose of spreading war contracts widely among the small factories capable of converting to war production.—*Newsweek. March 15, 1943. p. 57*

T-24, Cargo Carrier, Light: See Weasel

Tail-End Charlie: See Butt-End Charlie

Tailoring Job: See General Patch does a tailoring job

"Take Every Other Normal Precaution for the Protection of the Headquarters, but Let's Keep the Flag Flying": By General Douglas MacArthur. An officer on MacArthur's staff suggested that the American flag over the headquarters (Manila) might guide Japanese planes to the spot, and therefore perhaps should be taken down. MacArthur replied as above.—*New York Times. December 16, 1941. p. 1*

"Take Her Down": By Commander Howard W. Gilmore. A submarine skipper whose last gallant order, "Take her down," sealed his own death sentence was credited by the Navy today with successful attacks on three Japanese ships, the last of which the sub rammed in a dramatic night fight for life. It was in this final action somewhere in the distant Pacific that the officer rode the conning tower of his submerging submarine to his death rather than expose the craft or crew to enemy gunfire. He had been wounded a few moments before and knew that the time required to get him safely into the submarine might mean the sub's destruction.—*Times-Union. Rochester, N.Y. May 7, 1943. p. 1*

Tallyho: In radar code (the message going from the air to the ground) meant "The enemy has been sighted and recognized as hostile."—*Newsweek. September 10, 1945. p. 92*

Tank-Dozers: A new Allied break-through weapon consisting of a medium-sized tank to which was fitted a three-and-one-half-ton blade; combined lunging power of an M-4 Sherman tank with the slashing force of a bulldozer; capable of disposing of trees eighteen inches in diameter.—*New York Times. August 4, 1944*

Tank Horror: Latest German infantry anti-tank weapon. Shown in a picture of members of the Berlin Home Guard on parade, according to the German caption furnished to neutral countries with the picture.—*Democrat & Chronicle. Rochester, N.Y. February 7, 1945. p. 1*

Tanks, Not Talk: See "We Need Decisions. . . ."

TARFU: Things Are Really Fouled Up, variant of Snafu (q.v.). —*Time. November 30, 1942. p. 70*

Tarmac: British term for airport runway. Contraction of tarmacadam, of which the British built their runways.—*Democrat & Chronicle. September 8, 1940*

Task Force: A group of different types of naval vessels ordered to carry out a specific job. Also applied to other combined operations such as land and air.—*American Speech. October 1944. p. 226; October 1945. p. 225; Spectator (London). March 2, 1945. p. 198*

TBS: Talk Between Ships. Radio communication from one ship to another.—*American Speech. December 1946. p. 299*

TCC: Troop Carrier Command. See ATC

T-Day: The day when the War Production Board was to remove limitation orders on civilian production. The name "T-day" was based on the expected transition from a two-front to a one-front war.—*Printers' Ink. May 11, 1945. p. 11*

"Teach Your Troops Only What Is Necessary for War and under Conditions Closely Resembling the Actual Conditions of War": By Marshal Timoshenko (Russian Army).—*Mehring. Timoshenko, Marshal of the Red Army. p. 27*

Tear Off a Strip: See Shoot Down in Flames

Tedeschi: Italian word for Germans. Name sometimes given to the Germans by the GI's in Italy. Germans also called "Jerry" and "Kraut."—*Pyle. Brave Men. p. 242*

The **Tendency toward Democracy Is Capturing the Peoples** (of the World)": By Pope Pius.—*New York Times. December 31, 1944. p. 2E, 7E*

Ten-Ton Tessies: Name given by British press to 22,000-pound bombs, used in bombing German cities in February and March 1945.—*Newsweek. March 26, 1945. p. 36*

Terminal Leave: Accrued, unused leave granted an officer in the services between his relief from assignment and his separation from the service. In the case of enlisted men, the "Armed Forces Leave Act" of August 9, 1946, provided terminal leave pay for all enlisted men or members of the Armed Forces who served honorably in an enlisted status during the war service period, defined as from September 8, 1939, to August 31, 1946. Such terminal leave pay, if more than $50, was to be paid in $25 Treasury bonds, to mature in five years. In the summer of 1947, Congress passed a law to permit cashing of bonds after September 1, 1947. This law (public law 254) was signed by President Truman.—*American Speech. October 1946. p. 225; Mace. Army Times Veterans Guide. p. 4; Army and Navy Journal. August 2, 1947. p. 1258*

Test Able: Code name (Able for letter A) for the first atom bomb test at Bikini, an atoll in the Marshall Islands in the Pacific, July 1, 1946. The bomb was dropped from a B-29, to explode at surface level. Results of the test were issued in reports to the public on July 11, 1946.—*Encyclopedia Britannica. Ten Eventful Years. v. 1. p. 220*

Test Baker: Code name (Baker for letter B) for the second atom bomb test at Bikini July 25, 1946. In this test, the bomb was exploded well below the surface of the lagoon.—*Encyclopedia Britannica. Ten Eventful Years. v. 1. p. 221*

Test Charlie: Code name (Charlie for letter C) for what was to have been a third atom bomb test. In this test, it was planned that the bomb should explode in deep water. The test was scheduled for 1947, but was cancelled by President Truman on September 7, 1946.—*Encyclopedia Britannica. Ten Eventful Years. v. 1. p. 219*

TETA: Travelers Emergency Transportation Association. Founded by Howard Myles and Phil M. Kirtley in Moberly, Missouri, October 1942. Actually a glorified thumb-the-ride club for salesmen. Had chapters in cities in several states; membership of over 5,000. Every week members submitted to chapter secretaries a copy of their route lists. Lists were posted, and when routes were similar, salesmen doubled up.—*Newsweek. May 24, 1943. p. 67-9*

The **Teutonic Plague:** See World War II

Texan: (American plane) North American AT-6 SNJ trainer plane

"That Rubble Heap near Potsdam": Phrase that some Germans used in describing bombed-out Berlin.—*New York Times Magazine. September 24, 1944. p. 5*

Theateritis: Coined by General Marshall to describe difficulties caused by Allied theater commanders because of their insistent demands upon Joint Chiefs of Staff for additional men and supplies (Walter Lippmann in *New York Herald Tribune.* May 18, 1946).— *American Notes and Queries. July 1946. p. 54*

"There Are Many Roads That Lead Right to Tokyo, and We're Not Going to Neglect Any of Them": By Franklin D. Roosevelt. At the dinner of the White House Correspondents' Association, Washington, D.C., February 12, 1943, after his return from Africa.—*Vital Speeches. March 1, 1943. p. 293*

"There Are No Atheists in the Fox Holes": See No Atheists in foxholes

"There Are No Neutral Hearts": By Dorothy Thompson, newspaper columnist. Radio address to Canada, July 21, 1940.—*Vital Speeches. March 15, 1941. p. 347*

"There Is No Absenteeism in the Fox Holes in the Jungles": By Captain Eddie Rickenbacker. From speech delivered at a joint session of the legislature, Albany, New York, February 22, 1943.— *Vital Speeches. March 15, 1943. p. 327*

"There Is No Liberty without Security and No Security without Unity": By André Maurois (Emil Herzog). Speech at the 45th annual convention of the National Association of Manufacturers, Waldorf-Astoria, New York City., December 12, 1940.—*Vital Speeches. February 1, 1941. p. 238*

"There Is No Such Word as Capitulation": By Adolf Hitler, Reichsfuehrer of Germany. Address to arms workers in Berlin, December 10, 1940.—*Vital Speeches. January 1, 1941. p. 177*

"There Is Not Sufficient Room in the Area of the Pacific Ocean for a Peaceful America . . . and a Swashbuckling Japan": By The Honorable Joseph C. Grew, former Ambassador to Tokyo. Broadcast over Columbia Broadcasting system, from Washington, D.C., August 30, 1942.—*Vital Speeches. September 15, 1942. p. 715*

"There Will Be No Black-out of Peace in the United States": By Franklin D. Roosevelt. Radio address, September 3, 1939.—*Congressional Record. November 1939. App. p. 41*

There'll Always Be an England: Title of a popular song written by Ross Parker and Hughie Charles. It was written in March 1939, but had very little sale until after September 3, 1939. By mid-November, sales in England had reached 200,000. The song spread to Canada, and many automobiles bore stickers printed with the British flag, and the song title printed in red.—*Current History. October 22, 1940. p. 35*

They Give Their Lives—You Lend Your Money: War bond slogan for Second War Loan drive April 1943. One source attributed authorship of the slogan to Elizabeth Minsch, another to Shirley Ives, both with Young & Rubicam.—*Smith Alumnae Quarterly. August 1943. p. 209; New York Times Magazine. June 11, 1944. p. 20*

Things Are Rough in the ETO: This was a comment commonly heard among soldiers in the European Theater of Operations. It was applied to anything dangerous, difficult or unpleasant.—*American Speech. December 1946. p. 243*

"This Bloodthirsty Guttersnipe": By Winston Churchill, referring to Hitler, in a radio address, June 22, 1941.—*Vital Speeches. July 1, 1941. p. 552; Churchill. The Unrelenting Struggle. p. 171*

"This Is a Sad Day for All of Us; Everything That I Have Worked for Has Crashed into Ruins": By Neville Chamberlain; comment at the outbreak of war.—*New York Times. September 2, 1945. p. 2E, 7E*

"This Is It, Chaps": By Brendan ("Paddy") Finucane. Radioed above message to his squadron when he went down in the English Channel, July 18, 1942.—*Democrat & Chronicle. Rochester, N.Y. November 11, 1942. p. 16; Newsweek. July 27, 1942. p. 23; Reynolds. Wing Commander Paddy Finucane. p. 18, 74*

"This Is No Picnic": By General Kenneth A. N. Anderson, commanding the British First Army. Referring to the North African campaign.—*Time. November 23, 1942. p. 31*

This Is Our War. Join the WAAC: Poster caption

"This Is the Toughest War of All Time": By Franklin D. Roosevelt. Labor Day radio address, September 7, 1942.—*Newsweek. September 14, 1942. p. 31*

Three Bullets Laid on a Knife: Name given by army airmen to the P-38 Lockheed Lightning.—*Newsweek. April 5, 1943. p. 42*

Through the Storm: See "Let us move forward steadfastly. . . ."

Thunderbolt: (American plane) Republic P-47 fighter plane

Tickety-Boo: British slang meaning fine or okay.—*New York Times Magazine. February 17, 1946. p. 57*

Tie-in Sales: Forced purchase of an unwanted article in order to get even a small amount of a scarce one. First appeared in newspaper and magazine usage about June 1943.—*American Notes and Queries. July 1943. p. 54*

Tiffy: Nickname for Typhoon (q.v.)

Tiger: Code name for European operation—Canadian attack on D-Day.—*American Notes and Queries. September 1945. p. 87*

Tiger: Exclamation used by soldiers, meaning "shutup" or "zip your lip." Quoted by Lowell Thomas in a news broadcast, August 11, 1943

Tiger of Malaya: Nickname of Japanese General Tomoyuki Yamashita. On September 3, 1945, he surrendered his remaining forces to an Allied representative in northern Luzon. For his part in the responsibility for the March of Death (q.v.) he was condemned to death by hanging, December 1945.—*Newsweek. October 15, 1945. p. 54; December 17, 1945. p. 51*

Tiger Tank: German tanks. King Tiger, also called the Royal Tiger. Its official German designation was Panzérkampfwagen FDKFZ 182. See also Mark VI.—*Newsweek. February 26, 1945. p. 38*

Tigercat: (American plane) Grumman F7F fighter bomber plane

TIID: Technical Industrial Intelligence Division. An Allied Board was set up to send experts into Germany to ferret out Germany's war-developed scientific secrets and make them available. Reports have been printed and many may be purchased from the Government Printing Office in Washington, D.C.—*Newsweek. July 22, 1946. p. 56*

Timberwolves: Nickname for troops of Major General Terry Allen's 104th Division, which spearheaded the First Army's drive into Cologne.—*New York Times. March 11, 1945. p. 2E, 6E*

"The **Times Call for Clear, Lucid Thinking Rather Than Clare Luceish Thought**": By Bennett Cerf. In introducing Norman Angell, soon after Representative Clare Luce's speech in Congress. Quoted in *Saturday Review of Literature, March 6, 1943. p. 17.* See also Globaloney

Tin Fish: Nickname for torpedoes.—*Aviation. August 1943. p. 426 (ad)*

Tiny: Nickname of Sir William Edmund Ironside, British general. Stands 6'4" and weighs 258 pounds—which is why his troops nicknamed him "Tiny."—*Current Biography. 1940. p. 424*

Tiny Tim: Nickname given to a twelve-foot rocket-driven projectile, held by U.S. Army to be the most powerful missile in existence.—*American Notes and Queries. June 1946. p. 40*

Titeems: French nickname for the English people in general (from 'tea time'). The R.A.F. they called 'Les Rafs.'—*Nation. November 9, 1940. p. 447*

TNEC: Temporary National Economic Committee. Headed by Senator Joseph C. O'Mahoney, the TNEC studied the American economic system.—*America. July 24, 1943. p. 424*

"**Today There Is Only One Thing That Counts—Acts and Service to the Country**": By General Charles de Gaulle.—*New York Times. December 31, 1944. p. 2E, 7E*

"**Today We Are before a Sea Wall That Will Protect England Only so Long as It Suits Us**": By Walther von Brauchitsch, Field Marshal, German Army. Christmas Eve party, December 24, 1940.—*Newsweek. January 6, 1941. p. 23*

"**Today We Face the Greatest Task in Our History**": By Joseph C. Grew. Former United States ambassador to Japan (1932-41).—*Grew. Report from Tokyo. p. 25*

Tokyo Express: Originally referred to small forces of destroyer-transports which attempted, under cover of darkness, to reinforce and relieve pressure on isolated Japanese forces on Guadalcanal. Similar tactics were used by the Japanese on Leyte and Mindoro.—*New York Times. January 7, 1945. p. 2E, 7E*

Tokyo Rose: Name given by American soldiers in Pacific theater to woman announcer on a Japanese propaganda broadcast. She interspersed her comments with recorded American swing music. See also Enemy Ann.—*New York Herald Tribune. December 6,*

1944. In a UP dispatch from Yokohama September 4, 1945, "Tokyo Rose"—or at least one of the voices—was identified as a 29-year-old girl named Iva Togori, a California-born Nisei. Two other "Tokyo Roses" were named as Ruth Hayakawa, another Nisei, and June Suyama, of Canadian birth.—*American Notes and Queries. August 1945. p. 78; Newsweek. September 17, 1945. p. 96-7*

Tokyo Trolley: Name given at the Portland, Oregon, ship-yards of the Commercial Iron Works to what is said to be the world's largest side-haul marine railway. It brings ships in from anchorage to drydock. The damaged ship is nested in a steel cradle and hauled ashore on rails.—*Newsweek. June 25, 1945. p. 74*

Tomahawk: (American plane) Name given in the RAF to the Curtiss P-40 fighter plane

Tombstone Ridge: On southern Okinawa. Figured in the fighting there during the week of May 13-20, 1945. See also Chocolate Drop Hill, Conical Hill, Flat-top Hill.—*New York Times. May 20, 1945. p. 2E, 6E*

Tommy Gun: From the name of the Thompson submachine gun, but almost any type of portable automatic weapon was likely to be called a Tommy gun except the Browning Automatic rifle which was always a BAR.—*American Speech. December 1946. p. 246*

"Tomorrows That Sing": Last words of a French hostage about to be shot by the Nazis. Before he was shot (July 1942) in the Cherche Midi prison in Paris, Communist Deputy Gabriel Peri wrote: "I should like my friends to know that I have been faithful to my life-long ideal. I should like my fellow-countrymen to know that I am dying that France may live. . . In a few minutes I am going out to prepare the tomorrows that sing. (*Je vais préparer tout à l'heure les lendemains qui chantent.*)"—*New York Times Magazine. April 11, 1943. p. 15*

Tony: Name given by Allied pilots to a new Zero Japanese plane, the Mitsubishi 03.—*Newsweek. November 8, 1943. p. 27*

Too Little and Too Late: David Lloyd-George used this phrase in a speech of criticism of the British government's handling of the war, on the day after the fall of Finland: "It is the old trouble—too late. Too late with Czechoslovakia, too late with Poland, certainly too late with Finland. It is always too late, or too little, or both, and that is the road to disaster." This was in March 1940.

But earlier than this (May 1935), Allan Nevins expressed the same idea in an article in *Current History* on the subject "Germany disturbs the peace." "The former allies had blundered in the past by offering Germany too little, and offering even that too late, until finally Nazi Germany had become a menace to all mankind."—*American Notes & Queries. August 1942. p. 71; Current History. May 1935. p. 178; New York Times. March 1940. p. 1*

Tooey: Nickname of General Carl Spaatz.—*New York Times. August 20, 1944. p. 2E, 7E*

Top Secret: A security classification used by the armed forces and the diplomatic corps to denote material of the utmost secrecy.—*Britannica Book of the Year. 1946. p. 833*

Torch: Code name for operational plans for assault on North Africa.—*General Marshall's Report. 1945. p. 9*

Torpedo Boat: See E-Boat; Mosquito (boat)

Torpedo Juice: Pure alcohol used in torpedo engines; and, when mixed with pineapple juice, a drink.—*American Notes and Queries. December 1944. p. 135*

Torps: Commonly used abbreviation for torpedoes.—*Nation. November 9, 1940. p. 447*

Total: See All-out

Tovarich Voying: Means Comrade Warrior, and is the name given by soldiers of the Red Army to other soldiers in their midst who are unknown to them. Marshal Koneff is often called Tovarich Voying because at the front he often wears a greatcoat with no distinguishing epaulets.—*Newsweek. April 3, 1944. p. 27*

Trac: See L

Transcom Project: A joint undertaking of the Army Transportation Corps and the Air Transport Command by which homecoming combat troops were shuttled cross-country by air, to relieve railroads of part of the burden of troop movements.—*American Notes and Queries. August 1945. p. 71*

Traveller: (American plane) Beech C-43 GB transport plane

Tree-bursts: Name given by American soldiers to German anti-personnel shells. Timed to burst at tree-top level, they showered fragments down. Foxholes were no protection against these shells.—*Saturday Review of Literature. April 14, 1945. p. 10*

Trident Conference: Meeting held in Washington in May 1943, at which President Roosevelt, Prime Minister Churchill and combined Chiefs of Staff met to discuss plans of attack.—*General Marshall's Report. 1945. p. 10*

Triphibian: Applied to Lord Louis Mountbatten for his skill in land, sea, and air transportation, by Winston Churchill in a speech broadcast to the world, August 31, 1943.—*Churchill. Onwards to Victory. p. 230*

Triphibious: Involving the Army, Navy and Air Force. First used in 1941 in a speech in the House of Commons by Leslie Hore-Belisha, formerly Secretary for War. For a discussion of the term, consult article by Henry Louis Mencken.—*War Words in England.— American Speech. February 1944. p. 14*

Triple Seven: In China, the Chinese feared that the gloomiest day of the war would be "Triple Seven," the seventh anniversary of the Sino-Japanese war which began on the seventh day of the seventh month of 1937. See also China Incident.—*Newsweek. July 17, 1944. p. 24*

Truman Bread: To save wheat for the European countries, an 80 per cent wheat-flour bread replaced the usual white loaf. The flour was called Truman flour.—*American Notes and Queries. April 1946. p. 8*

TS Cards: "Beachhead chaplains are carrying a special 'tough stuff' ticket these days which they issue to guys with complaints about which nothing can be done. One ticket says 'this slip entitles the bearer to 15 minutes of crying time on a chaplain's shoulder for each question punched below.'" This is from a write-up by Kenneth L. Dixon on phases of life at Anzio beachhead.—*Democrat & Chronicle. Rochester, N.Y. April 11, 1944.* TS cards were present in the Pacific theater also, both on beachheads and in rear areas. They were supplemented by "Crying Towels" furnished by the chaplain instead of a shoulder. See also Weeping Slips

Tuba: A powerful transmitter developed in the United States (1943-1944) and set up in England, to jam the radar interceptors used by the German fighter planes. The German fighter planes used an air-borne interception radar known as "Lichtenstein" for close range location of their targets (the British bombers on night flights). The bombers themselves could not carry jamming equipment against the enemy planes, because the planes could follow the signal in and thus find their target. So a powerful transmitter was set up in England, from which there would be a blinding beam "shining" in the German "eyes" (i.e., their radar antennas), through which the bombers could fly to their bases in safety. Since the experimental model used a huge parabolic antenna, the project was promptly nicknamed "Tuba," to distinguish it from smaller projects already known as "Piccolo," "Flute," and the like.—*Joint Board, OSRD, War Dept., Navy Dept. Electronics Warfare. 1945. p. 34-5.* (Also a drink) See GI Liquor in the Pacific

Tunisgrad: Name given by the Germans to the Battle of Tunisia, because it was like the last stages of the battle for Stalingrad— a great delaying action fought by the Nazis to gain time.—*Newsweek. May 10, 1943. p. 17*

Turbojet: See Ramjet

Turnaround Time: See Pipeline Time

Tutor: (American plane) Timm N2T trainer plane

Typhoon: (British plane) Successor to Hurricane, this plane carried four rockets beneath each wing, giving it the broadside power of a light cruiser. Nicknamed "Tiffy" by the British.—*Newsweek. August 21, 1944. p. 28*

Tyrants' War: See World War II

UDA: Union for Democratic Action. Accused by the Dies Committee in June 1942 of being a Communist front organization.— *Newsweek. July 6, 1942. p. 31*

UDT: Underwater Demolition Teams. Underwater commando groups of expert swimmers who were trained to slip ashore from small boats to discover enemy defenses and to blow up obstacles to prepare the way for invasion in Europe and in the Pacific. The first school was trained in Bethesda, Maryland, by Commander Draper Laurence Kauffman. These "sailors in trunks" first proved their value in the Marshalls invasion. Sometimes called "Human Barracudas."—*Washington Post. September 1, 1945*

Ultimate Hope: See "We are the ultimate hope. . . ."

Umbrella: This very usual word acquired an added meaning in World War II. In war engagements, it came to mean air protection afforded to ground troops by a sufficient number of planes overhead, to fight off enemy planes and protect the ground troops from bombing and strafing. "Umbrella" was also used as a symbol of appeasement, because of Neville Chamberlain's custom of always carrying an umbrella. He carried one to the Munich conference when he went to confer with Hitler and Mussolini (in what proved to be a vain effort to maintain the peace) and signed the appeasement decree

Umtees: UMT (Universal Military Training) Demonstration Unit. A trial program put on by the United States Army at Fort Knox, Kentucky, as a demonstration of the way universal military training might work out.—*New York Times Magazine. February 23, 1947. p. 11*

UN: United Nations. This became the official designation at the San Francisco conference in June 1945. Previous to that it had been known as the UNO—United Nations Organization. The opening phrase of the charter read: "We the peoples of the United Nations. . ."—*Newsweek. June 18, 1945. p. 64*

UNCIO: United Nations Conference on International Organization.—*Newsweek. June 25, 1945. p. 62*

Uncle Joe: Nickname of Brigadier General John K. Cannon.—*Newsweek. June 14, 1943. p. 27*; also nickname of Lieutenant General Joseph W. Stilwell—*Current Biography. 1942. p. 810*

Uncle Sam: Radio voice planned to go on the air in March 1941, to help talk back at Lord Haw Haw (q.v.) and his fellow Nazi propagandists. As the program would be in a dozen tongues—a different one each day—the voice would belong to no single individual but to a group of linguists.—*Newsweek. March 10, 1941. p. 63*

Uncle Sugar: Expression used widely in the Pacific (and probably elsewhere) when referring to the United States. Derived from code words used in radio to transcribe the letters U S

Unconditional Resistance: Nazi authorities urged Germans not to desert their present leaders and demanded "unconditional resistance," as the military situation grew worse on both the western and eastern fronts.—*Democrat & Chronicle. Rochester, N.Y. February 6, 1945. p. 2*

Unconditional Surrender: At the conference of Roosevelt and Churchill at Casablanca in January 1943, plans for victory began to take shape. President Roosevelt told newspaper correspondents that this meeting would be known as the "unconditional surrender" conference, since those were the only terms considered for the surrender of the Axis powers. The phrase was borrowed from General U. S. Grant who used it in a message to General Buckner in 1862.—*Newsweek. February 1, 1943. p. 17*

Under-belly of the Axis: Phrase used by Winston Churchill. In a speech to the House of Commons on the war situation, November 11, 1942, Churchill said: "At the same time we make this wide encircling movement in the Mediterranean, having for its primary purpose the recovery of the command of that vital sea, but also having for its object the exposure of the under-belly of the Axis, especially Italy, to heavy attack." A similar phrase was used by Henry Taylor in a book published in April 1942, referring to the possibility of invasion of Europe from Africa: "Soft underside of the sprawling German turtle."—*Churchill. The End of the Beginning. p. 279; Taylor. Time Runs Out. p. 275*

Underground: An outlawed political or military movement or organization operating in secret. There was a very active underground movement against the Nazis in the European countries.—*Britannica Book of the Year. 1944. p. 770*

UNESCO: United Nations Educational, Scientific and Cultural Organization. "The purpose of the Organization is to contribute to peace and security by promoting collaboration among the nations through education, science and culture in order to further universal respect for justice, for the rule of law and for the human rights and fundamental freedoms which are affirmed for the peoples of the world, without distinction of race, sex, language or religion, by the charter of the United Nations." This statement of the purpose of UNESCO was printed and distributed by the Women's Action Committee for Lasting Peace of the American Association for the United Nations

Union in War of All Frenchmen: Joint statement of General Charles de Gaulle and General Henri Giraud, made during the conference at Casablanca, French Morocco, in January 1943. "We have met. We have talked. We have registered our entire agreement on the end to be achieved which is the liberation of France. . . This end will be attained by a union in war of all Frenchmen."—*Newsweek. February 1, 1943. p. 17*

Unite, Encircle, and Close In: Strategy set up by United Nations to oppose Hitler's strategy of "Divide and conquer."—*Newsweek. January 12, 1942. p. 21*

United We Conquer: Motto of Combined Operations (Commandos).—*Saunders. Combined Operations. p. viii*

UNO: See UN

Unotopia: Name suggested for the American home of the United Nations (Reuters dispatch to *Christian Science Monitor*).— *American Notes and Queries. May 1946. p. 24*

UNRRA: United Nations Relief and Rehabilitation Administration. This agency was not yet set up in July 1943, but a draft agreement had been approved by the United States, Britain, Russia, and China, and when operating, there would be a council representing all the united and associated nations working under a central executive committee composed of Big Four members. The UNRRA held its first conference in Atlantic City, New Jersey, November 1943.—*Newsweek. July 12, 1943. p. 11; November 22, 1943. p. 44*

U.P.: Rockets were first rejected by the War Department, but later developed in greatest secrecy. Scientists engaged on the project often did not know what they were working on. Even production blueprints were not labeled. Insiders never mentioned "Rocket"; they called it "U.P." (unrotated projectile).—*Newsweek. June 26, 1944. p. 17*

Upcats: See Cats

USAFE: U.S. Air Forces, Europe

USAFFE: (Pronounced you-SAW-fee) U.S. Army Forces, Far East, top headquarters (MacArthur's) in the Southwest Pacific Area. See also AFPAC

USAFI: United States Armed Forces Institute, Madison, Wisconsin.—*Britannica Book of the Year. 1946. p. 833*

USFET: United States Forces, European Theater. American headquarters for occupation of Germany after SHAEF was dissolved as of July 13, 1945. Explained by Raymond Gram Swing in a news broadcast July 12, 1945. Also noted in *Democrat & Chronicle. Rochester, N.Y. July 14, 1945. p. 3*

USO: United Service Organization. Under this head six well-known welfare organizations were to work in cooperation in the areas contiguous to training camps, naval stations and large defense production centers. More than 800 representatives of the Y.M.C.A., Y.W.C.A., Jewish Welfare Board, National Catholic Community Service, Salvation Army, and Travelers' Aid Association met in Washington, D.C., April 17, 1941, to hear Federal Security Administrator McNutt and others explain the plan.—*Christian Century. April 30, 1941. p. 597*

U.S.S. Blood and Guts.   See Ninth Army Navy

USSTAF: United States Strategic Air Forces (Europe)

Utah Beach: See Omaha beach

"The **Utmost Application of Exterminating Force**":   By Winston Churchill, in a speech on June 30, 1943, at the Guildhall on receiving the freedom of London.   His speech, entitled "Before the Autumn Leaves Fall," contained this phrase: "Our main attack is upon . . . the Ruhr . . . there is no industrial or military target in Germany that will not receive as we deem necessary the utmost application of exterminating force."—*Churchill.   Onwards to Victory. p. 167*

V-1:   A jet-propelled robot plane bomb, the first of the "V" or Vergeltungswaffen (Revenge weapons) with which Germany bombed England (especially London) after the Normandy invasion. V-1 looked like a small plane without a propeller.   See also Robot Bombs.—*New York Times Magazine.   November 19, 1944.   p. 6-7*

V-1 ½: Presumably smaller than V-2.   A rocket weapon used by the Germans against the Allies in Europe.   Major General Levin H. Campbell, Jr., of United States Ordnance said the weapon was either V-3 or V-4, but British experts called it V-1 ½.—*Newsweek. January 1, 1945.   p. 19*

V-2:   A jet-propelled rocket bomb.   Heavier and more complicated than V-1, it did approximately the same damage with about the same amount of explosive.—*Newsweek.   December 18, 1944. p. 31*

V-13:   A secret weapon flung by Americans into the German lines near Aachen in October 1944.   It was a street car loaded with 88mm. shells and dynamite.—*New York Times.   October 15, 1944. p. 2E, 7E*

Vackie: Slang term for an evacuated child or adult. See also Warphan.—*Reader's Digest. May 1940. p. 39*

Valiant: (American plane)   Vultee BT-13 and 15SNV trainer plane

Vanguard: (American plane)   Vultee P-48 fighter plane

Vanquish or Die: The Maquis (French underground) pennon bears General de Gaulle's Cross of Lorraine on a V-for-Victory and reads "Vaincre ou Mourir"—Vanquish or Die.—*Newsweek. March 27, 1944. p. 33*

Vansittartism: Lord Vansittart's theory of postwar treatment of Germany, involving primarily complete disarmament and reeducation.—*Nineteenth Century. May 1942. p. 203-8*

V-E Day; V-J Day: Designations suggested by James F. Byrnes, Director of War Mobilization, for the end of the war in Europe, and the surrender of Japan, respectively (UP dispatch from Washington, September 10, 1944).—*American Notes and Queries. October 1944. p. 102*

Velvet Curtain: Term used by the U.S.S.R. to describe British secrecy in British-occupied Europe and the middle east. See also Iron Curtain.—*Britannica Book of the Year. 1947. p. 841*

Vengeance: (American plane) Vultee A-31 light bomber plane

Ventura: (American plane) Vega B-34 PV medium bomber plane

Venus Fixers: Sixteen Allied officers (eight British, eight American) were given the title Allied Sub-Commission for Monuments, Fine Arts and Archives in Italy. Their job was to rebuild Italian towers, to furnish the air force and infantry with lists of Italian art treasures which must be spared if possible, to approve expenditures for rebuilding and restoring. Their long official title was shortened to "Venus Fixers" by the GI's.—*Time. April 16, 1945. p. 63*

Vetleggers: Word coined from 'veteran' and 'bootlegger' by the War Assets Administration to describe veterans who used their surplus-property certificates illegally to purchase property for resale.—*Newsweek. June 24, 1946. p. 17*

V-for-Victory: January 14, 1941, Victor de Laveleye, a member of the Belgian Parliament exiled in London, in a broadcast to his homeland, proposed the use of the letter V as a symbol of passive resistance in Nazi-occupied lands. He had heard that Belgian children were chalking the initials RAF (for Royal Air Force) on walls and sidewalks, but he thought one letter which could be chalked quickly would be safer. He chose the letter "V." See also "Colonel Britton." The V stood not only for "Victory" and for the French *Victoire* but also for *Vrieheid* and *Vrijheid*, the words for freedom in Flemish and Dutch respectively. The scheme rapidly evolved into the most ambitious British propaganda campaign of the war. On July 4, 1941, the British Broadcasting Corporation carried speeches in all European languages. These were sprinkled with the Morse code for V, three dots and a dash. The opening bar of Beethoven's C minor symphony, three short notes and a long note, known as the fate theme, was chosen as the leit-motif of the movement. July 20 was proclaimed by the British as "V day." V clubs were formed. Radio listeners were also told to open their Bibles to Daniel V, which contains the words written on the wall: "Mene mene tekel upharsin," or, "God hath numbered thy kingdom and finished it."—*Newsweek. July 28, 1941. p. 22-3; Democrat & Chronicle. Rochester, N.Y. April 26, 1945. p. 9.* See also Winston Churchill's broadcast to occupied countries on July 20, 1941.—*Churchill. The Unrelenting Struggle. p. 195*

Vichyate: Vichy (where the Nazi-dominated French government was set up) plus -ate, a pun on the word vitiate. To subject (France) to the regime of Vichy.—*American Speech. April 1942. p. 123*

Victory: The weekly magazine published by OEM (q.v.), formerly called "Defense", was rechristened "Victory" after the attack on Pearl Harbor, December 7, 1941.—*Newsweek. December 27, 1941. p. 7*

Victory Bonds: See Bonds

Victory Book Campaign: A National Defense Book Campaign was launched under the sponsorship of the American Library Association, the American Red Cross and the United Service Organizations, to collect donations of books for Army camps, Naval bases, U.S.O. clubs and other service centers. It started on January 12, 1942, under the name of Victory Book Campaign. Its slogan was "We Want Books."

A second drive for books for the Armed forces was carried on in 1943. No quota was set for this drive (the quota in the first drive was set at 10,000,000 books), but quality was stressed. The publicity campaign continued from January 5 to March 5, 1943. The Board of Directors of the Victory Book Campaign decided to close the campaign November 30, 1943 but offices were maintained until the following January and libraries continued to accept books.—*Publishers' Weekly. November 22, 1941. p. 1953; December 20, 1941. p. 2221; March 20, 1943. p. 1275; American Library Association. Bulletin. September 1943. p. 250*

Victory Circuit: USO Camp Shows had three circuits in the United States. The Victory Circuit presented full-size and full-dress musicals, revues, plays and concerts to all posts and naval stations with theater equipment large enough to accommodate them. See also Blue Circuit, Hospital Circuit and Foxhole Circuit.—*Newsweek. July 31, 1944. p. 60*

Victory Currency: Name given by Brigadier General Carlos P. Romulo, Resident Commissioner, to the currency issued by the Commonwealth Government of the Philippines for use by the invasion forces of General Douglas MacArthur (AP dispatch from New Guinea, October 20, 1944).—*American Notes and Queries. October 1944. p. 102*

Victory Gardens: A week after the bombing of Pearl Harbor, December 7, 1941, gardeners stopped talking of Defense gardens, and began calling them Victory gardens. As food prices went up and food became scarcer, and point rationing (q.v.) was instituted, more and more persons planted vegetables in their Victory Gardens, vegetables both for eating and for canning.

The American Institute of Food Distribution estimated that the Victory gardeners in 1943 whittled at least $1,250,000,000 from the country's total food bill with an estimated 4,500,000 tons of vegetables and fruit grown.—*House and Garden. August 1942. p. 65; New York Times. October 30, 1943. p. 17*

Victory Girl (V-Girl): One under sixteen who, without chaperon, became a pick-up for service men, especially in the amusement centers. In New York City, she was being taken into custody. In addition to "victory girl," other names applied to the girls by the soldiers and sailors were: khaki wackies, patriotutes, good-time Janes. —*Life. December 20, 1943. p. 101-2; American Notes and Queries. March 1944. p. 181*

Victory in 1944: In his first public statement as newly appointed commander of the main Allied invasion of Europe, General Dwight Eisenhower made the flat and carefully considered prediction that "we will win the European war in 1944." He went on to say: "The only thing needed for us to win the European war in 1944 is for every man and woman all the way from the front line to the remotest hamlet of our two countries [the United States and England] to do his or her full duty."—*New York Times. December 28, 1943. p. 1*

Vigilant: (American plane) Vultee L-1 liaison plane

Vindicator: (American plane) Vought-Sikorsky SB2U-3 light dive-bomber plane

Vinegar Joe: Nickname of General Joseph W. Stilwell. United States soldiers call him "Vinegar Joe" because of his acid tongue, but to Chinese army men Lieutenant General Stilwell is a figure to be compared with Frederick Townsend Ward, the almost-legendary American who helped their emperor put down the Taiping Rebellion 80 years ago.—*Democrat & Chronicle. Rochester, N.Y. July 4, 1943. p. 8D*

Viper: One of the unusual weapons which the Germans developed in the closing days of the war. It was a piloted, rocket-propelled midget plane designed to ram bombers. In operation the pilot climbs aboard when the Viper is on its launching ramp. In flight he aims it at a bomber and then bails out just before it strikes. The weapon made 620 miles an hour. Captured photographs of it were published in the Third Report of the Army Air Forces to the Secretary of War.—*Newsweek. November 19, 1945. p. 64*

Vipers (or Vips): Very Important Persons. Much superior to "Pipers" (Pretty Important Persons) and not supposed to mix with them. This nickname was given particularly to important persons traveling on planes in war areas.—*Newsweek. January 24, 1944. p. 31*

V-J Day: See V-E Day

V.L.R.: A very long range plane. Liberator bombers whose special fuel tanks allowed them a range of 2,000 miles. Winston Churchill in a speech given in the House of Commons on June 8, 1943, used the expression: "very long range air power—V.L.R. as it is called."—*Democrat & Chronicle. Rochester, N.Y. June 9, 1943. p. 2; Newsweek. June 21, 1943. p. 28*

V-Mail: Letters reduced in size by photography, to expedite handling of mail to and from servicemen.—*American Speech. October 1944. p. 226*

La Voix des Femmes: Publication of a French underground movement composed entirely of women. The movement grew out of food demonstrations; encouraged by success with that, the women throughout the unoccupied area formed groups, and in time branched out into providing sanctuary for fugitives. After coming into contact with the Fighting French and other underground groups, with their aid the women began publishing their paper.—*Newsweek. September 14, 1942. p. 16*

Volkssturm: The "People's Army" which Hitler established by decree when the Allied armies began beating against Germany from the west, east, southeast, and south; composed of every able-bodied man between sixteen and sixty and proclaimed a part of the German army under international law.—*New York Herald Tribune. October 19, 1944*

Volplane: Said of an airplane when it glides or coasts with motor power turned off

Voyager: (American plane) Beech C-45A JRB transport plane

Vrij Nederland: Weekly Dutch magazine in exile, published abroad.—*Saturday Review of Literature. July 17, 1943. p. 5*

VT Fuse: Variable Time Fuse. A secret weapon which the Army called "pozit" and the Navy called "Buck Rogers." The VT fuse is a self powered radio transmitter and receiver small enough to fit into the nose of an anti-aircraft shell and tough enough to stand the terrific shock of firing. The transmitter in the set broadcasts a continuous wave and when part of this wave is reflected back from an object seventy feet away, the shell is made to explode at the ideal distance for maximum effect. This device was perfected and produced in the United States and was very effective, among other uses, against the V-1 buzzbombs over England. VT Fuse was its technical name but it was more popularly termed 'proximity fuse' since it caused the shell to explode when near an object, rather than on direct contact.—*Time. October 1, 1945. p. 48; Radio News. December 1945. p. 51; American Speech. October 1946. p. 224, 226; Baxter. Scientists Against Time. p. 221-42*

WAA: War Assets Administration. For disposal of U.S. surplus war property

WAAAF: Women's Auxiliary Australian Air Force. Formed in 1939.—*Christian Science Monitor Magazine. September 23, 1939. p. 5*

WAAC: Women's Army Auxiliary Corps. Started May 1942. Established by act of Congress. Name later changed to WAC (q.v.).—*Time. May 18, 1942. p. 62; May 25, 1942. p. 72*

W.A.A.F.: British Women's Auxiliary Air Force. Formed in June 1939. Before that date the personnel of the Force had done duty for nearly a year in the R.A.F. companies of the A.T.S. Duties for women working for the R.A.F. were sufficiently different from those needed by the Army, so the W.A.A.F. came into being and functioned under the direct command of the R.A.F.—*Anderson. British Women at War. p. 21*

WAAMMS: Women's Auxiliary of the American Merchant Marine, Inc. Founded by Mrs. Ada Mae Roll and chartered in New York State in July 1943. Dedicated to the aid of merchant marine men and their families and will "carry on" after the war. Only wives of merchant marine personnel are eligible to enlist.—*New York Times. August 29, 1943. p. 6*

WAC: New abbreviation for WAAC (q.v.). President Roosevelt signed legislation renaming America's women soldiers and putting them under army regulations. The new law removed the "auxiliary" from the organization's name. A member of the WAC is known as a Wac.—*Democrat & Chronicle. Rochester, N.Y. July 5, 1943. p. 3*

WAC-I: Nickname for contingent of Wacs in India. It was an Indian Army Corps—no connection with American or British organizations. It included women of all ranks, races and creeds in India, from all provinces. Their insignia included an I for India, so they became known as "Wac-eyes."—*Item contributed by a friend from India*

WAC Nicknames: See Dovetails and G.I. Janes

Waffen SS: See SS

WAFS: Women's Auxiliary Ferrying Squadron. Part of Air Transport Command. Announced by Secretary of War Stimson September 10, 1942.—*Time. September 21, 1942. p. 58*

Wags: Nickname of K-9 Corps. See DFD: Dogs For Defense

Wait for me: Nickname of Commander David McCampbell, an air group commander in the Pacific. Tied with Marine Major Richard Bong (34 Japanese planes each) as America's ace of aces.— *New York Times Magazine. December 3, 1944. p. 21*

Walkie-Talkie: A portable radio. "The first portable two-way set was developed in 1933 in the laboratories of the Signal Corps. Walkie-Talkie was the nickname given by soldiers to the first sets made by Galvin Manufacturing Corporation, but as popularity of the device grew, "walkie-talkie" slipped into official Army jargon and is now applied to all similar sets."—*Fortune. October 1943. p. 62; American Speech. February 1941. p. 31; April 1946. p. 115*

Walkout Club: So many crews of American transport and battle planes, most of them flying along the air transport route into

China, had been rescued from the North Burma jungles, that they formed the Walkout Club. Membership was limited to all those on active service with American forces who spent time in the jungle after parachuting to the ground when their planes were forced down. Also called "Blister Club"—according to an Information Please broadcast March 26, 1945.—*Times-Union. Rochester, N.Y. January 17, 1944*

Walrus: (British plane) Supermarine amphibian reconnaissance flying boat, used chiefly as a submarine spotter

Wangenstein Alley: Name given by the nurses on the Normandy beachhead to the belly-wound ward. These wounds had priority on the operating tables. Term came from the inventor of a stomach suction device.—*Time. July 24, 1944. p. 54*

WAPS: Women of the American Press Service. Accredited American women war correspondents.—*Newsweek. March 8, 1943. p. 72*

"The War against the Japanese and Other Diseases of the Jungle Will Be Pressed Forward": By Winston Churchill in a speech "A Review of the War" to the House of Commons, September 28, 1944.—*Churchill. Dawn of Liberation. p. 243*

War Bonds: See Bonds

War Brides: Girls married overseas to U.S. service men. The first contingent arrived on the "Argentina" in New York City February 4, 1946. "Family Fleet," "Operation Mother-in-law," "Diaper Run" were some of the newspaper terms coined.—*American Notes and Queries. March 1946. p. 182*

War Fatigue: See Shell-shock

"War Is a Contagion": By Franklin D. Roosevelt. Speech in Chicago, October 5, 1937.—*Vital Speeches. October 15, 1937. p. 3*

"War, Like the Hurricane, Is the Result of Unbalanced Forces Which Continue until Stability or Equilibrium Is Restored": By Admiral Chester W. Nimitz in a broadcast, "Latest moves in Pacific," from Pearl Harbor to an American Legion convention in Chicago, Illinois, September 18, 1944.—*Vital Speeches. October 1, 1944. p. 746*

War Nerves: See Shell-shock

War of Survival: See World War II

War of the Dictators. See World War II .

The **War of the Free:** See World War II

War Time: Daylight saving time was officially called war time by President Roosevelt.—*Time. February 9, 1942. p. 12*

War Weariness: See Shell-shock

"The **War Will End Only When We Are Convinced That Hitler Has Had Enough":** By Winston Churchill. Radio address from London, October 1, 1939. "It was for Hitler to say when the war would begin; but it is not for him or for his successors to say when it will end. It began when he wanted it, and it will end only when we are convinced that he has had enough."—*Churchill. Blood, Sweat and Tears. p. 176*

Ward, E.D.: Mike name of Edward L. Delaney (taken from his first name, E D Ward), an American who did a great deal of broadcasting from Germany during the first year of the war. His specialties were glowing descriptions of the deeds of the Nazi army. Indicted for treason July 26, 1943, by the District of Columbia Grand Jury.—*Christian Science Monitor Magazine. July 18, 1942. p. 6*

Warhawk: (American plane) Curtis P-40 fighter plane

Warmonger: Webster's Dictionary gives as a definition of this: "a mercenary. Obs. One who stirs up war." It became far from obsolete during World War II when it was applied by appeasers and isolationists to anyone who suggested any determined stand against the Axis in its onward course of aggression

Warphan: War orphan. The term was used in World War I and revived in China around 1938. Though it was used in World War II, 'vackie' (from evacuée) became the more generally used term.—*American Speech. October 1939. p. 190; Nation. November 9, 1940. p. 447*

Warsages: Corsages made of War Savings Stamps. The Warsage Production Center of Rochester, N.Y. celebrated its second anniversary in August 1944. It was a war-aid agency run by volunteers who made and sold the corsages. It was the first such War Stamp accessory mass production center in the country and was the inspiration for the formation of similar groups in many other cities. In its first two years of activity, sales reached $37,817.45. Before the Center was organized, over 15,000 bouquets had been made by individuals in their homes and it was because of the great popularity of these that the

Center was started. Bouquets ranged from tiny 25 cent ones to those containing enough stamps for a $25 War Bond.—*Democrat & Chronicle. Rochester, N.Y. August 22, 1944. p. 10*

Warthog: See Privateer

Washing Machine Charlie: GI slang for early Japanese bombers, derived from the fact that when flying, their engines sounded like a washing machine

WASP: Women's Airforce Service Pilots. Director of this group was Jacqueline Cochran.—*Newsweek. March 12, 1945. p. 78*

Wasp: Flame thrower developed and used by the British. See also Crocodile.—*American Notes and Queries. September 1944. p. 85*

Wasps: Women's Auxiliary Service Platoon. On March 6, 1943 it was announced in Balboa, Canal Zone, that enlistments for a unit of the Women's Auxiliary Service Platoon would soon begin. The "Wasps" (first uniformed women's service group to be formed in the Canal Zone) was planned to furnish trained operators to relieve military personnel in the Army Air Force central control tower. The organization was sponsored by Lieutenant General George H. Brett, commanding the Caribbean Defense Area and Brigadier General Russell E. Randall, chief of the local fighter command.—*New York Times. March 7, 1943. p. 17*

The **Watch on the Channel (Die Wacht am Kanal)**: A German song which appeared on the radio in June 1944. With its emphasis on defending the Channel against the expected invasion from England, it showed that even German song writers had gone on the defensive.—*Newsweek. June 12, 1944. p. 29*

Water Bloke: Nickname of Major Peter W. Rainier, Chief Water Supply officer on the 2000-mile pursuit of Rommel from El Alamein to the Mareth Line and beyond.—*New York Times Book Review. February 20, 1944. p. 7*

Water Buffalo: Amphibious tank; so named because of a similarity to the animal. See L.—*New York Times Magazine. December 17, 1944. p. 20*

Water Weasel: A lightweight amphibious cargo carrier developed largely for use in swamp lands; capable of navigating in quagmire where the jeep cannot. See also Weasel.—*New York Times. September 3, 1944*

Wave Bombing: Fleets of bomber planes, sent out in successive waves to bomb a specified target

WAVES: Women Accepted for Voluntary Emergency Service. WAVES is the officially recognized title of the Women's branch of the United States Naval Reserve, established by an act of Congress on July 31, 1942.—*Ross. The Waves. p. 1*

"We Are Going to Strike—and Strike Hard": By Franklin D. Roosevelt. Annual message to Congress, Washington, D.C., January 7, 1943.—*Vital Speeches. January 15, 1943. p. 195*

"We Are Going to Win the War and We Are Going to Win the Peace That Follows": By Franklin D. Roosevelt. Radio address December 9, 1941. This was the first address directly to the people after the declaration of war on December 8, 1941.—*Baird. Representative American Speeches. 1941-42. p. 39*

"We Are Not Impressed": By Vice Admiral Thomas C. Kinkaid, commander of the Luzon task force. The waters of Lingayen Gulf were crowded with a huge U.S. convoy—fully 2,500,000 tons of shipping. Against this force 12 little Japanese swimmers ferrying explosives, paddled into the transport area. Some were captured and others shot as they resisted capture. Commenting on this Japanese trick, Vice Admiral Kinkaid (paraphrasing Queen Victoria's famous remark) said, "We are not impressed."—*Times-Union. Rochester, N.Y. January 11, 1945*

"We Are Not Yielding and We Do Not Propose to Yield": By Franklin D. Roosevelt. Message to Congress concerning the sinking by a Nazi submarine of an American ship, the Robin Moor.—*Vital Speeches. July 1, 1941. p. 548*

"We Are Now in This War. We Are All in It—All the Way": By Franklin D. Roosevelt. Radio address December 9, 1941. This was the first address directly to the people after the declaration of war on December 8, 1941.—*Baird. Representative American Speeches. 1941-42. p. 32*

"We Are Now Shutting Down. Good-bye till Better Times. Long Live the Queen": Official Dutch radio went off the air March 7, 1942, with these words, just before the fall of Java to the Japanese. Quoted in *Miller. General Douglas MacArthur, Fighter for Freedom. p. 277*

We Are the Menace, We Are the Hell, We Are the End of England: Song of the German U-boat crews.—*Newsweek. July 14, 1941. p. 26*

"We Are the Ultimate Hope and Sanctuary of Human Liberty": By Herbert Hoover. Address to Pennsylvania Society of New York, December 21, 1940.—*Vital Speeches. January 1, 1941. p. 183*

"We Are Wholly One in the Prosecution of the War to a Complete Victory": By Franklin D. Roosevelt. At dinner of the White House Correspondents' Association, Washington, D.C., February 12, 1943, after his return from Africa. The full quotation reads: "Lest there be any question in Nazi or Japanese minds that we are wholly one in the prosecution of the war to a complete victory over our enemies, the Prime Minister wished at Casablanca to make a formal agreement that if Germany should be conquered before Japan all British Empire resources and manpower would of course join with China and with us in an out-and-out final attack on Japan."—*Vital Speeches. March 1, 1943. p. 294*

We Build, We Fight: The Seabees' motto is Construimus Batuimus—"We build, we fight." Less formal and perhaps more popular is another of their slogans, "Can Do!"—*Cave. We Build, We Fight! p. 6.* Another slogan of the Seabees is "First to Land and Last to Leave."—*American Notes and Queries. January 1944. p. 149*

We Can ... We Must ... We Will: Slogan used on war poster. Taken from words of President Roosevelt: "This can be done; it must be done; it will be done." The quotation refers to delivering needed supplies to Britain. A radio address May 27, 1941.—*Vital Speeches. June 1, 1941. p. 511*

"We Cannot Be an Island": By Franklin D. Roosevelt. Radio address to those attending farm dinners to commemorate the eighth year of the New Deal Agricultural Program, March 8, 1941.—*Vital Speeches. April 1, 1941. p. 377*

"We Cannot Let Great Britain Down. If We Do—Hitler May Never Let Us Up": By James F. Byrnes. United States Senator from South Carolina. Radio address January 17, 1941.—*Vital Speeches. February 15, 1941. p. 268*

"We Can't Have the Luxury of Hate or the Stupidity of Contempt": By Charles P. Taft, Assistant Director, Office of Defense Health and Welfare Services. Speech delivered at Swarthmore College, Swarthmore, Pennsylvania, February 7, 1943.—*Vital Speeches. April 15, 1943. p. 408*

"We Do Not Covet Anything from Any Nation except Their Respect": By Winston Churchill. To the French people, an address broadcast in French and in English, October 21, 1940.—*Vital Speeches. November 1, 1940. p. 48; Churchill. Blood, Sweat and Tears. p. 403*

"We Do Not Retreat. We Are Not Content to Stand Still. As Americans We Go Forward, in the Service of Our Country, by the Will of God": By Franklin D. Roosevelt. Inaugural address, January 20, 1941.—*Vital Speeches. February 1, 1941. p. 227*

"We Do the Unexpected . . . We Expose Ourselves to Shore-based Planes. We Don't Stay behind the Battle with Our Carriers. But . . . Whatever We Do, We Do Fast." Admiral William F. Halsey once made this statement which is a condensed version of his tactics in the naval warfare against the Japanese.—*Newsweek. October 8, 1945. p. 60*

"We Expect to Be the Cause of Japan's Desperation": By Lieutenant General Millard F. Harmon, commander of Strategic Air Forces, Pacific Ocean areas. General Harmon was reported missing in March 1945.—*Democrat & Chronicle. Rochester, N.Y. March 3, 1945. p. 1*

"We Fight to Retain a Great Past—and We Fight to Gain a Greater Future": By Franklin D. Roosevelt. Annual message to Congress, Washington, D.C., January 7, 1943.—*Vital Speeches. January 15, 1943. p. 197*

"We Got a Hell of a Beating": By Lieutenant General Joseph W. Stilwell. "I claim we got a hell of a beating. We got run out of Burma and it is humiliating as hell. I think we ought to find out what caused it, go back and retake it."—*New York Times. May 26, 1942. p. 1*

"We Have a Savage Enemy and There's Plenty of Him": By Lieutenant General Joseph W. Stilwell.—*Democrat & Chronicle. Rochester, N.Y. June 16, 1943*

"We Have Sighted the Suburb of Pittsburgh and Have Taken It in Tow": The U.S.S. Pittsburgh had her entire bow ripped off by a thunderous sea in a typhoon southeast of the Ryukyus, June 5, 1945. The bow subsequently was recovered by a tug and towed to Guam for salvage. The tug sent the above message.—*Times-Union. Rochester, N.Y. July 13, 1945*

"We Have to Imitate Tarzan": General Orde Charles Wingate's slogan for his Chindits (q.v.).—*Rolo. Wingate's Raiders. p. 33*

"We Lift Our Battered Helmets in Admiration for Those Who Fought Magnificently against Overwhelming Odds and Drove the Enemy Back to Crushing Defeat": By Major General Alexander Archer Vandegrift, commanding general of the Marines in Guadalcanal. Message to Admiral Halsey, quoted by President Roosevelt, referring to the Solomons campaign. —*Vital Speeches. December 15, 1942. p. 131*

"We Must Be the Great Arsenal of Democracy": By Franklin D. Roosevelt. Radio address from Washington, D.C., December 29, 1940.—*Vital Speeches. January 15, 1941. p. 197*

"We Must Move on to a Great Social Offensive if We Are to Win the War Completely": By John G. Winant. In a speech on United Nations postwar aims given at Durham, England, on June 6, 1942.—*New York Times. June 7, 1942. p. 17*

"We Must Not Waste the Victory": By General George C. Marshall. In his valedictory message as Army Chief of Staff in October 1945, he asked "Are we already shirking the responsibility of victory? . . . Are we inviting the same international disrespect that prevailed before this war?" And then he gave his own answer: "We must not waste the victory."—*Time. March 25, 1946. p. 28*

"We Need a Whole-souled Devotion to the Building of a People's Peace": By Thomas E. Dewey in a speech at Oklahoma City, Oklahoma, September 25, 1944.—*Vital Speeches. October 1, 1944. p. 743*

"We Need Decisions, Not Discussions: We Need Planes, Not Predictions: We Need Tanks, Not Talk": By Wendell Willkie. Address at the annual dinner of the United States Conference of Mayors, Washington, D.C., January 13, 1942.—*Vital Speeches. February 1, 1942. p. 243*

"We See the Ridge Ahead": By Winston Churchill. Speech at Leeds May 16, 1942. "We have reached a period in the War when it would be premature to say that we have topped the ridge, but now we see the ridge ahead."—*Churchill. The End of the Beginning. p. 137*

"We Shall Drive on to the End, and Do Our Duty, Win or Die. God Helping Us, We Can Do No Other": By Winston Churchill. Radio address from London, May 10, 1942.—*Vital Speeches. May 15, 1942. p. 456*

"**We Shall Fight on Beaches, Landing Grounds, in Fields, in Streets and on the Hills**": By Winston Churchill. Speech before the House of Commons, June 4, 1940.—*Vital Speeches. June 15, 1940. p. 519*

"**We Shall Win or We Shall Die**": By General Douglas Mac-Arthur. Speech delivered at a dinner given in his honor at the Australian Parliament House, Canberra, Australia, March 26, 1942.—*Vital Speeches. April 15, 1942. p. 397*

"**We, the Peoples of the United Nations. . .**": Opening phrase in the charter of the United Nations

We Wanna Go Home: A song written in Frankfort by Army and Navy officers and expressing the general GI sentiment. It was being sung and whistled in Germany, a quick march, with catchy lyrics.—*Newsweek. January 7, 1946. p. 14*

We Want Books: Slogan of Victory Book Campaign (q.v.)

"**We Want to Break the Territorial and Military Chains That Confine Us**": By Benito Mussolini. Speech after declaration of war on England and France, June 10, 1940.—*Vital Speeches. June 15, 1940. p. 516*

"**We Will Gain the Inevitable Triumph—So Help Us God**": By Franklin D. Roosevelt. War address, December 8, 1941.—*Vital Speeches. December 15, 1941. p. 130*

"**We Will Never Cease to Strike**": By Winston Churchill. Speech at Mansion House, November 9, 1940. To the valiant Greek people: "We send from the heart of old London our faithful promise that, amid all our burdens and anxieties, we will do our best to aid them in their struggle, and that we will never cease to strike at the foul aggressor in ever-increasing strength."—*Churchill. Blood, Sweat and Tears. p. 424*

"**We Will Not Fail Mankind**": By Winston Churchill. In an impromptu speech at Glasgow during a tour of that city's civil defense organizations, January 17, 1941.—*Churchill. The Unrelenting Struggle. p. 23*

"**We Will Not Slow Down or Detour. Signs and Signals Call for Speed—Full Speed Ahead**": By Franklin D. Roosevelt. Address to the graduating class of the University of Virginia and over the radio to the world, June 10, 1940.—*Vital Speeches. June 15, 1940. p. 515*

Weasel: A caterpillar tread truck. Official designation for T-24, Cargo Carrier, Light. It made its first appearance on the Italian front. See also Water Weasel.—*New York Times Magazine. December 17, 1944. p. 20*

"Weed 'Em and Reap": "Louis Untermeyer writes that he is planning a Victory Garden book which he means to call 'Weed 'em and reap.'" Quoted from Bennett Cerf's column "Trade Winds."—*Saturday Review of Literature. March 27, 1943. p. 20*

Weeping Slips: Robert McCormick, NBC correspondent, reports an unofficially acknowledged custom of the Marines in the south Pacific. A Marine who complains too long and too loudly is given a "Weeping Slip," and when he collects ten such slips a special ceremony takes place in which he is formally presented with a Willkie button. See also TS cards.—*American Notes and Queries. February 1944. p. 166*

WEFT: See Wing, Engine, Fuselage, Tail

Wehrmacht: Term for German armed forces as a whole

We'll Hang Out the Washing on the Siegfried Line: Title of a popular song in London, October 1939. Quoted in *Gramling. Free Men Are Fighting. p. 38*

"We'll Take the Big Ones First": The cruiser San Francisco in the battle of the Solomons, November 13, 1942, raced between two formidable lines of Jap men-of-war, crippled a battleship and finished off a cruiser and a destroyer. "We'll take the big ones first!" was the challenge of Rear Admiral Daniel J. Callaghan as the battle joined. See also "Pick out the biggest one and fire."—*Democrat & Chronicle Rochester, N.Y. December 12, 1942*

"Well, We Got Here": By General Douglas MacArthur, as he arrived at the airport in Atsugi, Japan, after the Japanese surrender. "It's been a long hard road from Melbourne to Tokyo, but this looks like the payoff."—*Newsweek. September 10, 1945. p. 30*

Wellington: (British plane) Vicker's heavy bomber

"We're Battling Bastards from Bataan, No Mama, No Papa, No Uncle Sam": Slogan of 31st Infantry under Colonel Charles L. Steel, on Bataan.—*Time. March 9, 1942. p. 20*

Werewolf Song: Sung by a woman radio singer (German), "Lily the Werewolf."—*Newsweek. April 16, 1945. p. 61-2*

Werewolves: German underground movement; a secret group pledged to destroy both Allied invaders and German "traitors." Name comes from the medieval werewolves who fed on human flesh.—*Time. April 16, 1945. p. 40*

West Point on the Autobahn: Nickname for army group at Bad Nauheim, Germany. The staff and headquarters troops of the Fifteenth Army became the seat of the Theater General Board. With headquarters in the Grand Hotel, the Fifteenth seemed to draw rank like a magnet. Assigned to the staff were fifteen generals, eighty colonels, sixty lieutenant colonels, and many other officers reported in and out for brief periods. All these officers soon earned for the place the nickname "West Point on the Autobahn."—*Newsweek. December 24, 1945. p. 55*

WFA: War Food Administration. Established by executive order of President Roosevelt, March 26, 1943. War Food Administrator determined military, civilian, and foreign requirements for human and animal food, and for food used industrially; formulated and implemented a program that would supply food adequate to meet the requirements.—*United States Government Manual. Summer 1943. p. 330*

WFTD: Women's Flying Training Detachment. United States Army Flying School, headed by Jacqueline Cochran at Houston, Texas. Prepared women for the WAFS (q.v.). Miss Cochran was Director of women pilots in the Air Forces and special assistant to Chief of Air Staff Major General Barney M. Giles.—*New York Times. November 24, 1942. p. 21; Newsweek. July 19, 1943. p. 42*

"When the Hour of Action Strikes, We Will Let You Know. Until Then, Help Us by Following Our Instructions. That Is to Say: Keep Calm, Conserve Your Strength. We Repeat: When the Hour of Action Strikes, We Will Let You Know": By General Dwight Eisenhower. In a broadcast to the French people after Allied landings in Sicily, July 10, 1943.—*Democrat & Chronicle. Rochester, N.Y. July 10, 1943*

"When the Hour of Liberation Strikes in Europe, as Strike It Will, It Will Also Be the Hour of Retribution": By Winston Churchill. Speech to the House of Commons September 8, 1942.—*Churchill. The End of the Beginning. p. 218*

When You Are A.W.O.L. You're Working for the Axis: Poster caption. United States Production Board

"When You See a Rattlesnake Poised to Strike, You Do Not Wait until He Has Struck before You Crush Him": By Franklin D. Roosevelt in a radio broadcast September 11, 1941. This country was not yet at war with Germany but the Axis U-boats had made several attacks on American ships, including a United States destroyer. In his report to the nation, President Roosevelt said "It would be unworthy of a great nation to exaggerate an isolated incident. . . . But it would be inexcusable folly to minimize such incidents in the face of evidence which makes it clear that the incident is not isolated, but part of a general plan . . . the Nazi design to abolish the freedom of the seas and to acquire absolute . . . domination of these seas for themselves." The President's orders to the Navy and Air Forces were—not to wait for the Axis "snakes" to strike but to strike first if they entered waters the protection of which would be necessary for American defense.—*Newsweek. September 22, 1941. p. 13-14*

Whirley: See Robot Bombs

Whirlwind: (British plane) Westland fighter plane, also used for fighter-bomber purposes

White Ball: See Com Z

White Noise: White noise is to sound what white light is to light. It is heard when all sound frequencies are added together, just as white light is seen when all colors, or light wave frequencies are added together. As faster air planes are built, the white noise becomes worse. It is apt to produce temporary deafness and interfere with communications. Therefore, scientists are working on problems of eliminating or reducing the noise.—*Science News Letter. July 31, 1943. p. 67-8*

Whitey: Nickname of Lieutenant General Lesley J. McNair (United States Army).—*Current Biography. 1942. p. 553*

Whitley: (British plane) Armstrong-Whitworth heavy bomber

Whizzbangs: See Robot Bombs

WHO: World Health Organization, a United Nations affiliate with sixty-three member nations.—*New York Times. July 28, 1946. p. 6E*

"Who Says a Wasp Cannot Sting Twice?": By Winston Churchill. Message of thanks to the United States Navy acknowledging aid given by the air craft carrier Wasp to the Island of Malta.—*Churchill. The End of the Beginning. p. 169*

Wichita: (American plane)   Beech AT-10 trainer plane

Widgeon: (American plane)   Grumman J4F transport plane

Wilco: Radio term for "will comply."   Used throughout the services and also taken up by civilians.   "Roger—wilco" means "O.K. I'll do it"

The Wild Man: Nickname of Major General Terry Allen (United States Army).—*Newsweek. March 29, 1943. p. 19*

Wildcat: (American plane)   Grumman F4F fighter plane

Will to Die: "How were the Marines able to take Tarawa in 76 hours? 'Gentlemen, it was our will to die,' Major General Holland McTiere Smith, commander of the amphibious forces (assault troops), said at a press conference yesterday."—*Democrat & Chronicle. Rochester, N.Y. November 30, 1943*
A conflicting account says "Tarawa was taken, said Major General Julian C. Smith, only because men 'showed a willingness to die.' "—*New York Times Magazine. December 12, 1943. p. 18*

"Willkie": Because of Wendell Willkie's lightning trip to Great Britain, the English language is enriched with a new word. Now, when a young flier of the Royal Air Force is ordered out for a quick reconnaissance, he is likely to say, "I'm off to give Havre a Willkie. Be back in an hour."—*New York Times Book Review. May 25, 1941. p. 21.* In a British publication, 1943, "Service Slang" compiled by members of the RAF, the term "Willkie" was not included. It therefore presumably never came into general usage, though a temporary use was picked up by the *New York Times,* as noted

Willow Run: Name given to officers' mess at Grosvenor House, London.—*American Speech. April 1945. p. 151*

Wimpy Special: In Army canteens in Australia hamburgers were given the name Wimpy Special (after Popeye the Sailor's hamburger-loving friend Wimpy).—*Newsweek. June 15, 1942. p. 26.* Though this term originated in Australia, it went far afield and was in common usage the length and breadth of the Pacific (according to a letter from a serviceman)

WIMS: Wartime Instruction Manual for Merchant Ships, a volume which had to be studied and known by all deck officers of the United States Merchant Marine. It was known as the "Convoy Bible." —*New York Times. December 24, 1944. p. 2E, 6E*

Wind Messages: Japanese code messages contained in weather reports telling of Japan's decision to enter the war. They figured in the testimony in Congress' Pearl Harbor investigation in December 1945.—*New York Times. December 16, 1945. p. 2E, 7E*

Window: See Radar Countermeasures

Wing: See Air Force

Wing, Engine, Fuselage, Tail: WEFT was a system for aircraft recognition. Poster caption. United States Army. Army orientation course

Wingate's Raiders: See Chindits

Wingco: R.A.F. slang for Wing Commander.—*Nineteenth Century. April 1944. p. 182*

Winged Comet: See Robot Bombs

Wingman: A wingman was the second man in a team of two, each flying a fighter plane. The wingman flew his plane to one side and just back of the leader. His job was to protect the leader.—*American Speech. April 1946. p. 145*

Winnie: Nickname of Winston Churchill, Prime Minister of England.—*Newsweek. August 31, 1942. p. 22*

WINS: Women in National Service. Twenty million American housewives and their teen age daughters received a name from the *Ladies Home Journal,* which also dedicated a wartime housekeeping manual to the WINS, "the greatest reserve strength of America."—*Ladies Home Journal. March 1943. p. 24*

WIPS: Women in Production Service. A voluntary, semimilitary organization of women employees at the E. I. DuPont de Nemours & Co., at Richmond, Virginia. Plant duties were tied directly into the war effort. WIPS was incorporated in Virginia, but the scheme was available for any war plant.—*Business Week. May 22, 1943. p. 114*

Wires: Girls were used to send and receive messages at army posts scattered across the country. At one of the Southern posts these feminine radio operators dubbed themselves the Wires.—*Independent Woman. April 1943. p. 105*

Wizard: Nickname of General Sir Alan Francis Brooke, commander in chief of the British Home Forces. He was knighted for his efficiency in carrying out the retreat from Dunkirk.—*Current Biography. 1941. p. 105*

The **Wizard**: Nickname of General Sir Archibald Wavell (British Army).—*Current Biography. 1941. p. 902*

WLA: Women's Land Army. **Part of the United States Crop** Corps.—*Newsweek. July 19, 1943. p. 61*

WLB: See NWLB

WMC: War Manpower Commission. Established within the Office of Emergency Management by executive order of President Roosevelt, April 18, 1942. Formulated programs and policies to assure maximum effectiveness in the utilization of the nation's manpower. Weighed the needs of industry, agriculture and the armed forces.— *United States Government Manual Summer 1943. p. 100*

Wolf Line: Slang for the overseas "stag line" of soldiers and sailors waiting to "date up" the WACs in North Africa.—*New York Herald Tribune. September 16, 1943*

Wolfpack: Name given to bands or groups of German submarines raiding Allied convoys in the Atlantic. This term was also used in World War I

Wolf's Teeth: Term used to designate concrete anti-tank obstacles laid by the Finns along the Russian lines.—*American Notes and Queries. June 1944. p. 39*

Wop: See Op

World War II: Officially designated as name for the war 1939-1945. This name was used by *Time* magazine as early as September 1939. After many other names were suggested, retiring War Secretary Stimson and Navy Secretary Forrestal wrote a joint letter to President Truman recommending the term World War II. Truman approved, and the letter appeared in the official Federal Register, September 1945.—*Time. October 1, 1945. p. 60.* Other names suggested at various times were "Tyrants' War" (submitted by J. F. Snyder of Murfreesboro, Tennessee) ; "War of Survival" ; "War of the Dictators" (used by C. J. Haines and W. B. Walsh in their *Development of Western Civilization* published in New York in 1941) ; "The War of the Free" (suggested by W.W.R. of Lynn, Massachusetts, in *New York Times Magazine. July 2, 1944.* p. 2) ; "The Last War" and "The Second Phase of the World War" (Lucian Heichler of New York in *New York Times. June 18, 1944.* p. 8E) ; "The Teutonic Plague" (Irving Virgil Gellis of New York in *New York Times. May 17, 1942*) ; "People's War" (originally suggested by Prime Minister Curtin of Australia and used by William Green in

1942 in *New York Times.* June 28, 1942); "Crusade for Living" (Major General Russell P. Hartle in an order of the day from his Ulster headquarters, reported in *New York Times.* April 12, 1942); "Liberty War" and "Gips" (allegedly a contraction of Germany, Italy, Japan) were submitted to President Roosevelt in April 1942.— *New York Times. April 19, 1942.* A Russian designation has been translated as Patriotic War, though perhaps Fatherland War would be a more accurate translation of the Russian original.—*American Notes and Queries. June 1944. p. 42; August 1944. p. 75; July 1945. p. 64*

WOWS: Women Ordnance Workers. WOW, Inc., started in Electric Household Utilities Corp., Chicago, Illinois in August 1942. By May 1943, it had become a national organization of 33,000.—*Business Week. May 1, 1943. p. 91; Reader's Digest. March 1943. p. 47-50*

WPB: War Production Board. Established within the Office of Emergency Management by executive orders of President Roosevelt, January 24, 1942, and April 7, 1942. To exercise general direction over the war procurement and production program, determine policies, supervise the OPM, etc. Supply Priorities and Allocations Board (SPAB) was abolished by the order creating the WPB. Office of Production Management (OPM) was also abolished and its duties taken over by WPB. See also CPA.—*United States Government Manual. Summer 1943. p. 117-18*

WRA: War Relocation Authority. Established within Office of Emergency Management by executive order of President Roosevelt, March 18, 1942. To provide for the removal from designated areas of persons whose removal seemed necessary in the interest of national security, and for their relocation, maintenance and supervision.— *United States Government Manual. Summer 1943. p. 127*

W.R.C.N.S.: Women's Royal Canadian Naval Service. Canada's WRENS were organized in 1942.—*Whitton. Canadian Women in the War Effort. p. 18*

Wrens: Nickname applied to the W.R.N.S. (Women's Royal Naval Service), British service organized in 1917, demobilized in 1919, and reorganized in 1939.—*Scott. British Women in War. p. 15*

WSA: War Shipping Administration. Established within the Office of Emergency Management by executive order of President Roosevelt on February 7, 1942. Transferred to the Administrator the functions, duties, and powers of the United States Maritime Commission.—*United States Government Manual. Summer 1943. p. 129*

WTS: War Training Service of the Civil Aeronautics Administration. Until December 1942, it was known as the CPT (Civilian Pilot Training).—*Democrat & Chronicle. Rochester, N.Y. December 13, 1942*

Wunderwaffe: Wonder weapons. Nicknamed Wuwa. Before the invasion of Europe, there was a great deal of German propaganda about the wonderful new secret weapons. Came the invasion, and the German people were perhaps even more surprised than the Allies, by the absence of Goebbels much vaunted "Wuwa." When the robot bombs (q.v.) were launched against London, these became known among the German people as Wuwa.—*Newsweek. June 19, 1944. p. 20; June 26, 1944. p. 24*

Wurzburgs: Nazi radars shaped like giant electric heaters. Thousands of these were spread over Europe and along the coast.—*Time. December 3, 1945. p. 52*

Wuwa: See Robot Bombs; Wunderwaffe

W.V.S.: Women's Voluntary Services (British). Started in 1938. Its aim was to coordinate the work of women for national service, working in cooperation with existing women's services.—*Anderson. British Women at War. p. 47-56*

X-Hour: Designation given by the Nazis to the day when Russia would attack Berlin.—*Newsweek. March 26, 1945. p. 38*

Yale: (American plane) North American BT-9, BT-14 trainer plane

Yank: United States Army newspaper. v. 1 no. 1 appeared June 17, 1942.—*Newsweek. May 18, 1942. p. 48; June 22, 1942. p. 74; Time. June 22, 1942. p. 53*

Yankee Doodle: (American plane) Fairchild AT-13 and 14 trainer plane

Yehudis: See Gremlins

Yellow Diamond: The name of a large-scale trucking operation by which CONAD (q.v.) supplied the Sixth Army Group during the latter part of March and through April and May 1945, in the sustained drives of these armies through Germany and Austria.—*U.S. Army. ETO. CONAD History. p. 188, 379*

Yellow Seal Dollars: Unlike other invasion currencies, these, used in the invasion of North Africa, were regular American money, with yellow ink substituted for blue in printing the U.S. seal; Hawaiian dollars fall into this same class—regular currency with the word "Hawaii" overprinted.—*American Notes and Queries. April 1945. p. 8*

Y-Gun: Gun with Y-shaped firing arms, for simultaneous discharge of depth bombs from destroyer or other warcraft.—*Democrat & Chronicle. Rochester, N.Y. September 8, 1940*

You: See Plane nicknames

You Buy 'Em—We'll Fly 'Em: Poster caption. United States Treasury Department. Poster for sale of Defense bonds and stamps

"You Do Your Worst—and We Will Do Our Best": By Winston Churchill. Speech delivered at a luncheon given by the London County Council, July 14, 1941. "The people of London with one voice would say to Hitler. . . 'You do your worst—and we will do our best.' "—*Churchill. The Unrelenting Struggle. p. 186*

"You Have Met the Enemy and the Enemy Is Yours": Admiral Chester W. Nimitz used the above words (paraphrasing Oliver Hazard Perry) in commending the submarine successes in the Pacific. Submarines at that time had destroyed 4,500,000 tons of Japanese shipping.—*Democrat & Chronicle. Rochester, N.Y. May 28, 1945. p. 1*

You Have Never Lived until You Have Been Cussed Out by General Patton: Said of Lieutenant General George S. Patton Jr., by his men.—*New York Times Magazine. April 4, 1943. p. 8*

"You Supply the Sweat, We'll Supply the Blood and Tears": Suggested as a message from the Armed Forces to the United Mine Workers, by Walter Winchell, in a radio broadcast June 13, 1943. In connection with the coal strike

"You Will Be Present at the Peace if You Are Still Alive. That Peace Will Be in the White House, but the White House Will Not Be as You Envisaged": By Admiral William Halsey, commander of American naval forces in the South Pacific. In an interview in December 1942, Halsey thus dealt with Admiral Yamamoto's (Japanese Fleet commander) boast that he would make peace in the White House.—*Newsweek. January 11, 1943. p. 22.* In a speech in January 1946, Admiral Nimitz declared that the reported boast of Yamamoto about making peace in the White House was

Japanese militaristic propaganda. Speaking before the Associated Press Managing Editors Association, Admiral Nimitz said: "Admiral Yamamoto was reputed to have bragged he would dictate peace in the White House. . . . We believed he made that boast; more importantly, the Japanese people believed he made that boast. But since the end of the war, we have learned from Japanese sources that Yamamoto never said anything of the kind; in fact, he had such a healthy respect for the United States that he said quite the opposite."—*Democrat & Chronicle. Rochester, N.Y. January 11, 1946. p. 3*

"You Will Not Falter. You Cannot Fail": By Henry L. Stimson, Secretary of War. Radio address to selectees, August 15, 1941.— *Vital Speeches. September 1, 1941. p. 688*

You've Done Your Bit. Now Do Your Best!: Slogan for sale of War Bonds, 1943

You've Had It: R.A.F. slang. For example, "Can I get a taxi?" asks an American outside the Savoy. "You've had it," says an R.A.F. flyer, meaning "You haven't got it and the chances are you won't get it."—*Time. March 22, 1943. p. 52*

Zaibatsu: See Gumbatsu

Zebra: Air Force slang for a cadet officer in the Air Force training plan; he was usually very conscious of his stripes.—*American Speech. December 1946. p. 310*

Zeroitis: See Shell-shock

Z-Guns: Anti-aircraft rocket guns (British).—*Newsweek. April 17, 1944. p. 38*

ZI: Zone of the Interior, the Army term for the continental United States

Zip Your Lip: See Tiger

Zipper Ships: Airplane cargo carriers, ZEC-2's, modified Liberty ships, which were designed to carry crated aircraft.—*New York Times. June 17, 1945. p. 27*

Zombies: Home Defense Army (Canada). Under a new modified government conscription policy, the Zombies were to be sent abroad for overseas service. Many went AWOL from embarkation points.—*Newsweek. December 4, 1944. p. 66; January 29, 1945. p. 56*

Zoom: Aviation term, meaning upward flight. To say a plane "zoomed down" would be incorrect, because zoom always means upward flight.—*Word Study. October 1945. p. 6*

Zoomies: Nickname of fliers in the Aleutians.—*Saturday Review of Literature. July 31, 1943. p. 18*

Zweiglager: A branch camp. See also Lager.—*Red Cross Courier. June 1943. p. 11*

WAR SONGS

A LIST OF TITLES

Tin Pan Alley worked hard trying to write for World War II a song hit that would sweep the country in somewhat the way of George M. Cohan's "Over There" in the war of 1914-1918. Several songs had intensive "runs" for short periods, notably "White Cliffs of Dover," "Praise the Lord and Pass the Ammunition," "Comin' in on a Wing and a Prayer," "Johnny Zero," "Rodger Young," "Lili Marlene," and some others, but never one that seemed to be THE SONG. There were songs for the various branches of the service, songs for various battle areas and incidents, songs about life on the home front, songs for America, for Britain, songs lauding freedom and patriotism, and songs expressing personal longing. Perhaps the field was too vast to be crystallized into one song, or perhaps the radio offered too many outlets for a multitude of songs to be too continuously heard, making it impossible for one alone to stand out. Whatever the reason, both V-E Day and V-J Day came and went and we still had no song that was as typically the song of World War II, as "Over There" was the song of World War I.

It seemed worth while to include song titles in this book on the language of World War II, since so many of them reflected trends in thinking and ways of speaking during the war, and many were based on slogans or on much used phrases, for example, "Remember Pearl Harbor," "Any Bonds Today," "Got Any Gum, Chum," "God Is My Co-Pilot," and many others.

This list in the main was compiled from a collection of war songs in the Sibley Music Library of the Eastman School of Music of the University of Rochester. Miss Barbara Duncan, Librarian, had a standing order with music publishers for copies of war songs, as they were published, so the list as here given, is as complete as I was able to make it. Titles marked * are included (with further information) in the body of the book.

Abe Lincoln had just one country
After it's over
The airmen are flying
Alaska's flag
All hail to thee, America!
All out for America (Marching song of the U.S.A. Dedicated to "our Commander in Chief")
All out for freedom
All together (for your country and mine)
America! America!
America calling
America calls
America farewell
America! Let's go!

America, my home
America, my own, my native land
America, thou blessed land
America United (is rolling along)
America wake up!
American anthem (Americanism set to music)
The American doughboy
American eagles (from the all-soldier show "This is the army")
American lullaby
American prayer
The American way
American women for defense (A.W.V.S. marching song)
The American's creed
America's call
America's on the march
And still the Volga flows
Angels of mercy (written expressly for and dedicated to American Red Cross, by Irving Berlin)
*Any bonds today?
Arm in arm (from Tars and Spars, a recruiting revue presented by the United States Coast Guard)
Arms for the love of America (Army Ordnance Song, dedicated to Major General C. M. Wesson, Chief of Ordnance. Words and music by Irving Berlin)
Army Air Corps (official song of the United States Army Air Corps)
Army hymn (a prayer for soldiers)
The Army mule, the Navy goat and the kick of the kangaroo (dedicated to the 52nd Coast Artillery, U.S. Army)
The army service forces (from the all-soldier musical show, "Stars and Gripes," produced by Special Service Theatre Section, Fort Hamilton, N.Y.)
The army's made a man out of me (From the all-soldier show "This is the army")
At mail call today

Back home for keeps
Back the red white and blue with gold
Be a good soldier (while your daddy's away)
Be brave, beloved
Be glad you're an American
Because we are Americans
*Berlin will rise again
Better not roll those blue, blue eyes (at somebody else)
Bill of Rights

Bless 'em all
The blond sailor
Blue bugle call
Bombardier song (Dedicated to the bomber crews of the U.S. Army Air Forces)
Bomber command
Born to the sky (song of the Army Air Forces, Air Transport Command, dedicated to Major General Harold L. George and the men of the Air Transport Command)
A boy in khaki—a girl in lace
Boy, oh boy!
Boys of the U.S.A.
Brave Britain
Brave men of the infantry (dedicated to the Infantry of the U.S. Army)
British children's prayer
Buckle down buck private
Buddy boy
Bugles in the sky
Buy a bond today
Buy war bonds (dedicated to the Armed Forces of the United States)
Bye, bye, Benito
Bye bye Bessie

Call of America
Call out the Marines
Captains of the clouds (Official song of the Royal Canadian Air Force)
Captains on high
Carlson's Raiders (as sung by U.S. Marine Raiders under the command of Lieutenant Colonel Evans F. Carlson)
Carry him back (to his folks and his home and mine)
Chin up! Cheerio! Carry on!
Citizens song
Civilian (from "Tars and Spars," a recruiting revue presented by the United States Coast Guard)
Clancy's gone and joined the army
Cleanin' my rifle (and dreamin' of you)
Coast Guard victory song
*Comin' in on a wing and a prayer
Coming home
The conquering Marines (dedicated to the late General Smedley D. Butler)
Conversion, "Look God, I have never spoken to You"
Corns for my country (from the Warner Brothers picture "Hollywood Canteen")

Cranky old Yank (in a clanky old tank)

Daddy's letter
"Damn the torpedoes. Full speed ahead!"
A dash of the red, white and blue
The daughter of Mademoiselle from Armentieres
Dear Arabella
Dear Mom
Defend your country
Dig down deep (song in behalf of the United States Treasury War Bonds and Stamps Campaign)
Dip your pen in sunshine (and drop the boys a line)
Don't be blue, little pal, don't be blue
Don't change horses
Don't cry
Don't cry sweetheart
Don't forget your buddy (the only Buddy, Mother, Sweetheart song)
Don't let my spurs get rusty
Don't sit under the apple tree (with anyone else but me)
Don't steal the sweetheart of a soldier
Don't worry mom
Dunkirk, a ballad
Duration blues
The dying soldier

Ee-nie mee-nie A.P.O. (where did my G.I. Johnny go?)
The Ernie Pyle infantry march (from the Lester Cowan production, Ernie Pyle's "Story of G.I. Joe," with appreciation to Lieutenant Colonel Edward Hope Coffey, Infantry)
Eventually comes love
Every soldier has an angel by his side
Every state has answered the call
Everybody's seen him but his daddy
Ev'ry one's a fighting son of that old gang of mine
Ev'rybody ev'ry payday
Ev'rything will be like home in Ireland

The farmer's son
A fellow on a furlough
Fight to victory (combat song of the infantry)
Fightin' Doug MacArthur
Fighting amphibians (official force song, Amphibious Training Command U.S. Atlantic Fleet)
Fighting man
Fighting men of Uncle Sam

Fighting on the home front, WINS (national war song of the American housewife)
The fighting Quartermaster Corps
Fighting sons of the Navy blue
Flying flag
Follow the president
For peace and freedom (official song, World's Fair of 1940 in New York)
For the flag, for the home, for the family (for the future of all mankind)
For victory! for liberty!
Forever and a day
Forgive me, silent soldier
Forward America (dedicated to our Armed Forces everywhere)
Forward, forces of the red, white and blue
Four buddies
Free for all
Freedom for the world
Freedom ring!
Freedom's land
Freedom's morning
From Broadway to Tokyo
From D-Day to V-Day (my prayers are all for you)
From the Coast of Maine to the Rockies
From the hills above Pearl Harbor dedicated to Lieutenant Commander H. F. Hanson and the choir of the Great Lakes Naval Training Station, Great Lakes, Ill.)
Der Fuehrer's face
Fun to be free

Gee isn't it great to be an American!
Gentlemen, the toast is: Our land!
Get out and dig, dig, dig (the Victory garden theme, a feature of the Blue Network's National Farm and Home hour)
Get your gun and come along
G.I. blues
G.I. jive
The girl behind the boy behind the gun (Red Cross nurse)
Girl scouts are we
Girl scouts together
Girls of the U.S.A.
Give us the tools
Glide, glider, glide
Go back where you belong (If you can't be true to the red, white and blue, then go back where you belong)

Gobs of love
*God bless America
God bless my darling, he's somewhere
God bless our fighting boys
God bless our land
God bless our president
God is my co-pilot (a hymn dedicated to the U.S. Air Forces)
God must have loved America
God of battles (give us victory, Lord). Poem written by Lieutenant General George S. Patton, Jr., musical setting by Peter de Rose)
God save our men
God's country (Hi there, neighbor)
Goodbye dear, I'll be back in a year
Goodbye mama (I'm off to Yokohama)
Good-for-nothing (is good for something now)
Goodnight Captain Curly-head
Goodnight mother
Goodnight soldier
Goodnight, wherever you are
Got any gum, chum?
Great news is in the making (from the RKO-Radio picture "Around the world")
Guardian of the colors
Guns in the sky (a tribute to the aerial gunner)
A guy 24 and a B-29

Hail to America
Hail to the Merchant Seamen
Hallelu (Judgment day is comin')
Hallelujah! Hallelujah! We'll pull together
*Hats off to MacArthur! and our boys down there
He wears a pair of silver wings
Heave ho! my lads, heave ho! (Song of the Merchant Marine)
He'll have to cross the Atlantic (to get to the Pacific)
Hello! Broadway, London calling
"Hello Central: call Berlin!"
Hello mom
Hello Private Doe
Here come the Engineers (dedicated to the United States Army Corps of Engineers)
Here comes the Navy (adapted to melody of "Beer Barrel Polka")
Here we come through the rainbow
Here's to the flag! (keep it flying over here—over there—everywhere)
Here's to you, MacArthur
He's a great American

He's a real All-American now
He's got a wave in his hair (and a Waac on his hands)
He's home for a little while
He's my uncle
He's 1-A in the Army (and he's A-1 in my heart)
Hey, Tojo! Count yo' men!
Hey! Zeke (your country's callin')
Hip hip hooray
Hit the leather (Cavalry song. Dedicated to the Cavalry School at Fort Riley, Kansas)
Hitler's funeral march
Hitler's reply to Mussolini
Hi'ya chum (where 'ya from?)
Hold your hats on!
Hollywood canteen
Home to the arms of mother (from the Paramount picture "Hail the conquering hero")
The house I live in
How about a cheer for the Navy (from the all-soldier show "This is the Army")
Hup! Tup! Thrup! Four (from the all-soldier musical show "Stars and Gripes")
Hut! 2-3-4 (I love the marching song)
Hymn to the United States Navy (dedicated, by permission, to the Class of 1944, U.S. Naval Academy, Annapolis, Md.)

I am an American (2 songs appeared with this title)
I dreamt the war was over
I feel a draft coming on
I had a little talk with the Lord
I hear America calling
I hear America singing
I left my heart at the stage door canteen (from the all-soldier show "This is the army")
I lost my job again
I love coffee (I love tea)
I pledge allegiance
I sent a letter to Santa (to watch over Daddy for me)
*I threw a kiss in the ocean
I wanna dance with a sailor
I was here when you left me (I'll be here when you get back)
I wish, I wish, I wish
I wish that I could hide inside this letter
I'd like to give my dog to Uncle Sam (the blind boy and his dog)
I'll be back

I'll be back in a year, little darlin'
I'll be marching to a love song
I'll pray for you
I'm a convict with Old Glory in my heart
I'm a son of a son of a Yankee Doodle Dandy
I'm all that's left of that old quartette
I'm getting tired so I can sleep (from the all-soldier show "This is the Army")
*I'm gonna get lit-up when the lights go up in London
I'm in the army now
I'm living now in Ireland
I'm proud to be an American
I'm wearing my heart on my sleeve for you
In God's name and for liberty
In London town at night
In my arms (featured in the M-G-M motion picture "See here, private Hargrove")
The Infantry (doughboy war song)
The Infantry—kings of the highway (the U.S. Infantry Association marching song)
It's great to be an American
I've been drafted (now I'm drafting you)

Jerry, my soldier boy
Johnny Doughboy found a rose in Ireland
Johnny the one
Johnny zero
Johnny's got a date with a gal in New York
Jumpin' with a G.I. gal
Jumping to the jukebox (from the all-soldier musical show "Stars and Gripes")
Junk ain't junk no more ('cause junk will win the war) (theme song of the National Salvage campaign)
Just a blue serge suit
Just a prayer

Keep a star in the window and a prayer in your heart
Keep 'em flying! (dedicated to U.S. Army Air Corps)
Keep 'em smiling
Keep ole Glory flying
Keep the flag a'flying, America
Keep the star spangled banner unfurled
Keep the stars and stripes together

Keep your powder dry
Ke-Toky-i-o
The King is still in London
The K-9 corps (official march of "Dogs for defense," Inc.)
Knit one purl two
K.P. serenade

Lalapaluza Lu
Land of the free
The last time I saw Paris
Left-right
Let freedom ring
Let our white house be our lighthouse
Let us all sing auld lang syne
Let your mother be your sweetheart
Let's all say a prayer tonight
Let's be true to the U.S.A.
Let's bring new glory to Old Glory
Let's get goin'
Let's get off
Let's get together
Let's go! U.S.A.
Let's keep a V in ev'ry heart (official theme song of the "V" Club of America sponsored by the British-American Ambulance Corps, New York)
Let's put the axe to the Axis
Let's say a prayer (for Somebody's boy)
Let's sing a song of America
Let's sing a victory song
Liberty under God
*Lili Marlene
Little Bo-Peep has lost her jeep
The little brown suit my uncle bought me (from the all-soldier musical show "Stars and Gripes")
A little old church in England
Little war child
London pride
Long live America
Long live America, the savior of democracy
Look homeward, America
Look out below
Lords of the air
Love sometimes has to wait (from the all-soldier musical show "Stars and Gripes")

Ma, I miss your apple pie
Major and the minor
Make with the bullets, Benny
Making hay for the U.S.A.
March for the new infantry
March of the volunteers, a song of fighting China

March of the women marines (official march of the Marine Corps Women's Reserve)

March on, America

Marching song of freedom

Marching through Berlin (from the moving picture "Stage door canteen")

Marching to Berlin and to Tokyo

May the angels be with you

Me and my Uncle Sam

Mechs of the Air Corps

Mem'ry of this dance

Men, come along

Men of the Merchant Marine

Men of the open sea

Merchantmen (to all merchantmen of the Allied nations)

A merry American Christmas

Military polka

Modern cannon ball

Move it over

Mow the Japs down!

Mud in his ears

Mussolini's letter to Hitler

My beloved is rugged

My boy's prayer (dedicated to the mother of every soldier, sailor, marine, flyer, and man in the armed forces of Uncle Sam and the United Nations)

My British buddy (written by Irving Berlin for the overseas production of "This is the army")

My daddy (You're just my daddy to me)

My great, great, grandfather

My guy's come back

My heart belongs to a sailor

My heart's in America

My kind of people

My old American home

My own America

My pin-up girl (from the all-soldier musical show "Stars and Gripes")

My pledge of allegiance

My sergeant and I are buddies (from the all-soldier show "This is the Army")

My soldier boy so far away

Navy airmen

The Navy hymn (Eternal Father, strong to save)

Navy wings

Nimitz and Halsey and me!

1942 Turkey in the straw

No love, no nothin' (from the 20th Century-Fox picture "The gang's all here")

No more toujours l'amour

O sailor boy

Ode to a marine

Ode to the statue of liberty

Off the shores of somewhere

"Oh! my achin' back"

Oh, pray for peace

Oh! They're makin' me all over in the army

Old Father Neptune (dedicated to the men of the Navy, Coast Guard and Merchant Marine)

Old Glory, I salute you

Old Glory, you're the grandest flag

On freedom's wings

On, on, to victory

On the old assembly line

One for all—all for one

Our country

Our faith shall live (a prayer for a new world. Dedicated to Captain Eddie Rickenbacker)

Our glorious America

Our soldiers

Over here

Paris will be Paris once again

Patriotic rhythm

Please touch my daddy's star again and change it back to blue

Pledge ("I pledge allegiance to the flag")

Pledge of allegiance

Pledge to the flag

Pony boy is in the army now

*Praise the Lord and pass the ammunition

A prayer for General Eisenhower and his men

Prayer for the men who fly

Private Buckaroo

The private's song

Put another chair at the table

Put another nail in Hitler's coffin

Ramparts we watch

A real American

Red, white and blue (official theme song of Red, White and Blue network)

The regimental polka

Remember Hawaii

Remember Pearl Harbor

The rhythm is red an' white an' blue (from the RKO Radio picture "They meet again")

Ridin' herd on a cloud

Ring out Big Ben

The road to victory (published by request of the United States Treasury Department in connection with the Third War Loan)

*Rodger Young

Roll tanks roll

A rookie and his rhythm (from Sol Lesser's production "Stage door canteen," a United Artist release)

Rose Ann of Charing Cross

Rosie the riveter

Sailor with the Navy blue eyes

Sailors of the sky

Savin' myself for Bill

Say a prayer for the boys over there

Seeds for victory and peace

Semper paratus (official Coast Guard marching song)

The sentry's prayer

She'll always remember

Shelter lullaby

She's my commanding general

Shhh ! ! ! it's a military secret

Shootin' the works for Uncle Sam

Shout ! wherever you may be—I am an American

Show your medals, Mother Malone

Shut my mouth (I ain't talkin')

Silver wings in the moonlight

Sing ! Sing ! Sing ! (Sing so they can hear you)

Six jerks in a jeep

Sky anchors (Naval aviation song)

A slip of the lip (can sink a ship)

Smoke on the water

A soldier dreams (of you tonight)

Soldier let me read your letter

A soldier speaks

Soldier, what did you see?

A soldier's leave

Soldiers of God (official chaplains' march)

A soldier's prayer

Some chicken (marching song, based on Prime Minister Churchill's Ottawa speech)

Something for the boys

Son o' mine

Son of a gun who picks on Uncle Sam

Song of America

Song of freedom

The song of liberation

Song of the A.A.A. (marching song of the Anti Aircraft Artillery)

Song of the Army Nurse Corps (official anthem of the Army Nurse Corps)

Song of the Army Transportation Corps (official song of the Transportation Corps, Army Service Forces)

Song of the bombardiers

Song of the devil dogs (the enemy hates United States Marines)

The song of the fighting marines (dedicated to Major General John H. Russell, Commandant, United States Marine Corps)

Song of the free

Song of the G S O (officially approved by the Girls Service Organization of junior USO hostesses)

Song of the Infantry

Song of the refugee

The song of the Seabees (dedicated to the Seabees construction and fighting men of the United States Navy)

Song of the Signal Corps (dedicated to the United States Signal Corps)

Spirit of Aberdeen

Spread your wings

Stalin wasn't stallin' (a modern spiritual)

Stand by America

Stand by the Navy (official song of the National Women's Council of the Navy League)

Stars and stripes of liberty

Stars and stripes on Iwo Jima

Straighten up and fly right

Sweethearts' manual of arms

Tank destroyer men (the song of the tank destroyers, officially approved September 1944. Dedicated to Tank Destroyer Battalions everywhere)

Taps (prayer for repose)

Tell it to the marines

Ten days with baby

Ten little Gremlins

Ten little soldiers (on a 10-day leave)

Tess's torch song (I had a man)

Thank you America

Thank your lucky stars and stripes

Thanks to the Yanks (theme song of the Bob Hawk radio program "Thanks to the Yanks")

That Old Glory may keep flying

That Russian winter (from the all-soldier show "This is the Army")

That soldier of mine

That star-spangled baby of mine

That's the infantry ("We're marching God knows whither, and we'll get there God knows when")

Then — now — forever (respectfully dedicated to the United States Army)

There are no wings on a fox-hole (dedicated to the Infantrymen of the United States Army)

There is a fellow worth waiting for

There won't be a shortage of love

There'll always be a U.S.A. (official song of United Youth for Defense)

*There'll always be an England

There'll be a hot time in the town of Berlin (when the Yanks go marching in)

There'll be a jubilee

There'll be a Yankee Christmas

There'll never be a black-out in my heart for you (to all members of the Allied armed forces from their women folks back home)

There's a blue star shining bright (in a window tonight)

There's a cowboy ridin' thru the sky

There's a fella waitin' in Poughkeepsie (from the Paramount picture "Here come the Waves")

There's a flag that I love (dedicated to the military and naval forces of the United States)

There's a new flag on Iwo Jima

There's a star-spangled banner waving somewhere

There's an F D R in freedom

There's no ceiling on love

There's no yellow in the red white and blue

There's somebody waiting for me

They live forever

They looked so pretty on the envelope

They started somethin' (but we're gonna end it)

They're either too young or too old (from the Warner Brothers picture "Thank your lucky stars")

The things that make a soldier great

The things that mean so much to me

Think of the joy when the boys come home

This is God's war

This is my country

This is our side of the ocean

This is the army, Mr. Jones (written by Irving Berlin for his all-soldier show "This is the Army"; opened on Broadway July 4, 1942)

This is worth fighting for

This time

Three cheers for our president (march song, respectfully dedicated to President Franklin Delano Roosevelt)

Three little sisters

'Til Reveille

Till the lights of London shine again (dedicated to Quentin Reynolds and our other brave foreign correspondents who are America's shining lights in London)

Till the sun shines thru again

Till then

The time is now

Time's a-wastin'

A tiny little voice (in a tiny little prayer)

To mother (dedicated to the mothers of boys in the armed forces)

Treat 'em rough, soldier boy!

Trek song

$21 a day—once a month

Uncle Sam gets around (from the 20th Century-Fox picture "Cadet girl")

Uncle Sam goes to town

Uncle Sammy here I am

Uncle Sam's lullaby

United Nations

The unknown soldier's song (Handel's Largo)

The U.S. Engineers

U.S. Engineers "Fight" song (dedicated to the Army Engineers)

"V" calls for victory (victory march based on Beethoven's main theme of the V Symphony)

V for victory

The "V" song (official song of "Bundles for Britain")

"V" to victory

Victory cavalcade (introduced and featured by "Ritzin' the blitz," all-soldier revue)

Vict'ry polka

Viva Roosevelt

Voice of America

The Wac hymn

Wait for me Mary

Wake up, America

Waltzing Matilda ("The unofficial national anthem of Australia")

*The watch on the Channel

Watch your uncle

Wave that flag, America
Wave the flag
We are Americans too
*We are the menace, we are the hell, we are the end of England
We did it before and we can do it again
We fight for peace
We hate to leave (from the M-G-M picture "Anchors aweigh")
We like it over here
We must be vigilant
We mustn't say goodbye
We oughta have the girls
*We wanna go home
Weep no more, my darlin' (I'm comin' home to you)
Welcome home
We'll always remember Pearl Harbor
We'll be singing hallelujah marching thru Berlin
*We'll hang out the washing on the Siegfried line
We'll meet again
We'll win through—we always do
We're all Americans (all true blue)
We're all in it
We're all together now
We're gonna have to slap, the dirty little Jap (and Uncle Sam's the guy who can do it)
We're in the Navy
We're in to win
We're on our way (Infantry song)
We're the girls of Uncle Sam (dedicated to the women of our armed forces)
We're the guys who shoot supplies (the song of the Supply Corps of the United States Navy. Dedicated to Rear Admiral "Brent" Young)
*Werewolf song
We've got a job to do
We've got the Lord on our side
We've got to do a job on the Japs, baby
We've just begun to fight, (Hallelujah)
Whaddaya say we're on our way
What a day
What does a soldier dream of?
When my boy comes home
When that man is dead and gone
When the boys and girls come marching home
When the boys come home
When the Empire gets together
When the lights go on again (all over the world)

When the roses bloom again
When the Yanks come sailing home
When the Yanks go marching in
When they sound the last all clear
When this crazy world is sane again
When you hear the sirens blow
When you put on that old blue suit again
White cliffs of Dover
Who wants war?
Why do they call a private a private? (from the Army Special Services revue "About face")
Winged victory
Wings of gold (dedicated to U.S. Naval Aviation)
Wings over America
Wings to victory (song of the soldiers of the sky. Dedicated to and adopted by the 119th Observation Squadron U.S. Army Air Corps and 44th Division, Aviation)
With a pack on his back (and a girl on his mind)
With my head in the clouds (from the all-soldier show "This is the Army")
Women of the year
Wonder when my baby's coming home
Wrap your dreams in the red, white and blue

A Yank and a tank (song of the Armored Command. In honor of the gallant men of the armored services)
Yankee Doodle ain't doodlin' now
Yankee Doodle polka
Yankee Doodle spirit (from the Walt Disney motion picture "The new spirit" produced for the U.S. Treasury Department)
Yankee Doodle tan
Yankee mother's prayer (for her soldier over there)
The Yankees are coming
Yanks are comin' again
Yanks are coming
You buy 'em, we'll fly 'em (song of the Air Forces)
You can always tell a Yank (from the Warner Brothers picture "Hollywood canteen")
You can't get that no more
You can't say no to a soldier (from the 20th Century-Fox picture "Iceland")

You'll be sorr-ee!

You'll never be blue in a blue uniform (written at and dedicated to United States Naval Training Station, Sampson, New York)

Your flag and mine

You're a lucky fellow Mr. Smith

You're a sap, Mister Jap

You're on the right side of the ocean

Youth on parade

LIST OF BOOKS REFERRED TO AS SOURCES
OF INFORMATION IN THE TEXT

Anderson, Mary Désirée (Mrs. Trenchard Cox). British Women at War. Murray. 1941

Bailey, Gilbert P. Boot, a Marine in the Making. Macmillan. c1944
Baird, A. Craig. Representative American Speeches: 1939-40; 1940-41; 1941-42. H.W. Wilson
Ballou, Robert Oleson. A History of the Council on Books in Wartime. Garden City. 1946
Baxter, James Phinney. Scientists against Time. Little. c1946
Beveridge, Sir William Henry. Social Insurance and Allied Services. Macmillan. c1942
Biographie Universelle, Ancienne et Moderne. Michaud Freres. 1812
Britannica Book of the Year. 1944; 1945; 1946

Cave, Hugh Barnett. We Build, We Fight! the Story of the Seabees. Harper. c1944
Chase, Allan. Falange; the Axis Secret Army in the Americas. Putnam. c1943
Chiang Kai-shek. All We Are and All We Have. John Day. c1943
China. Ministry of Information. China Handbook: 1937-1943: A Comprehensive Survey of Major Developments in China in Six Years of War. Macmillan. c1943
Churchill, Winston Leonard Spencer. Blood, Sweat and Tears. Putnam. c1941
Churchill, Winston Leonard Spencer. The Dawn of Liberation. Little. c1945
Churchill, Winston Leonard Spencer. The End of the Beginning; War Speeches. Little. c1943
Churchill, Winston Leonard Spencer. Onwards to Victory. Little. 1944
Churchill, Winston Leonard Spencer. The Unknown War; the Eastern Front. Scribner. c1931
Churchill, Winston Leonard Spencer. The Unrelenting Struggle; War Speeches. Little. c1942
Colby, Elbridge. Army Talk. Princeton. c1942
Considine, Robert. MacArthur the Magnificent. McKay. c1942

Desmond, Robert W. The Press and World Affairs. Appleton. c1937
Dunlap, Orrin E. Jr. Radar, What Radar Is and How It Works. Harper. c1946

Eastman Kodak Company. Kodak Flies the Battle Flag of War Production. n.d.
Encyclopaedia Britannica, Inc. Ten Eventful Years, 1937 through 1946. Author. c1947

Ford, Harvey Seabury. What the Citizen Should Know about the Army. Norton. 1941
Fox, Monroe L. Blind Adventure. Lippincott. c1946

Gramling, Oliver. Free Men Are Fighting; the Story of World War II. Farrar. c1942
Grew, Joseph Clark. Report from Tokyo; a Message to the American People. Simon. c1942
Gunther, John. Inside Latin America. Harper. c1940

Hart, W. E. (pseud.) Hitler's Generals. Doubleday. c1944

Hemingway, Ernest. The Fifth Column. Scribner. c1938

Hersey, John Richard. A Bell for Adano. Knopf. c1944

Hersey, John Richard. Into the Valley; a Skirmish of the Marines. Knopf. c1943

Hodgson, Stuart. The Man Who Made the Peace: Neville Chamberlain. Dutton. c1938

Hoffmann, Eleanor. Feeding Our Armed Forces. Nelson. c1943

Huie, William Bradford. Can Do! the Story of the Seabees. Dutton. c1944

Johnston, Stanley. Queen of the Flat-Tops; the U.S.S. Lexington and the Coral Sea Battle. Dutton. c1942

Latzko, Adolf Andreas. Lafayette. Doubleday. c1936

Lawson, Ted W. Thirty Seconds over Tokyo. Random. c1943

Lippmann, Walter. U.S. Foreign Policy: Shield of the Republic. Little. c1943

Lucas, Jim G. Combat Correspondent. Reynal. c1944

McCracken, Kenneth. Baby Flat-top. Farrar. c1944

Mace, Don. Army Times Veterans Guide, rev. ed. Army Times. c1946

Mehring, Walter. Timoshenko, Marshal of the Red Army. Unger. c1942

Meyer, Franz Sales. A Handbook of Ornament. Architectural Book Pub. Co. n.d.

Miller, Francis Trevelyan. General Douglas MacArthur, Fighter for Freedom. Winston. c1942

Miller, Francis Trevelyan. History of World War II. Winston. c1945

National Geographic Society, Washington, D.C. Insignia and Decorations of the U.S. Armed Forces. Author. c1943-45

Oxford Dictionary of Quotations. Oxford. 1941

Parsons, Robert Percival. Mob 3, a Naval Hospital in a South Sea Jungle. Bobbs. c1945

Philco Corporation. Radar on Wings (pam.) Author. 1945

Pinchon, Edgcumb. Zapata the Unconquerable. Doubleday. c1941

Princeton University. Dept. of Economics and Social Institutions. Industrial Relations Section. Hours Administration as Influenced by the Defense Program; by Edward P. Moore. (Research report ser. no. 64) c1941

Princeton University. Dept. of Economics and Social Institutions. Industrial Relations Section. Re-organization of Hour Schedules (Part III of Industrial Relations Digests . . .) c1941

Pyle, Ernest Taylor. Brave Men. Holt. c1943-44

Reynolds, James. Wing Commander Paddy Finucane [Brendan Finucane] a memoir. Hackett. c1942

Rolo, Charles James. Wingate's Raiders; an Account of the Fabulous Adventure that Raised the Curtain on the Battle for Burma. Viking. c1944

Romulo, Carlos Penna. I Saw the Fall of the Philippines. Doubleday. c1942

Roosevelt, Franklin Delano. Looking Forward. John Day. c1933

Roosevelt, Franklin Delano. The Public Papers and Addresses of Franklin D. Roosevelt. Random. c1938

Roosevelt, Theodore. The Great Adventure. Scribner. c1918

Ross, Nancy Wilson. The Waves; the Story of the Girls in Blue. Holt. c1943

St. John, Robert. From the Land of Silent People. Doubleday. c1942

Saunders, Hilary Aidan St. George. Combined Operations. Macmillan. c1943

Schwarzwalder, John. We Caught Spies. Duell. c1946
Scott, Peggy. British Women in War. Hutchinson. n.d.
Shridharani, Krishnalal Jethalal. My India, My America. Duell. c1941
Smith, Robert Aura. Divided India. McGraw. c1947
Snow, Edgar. People on Our Side. Random. c1944

Taylor, Henry J. Time Runs Out. Doubleday. c1942
Trumbull, Robert. The Raft. Holt. c1942

U.S. Army. European Theater of Operations. CONAD History. 1945
U.S. Army Air Forces. Official Guide to the Army Air Forces, AAF; a Directory, Almanac and Chronicle of Achievement. Simon. c1944
U.S. Civil Aeronautics Administration. Army-Navy-CAA Standard Airport Traffic Control Procedures (pam.). 1945
U.S. General Staff. Omaha Beachhead (6 June-13 June 1944) U.S. War Department. Historical Division. 1945
U.S. General Staff. ¡General Marshall's Report¡. The Winning of the War in Europe and the Pacific; Biennial Report of the Chief of Staff of the United States Army July 1, 1943 to June 30, 1945, to the Secretary of War. Simon. 1945
U.S. Office of Scientific Research and Development. Electronics Warfare. . . ¡Released by Joint Board on Scientific Information Policy for Scientific Research and Development Office, War Department, Navy Department¡. U.S. Government Printing Office. 1945
U.S. Office of War Information. Division of Public Inquiries. United States Government Manual: Summer 1943. Washington, D.C.

Vernadskii, Georgii Vladimirovich. Ancient Russia (History of Russia, v. 1) Yale. c1943
Voices of History; Great Speeches and Papers of the Year. Watts. 1944-1945

Wallace, Henry Agard. Price of Free World Victory; with Some Comments by Raymond Clapper [and Others]. Fischer. c1942
Warplanes of the World (pam.) Dell. c1943
Webster, Noah. Webster's New International Dictionary of the English Language. 2nd ed. Merriam. 1943 (c1939); also 1944 (c1939)
Welles, Sumner. The Time for Decision. Harper. c1944
Wells, Albert Wade. Hail to the Jeep; a Factual and Pictorial History of the Jeep. Harper. c1946
White, William Lindsay. They Were Expendable. Harcourt. c1942
Whitton, Charlotte Elizabeth. Canadian Women in the War Effort. (Macmillan War Pamphlets. Canadian series). Macmillan. 1942
Willkie, Wendell Lewis. One World. Simon. c1943
Wolfert, Ira. American Guerrilla in the Philippines. Simon. c1945
Wolfert, Ira. Torpedo 8; the Story of Swede Larsen's Bomber Squadron. Houghton. c1943
World Almanac and Book of Facts for 1943, 1944; ed. by E. Eastman Irvine. New York World-Telegram. c1943, 1944
Wright, Joseph, ed. The English Dialect Dictionary. Putnam. 1898-1905

INDEX